A SOCIAL HISTORY OF KNOWLEDGE

PETER BURKE

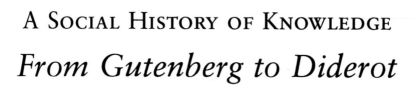

A SOCIAL HISTORY OF KNOWLEDGE

From Gutenberg to Diderot

Based on the first series of Vonhoff Lectures given at
the University of Groningen (Netherlands)

POLITY

The right of Peter Burke to be identified as author of this work has been asserted in accordance with the Copyright, Designs and Patents Act 1988.

First published in 2000 by Polity Press in association with Blackwell Publishers, a Blackwell Publishing Company.

Reprinted 2002, 2004, 2007, 2008

Polity Press
65 Bridge Street
Cambridge CB2 1UR, UK

Polity Press
350 Main Street
Malden, MA 02148, USA

A catalogue record for this book is available from the British Library.

Library of Congress Cataloging-in-Publication Data
Burke, Peter.
    A social history of knowledge: from Gutenberg to Diderot / Peter Burke.
        p.   cm.
    'The Vonhoff lectures, 1998–9.'
    Includes bibliographical references and index.
    ISBN: 978-0-7456-2484-6
    ISBN: 978-0-7456-2485-3 (pbk)
    1. Knowledge, Sociology of—History.   I. Title.

  BD175.B86   2000
  306.4'2'0903—dc21   00–039973

Typeset in 10.5 on 12pt Sabon
by Graphicraft Limited, Hong Kong
Printed and bound in United States by Odyssey Press Inc., Gonic, New Hampshire

This book is printed on acid-free paper.

For further information on Polity, visit our website: www.polity.co.uk

CONTENTS

PREFACE AND ACKNOWLEDGEMENTS

This book is based at least as much on forty years' study of early modern texts as it is on secondary works. The footnotes and bibliography, however, are confined to the works of modern scholars, leaving the primary sources to be discussed in the text itself. Although the focus of the study is on structures and trends rather than on individuals, it is impossible to discuss a topic such as this without introducing hundreds of names, and readers are advised that the dates as well as brief descriptions of each person mentioned in the text will be found in the index.

The study published here is the result of a long-term project which has led to a number of articles as well as to lectures and seminar papers given at Cambridge, Delphi, Leuven, Lund, Oxford, Peking, São Paulo and St Petersburg. After long simmering, the project was finally brought to the boil by the invitation to deliver the first series of Vonhoff lectures at the University of Groningen.

My special thanks to Dick de Boer for looking after me at Groningen and reminding me of the importance of changes in the knowledge system in the thirteenth and fourteenth centuries. Thanks also to Daniel Alexandrov, Alan Baker, Moti Feingold, Halil Inalcik, Alan Macfarlane, Dick Pels, Vadim Volkoff and Jay Winter for help of different kinds, and to Joanna Innes for letting me see her classic – though still unpublished – paper on the use of information by the British government.

For commenting on parts of the manuscript I am indebted to Chris Bayly, Francisco Bethencourt, Ann Blair, Gregory Blue, Paul Connerton, Brendan Dooley, Florike Egmond, José Maria González García, John Headley, Michael Hunter, Neil Kenny, Christel Lane, Peter Mason, Mark Phillips, John Thompson and Zhang Zilian. My wife Maria Lúcia read the whole manuscript and asked some usefully awkward questions as well as suggesting improvements. The book is dedicated to her.

1

SOCIOLOGIES AND HISTORIES OF KNOWLEDGE: AN INTRODUCTION

Whatever is known has always seemed systematic, proven, applicable
and evident to the knower. Every alien system of knowledge has likewise
seemed contradictory, unproven, inapplicable, fanciful or mystical.

Fleck

TODAY we are living, according to some sociologists at least, in
a 'knowledge society' or 'information society', dominated by
professional experts and their scientific methods.[1] According
to some economists, we live in a 'knowledge economy' or 'information economy', marked by the expansion of knowledge-producing or
knowledge-disseminating occupations.[2] Knowledge has also become
a major political issue, centred on the question whether information
should be public or private, treated as a commodity or as a social
good.[3] Historians of the future may well refer to the period around
2000 as the 'age of information'.

Ironically enough, at the same time that knowledge has entered
the limelight in this way, its reliability has been questioned by philosophers and others more and more radically, or at least more and
more loudly than before. What we used to think was discovered is
now often described as 'invented' or 'constructed'.[4] But at least the
philosophers agree with the economists and sociologists in defining
our own time in terms of its relation to knowledge.

We should not be too quick to assume that our age is the first to
take these questions seriously. The commodification of information
is as old as capitalism (discussed in chapter 6). The use by governments of systematically collected information about the population
is, quite literally, ancient history (ancient Roman and Chinese history

---

[1] Wiener (1948), 11; Bell (1976); Böhme and Stehr (1986); Castells (1989); Poster
(1990); Stehr (1994); Webster (1995).
[2] Machlup (1962, 1980–4); Rubin and Huber (1986).
[3] Schiller (1986, 1996).
[4] Berger and Luckmann (1966); Mendelsohn (1977); Ziman (1978); Luhmann (1990).

1

in particular). As for scepticism about claims to knowledge, it goes back at least as far as the ancient Greek philosopher Pyrrho of Elis.

The point of these remarks is not to replace a crude theory of revolution with an equally crude theory of continuity. A major aim of this book is to try to define the peculiarities of the present more precisely by viewing it in the perspective of trends over the long term. Current debates have often stimulated historians to ask new questions about the past. In the 1920s, growing inflation encouraged the rise of price history. In the 1950s and 1960s, a population explosion encouraged research into demographic history. In the 1990s, there was increasing interest in the history of knowledge and information.

From the knowledge element in society let us turn to the complementary opposite theme of the social element in knowledge. One purpose of this book may be described in a single word: 'defamiliarization'. The hope is to achieve what the Russian critic Viktor Shklovsky described as *ostranenie*, a kind of distanciation which makes what was familiar appear strange and what was natural seem arbitrary.[5] The point is to make us (writer and readers alike) more conscious of the 'knowledge system' in which we live, by describing and analysing changing systems in the past. When one inhabits a system, it generally looks like 'common sense'. Only by comparison can one see it as one system among others.[6] As the Polish scientist Ludwik Fleck once put it, 'Whatever is known has always seemed systematic, proven, applicable and evident to the knower. Every alien system of knowledge has likewise seemed contradictory, unproven, inapplicable, fanciful or mystical.'[7]

The suggestion that what individuals believe to be truth or knowledge is influenced, if not determined, by their social milieu is not a new one. In the early modern period – to mention only three famous examples – Francis Bacon's image of the 'idols' of the tribe, cave, market-place and theatre, Giambattista Vico's remarks on the 'conceit of nations' (in other words, ethnocentrism) and Charles de Montesquieu's study of the relation between the laws of different countries and their climates and political systems all expressed this fundamental insight in different ways which will be discussed in more detail below (210).[8] All the same, the shift from insight to organized and systematic study is often a difficult one which may take centuries to accomplish. This was certainly the case for what is now described as the 'sociology of knowledge'.

---

[5] Bourdieu (1984); cf. Ginzburg (1996, 1997).
[6] Geertz (1975); cf. Veblen (1918).
[7] Fleck (1935), 22; cf. Baldamus (1977).
[8] Mannheim (1936); Stark (1960).

THE RISE OF THE SOCIOLOGY OF KNOWLEDGE

As an organized enterprise, the sociology of knowledge goes back to the early twentieth century.[9] More exactly, at least three similar enterprises were begun in three different countries: France, Germany and the USA. Why there should have been a special concern with the relation between knowledge and society in these three countries in particular is itself an interesting problem in the sociology of sociology.

In France, where Auguste Comte had already advocated a social history of knowledge, a 'history without names', Emile Durkheim and his followers, notably Marcel Mauss, studied the social origin of fundamental categories or 'collective representations', such as space and time, the sacred and the profane, the category of the person, and so on, in other words attitudes which are so fundamental that people do not know they hold them.[10] What was new here was the systematic examination of 'primitive' categories on which travellers and philosophers had sometimes commented in earlier centuries, as well as the general conclusion that social categories are projected onto the natural world, so that the classification of things reproduces the classification of people.[11]

Out of this Durkheimian concern with collective representations came a number of important studies, including several on ancient Greece as well as a book about the fundamental categories of Chinese thought by the French Sinologist Marcel Granet.[12] In similar fashion the historians Marc Bloch and Lucien Febvre produced famous analyses of 'collective mentalities' or shared assumptions. Bloch adopted this approach in his study of the belief in the healing powers of the kings of France and England, Febvre in his examination of the so-called 'problem of unbelief' in the sixteenth century, arguing that atheism was unthinkable at this time.[13]

In the United States, Thorstein Veblen, best known for his theories of conspicuous consumption and the 'leisure class', was also interested in the sociology of knowledge. As befitted a former student of Charles Peirce and a colleague of John Dewey, two pragmatist philosophers who had been criticizing assumptions of 'correspondence' between reality and what we say about it, Veblen was interested in the sociology of truth. He was especially concerned with the relation

---

[9] Merton (1941).
[10] Durkheim and Mauss (1901–2).
[11] Worsley (1956); Lukes (1973); Lamo de Espinosa, González Garcia and Torres Albero (1994), 205–26.
[12] Granet (1934); cf. Mills (1940).
[13] Burke (1990), 17–19, 27–30.

to knowledge of specific social groups and institutions. In this area he made three important contributions.

The first of these contributions, published in 1906, considered the place of science in modern civilization, and argued that the modern 'cult of science', as he called it, including the penchant for impersonal explanations instead of anthropomorphic ones, was a consequence of the rise of industry and machine technology. In a study of the American academic establishment, Veblen went on to shine his sociological torch on the dark places in the university system, comparing academics to other 'keepers' of 'esoteric knowledge' such as 'priests, shamans, medicinemen', and noting that within the group this esoteric knowledge is regarded as universal truth, 'although it is evident to any outsider that it will take its character and its scope and method from the habits of life of the group'.

Finally, in an essay on 'the intellectual pre-eminence of Jews in modern Europe' (1919), Veblen suggested that this pre-eminence or creativity was greatest in the nineteenth century, at just the time when many Jews were becoming assimilated to Christian culture. His point was that this assimilation was still incomplete, that many Jewish intellectuals were rejecting their own cultural heritage without completely taking over that of the Gentiles. Their position on the border of two cultural worlds made them sceptics 'by force of circumstances' (below, 32), since the idols of their own tribe had 'crumbled', while they had no particular incentive to accept the idols of the Gentiles. Their detachment from the ideas taken for granted in the culture around them encouraged these intellectuals of Jewish extraction to become intellectual innovators.

In this last case, Veblen's insight doubtless stemmed from his own marginal position, in part deliberately chosen but in part the result of his being the son of Norwegian peasant immigrants, an ethnic and social background unusual among the American intellectuals of his day.[14] Typically, the outsider Veblen left no school in the strict sense, though he did inspire successors, as we shall see (below, 9).[15]

In Germany at this time, there was more interest in the sociology of ideas, sometimes following and sometimes diverging from the ideas of Karl Marx. Max Weber's study of what he called the 'Protestant Ethic', for example (first published in 1904), placed this value-system in social context as well as putting forward a theory about its economic consequences. His theory of bureaucracy (below, 118) was also

---

[14] Veblen (1906, 1918, 1919); cf. Lamo de Espinosa, González Garcia and Torres Albero (1994), 380–6.
[15] Veblen (1918) 1–2.

a contribution to the sociology of knowledge, even if it was not presented as such. Other sociologists in Germany, notably Max Scheler and Karl Mannheim (who began his career in Hungary and finished it in England), were arguing at about the same time as Weber that ideas are socially 'situated' and shaped by world-views or 'styles of thought'. These styles of thought were associated with periods, with nations and (for Mannheim, though not for Scheler), with generations and with social classes.

For example, Mannheim contrasted two European styles of thought which developed in the eighteenth and nineteenth centuries. On one side the French style, liberal and universalist, judging society from the standpoint of an unchanging reason. On the other the German style, conservative and 'historicist', in the sense of experiencing the world as change and using history rather than reason or religion to give meaning to experience. Mannheim's point was not to praise or condemn either style but simply to note that the social interests of a given group make the members of that group sensitive to certain aspects of social life. On this basis they develop a particular 'ideology'.[16]

All the same, according to Mannheim, intellectuals are a 'relatively classless stratum'. They were a 'free-floating intelligentsia' (freischwebende Intelligenz), a phrase Mannheim borrowed from Alfred Weber, brother of the more famous Max but an important sociologist in his own right. The fact that they are relatively detached from society – the qualification 'relatively' is sometimes forgotten by Mannheim's critics – allows intellectuals to see social trends more clearly than other people can.[17]

It was the German group who christened their enterprise 'sociology of knowledge' (Soziologie des Erkennens, Wissensoziologie), a description with an odd ring to it and one which was doubtless intended to shock the public. It is relatively easy to accept the idea of a history or a sociology of ignorance, even though there are still relatively few studies in this area.[18] A social analysis of the obstacles in the way of our discovering the truth, in the style of Francis Bacon, is not difficult to accept either. What is more disturbing is the idea of a sociology of knowledge, since knowing is what philosophers call a 'success verb': what we know, as opposed to what we believe, is true by definition. The idea of a social explanation of the truth, of the kind put forward by Karl Marx and Friedrich Nietzsche, still has the power to shock, as the case of Michel Foucault's discussion of

---

[16] Mannheim (1927).
[17] Mannheim (1925); cf. Scheler (1926).
[18] Moore and Tumin (1949); Scott (1991).

'regimes of truth' in the 1980s demonstrated. In the 1990s, to entitle a book on seventeenth-century science 'the social history of truth' was still a deliberate provocation.[19]

THE REVIVAL OF THE SOCIOLOGY OF KNOWLEDGE

After these remarkable beginnings, the study of knowledge virtually dried up or at any rate became less productive than other fields of sociology in all the three countries discussed above. The one outstanding figure between the 1930s and the 1960s was the American Robert Merton, and his work on the relation between Puritanism and science, despite its greater concern with institutions such as the Royal Society, was essentially a development of the ideas of Max Weber on Puritanism and capitalism.[20] The Polish sociologist Florian Znaniecki, who migrated to the USA, followed in the footsteps of Veblen and published a study of *Social Role of the Man of Knowledge* (1940), but then turned to other things. In Paris, the Russian *émigré* Georges Gurvitch seemed poised to revive the subject in the early 1960s, but he died before he could do more than outline his programme.[21] *The Social Construction of Reality* (1966), a collaborative work by an American and an Austrian scholar, Peter Berger and Thomas Luckmann, was well received and may have been influential, but the authors did not follow it up with substantive studies in the broad approach to the sociology of knowledge which they advocated. The main stimulus for renewal came from outside sociology, notably from Claude Lévi-Strauss in anthropology, from Thomas Kuhn in the history of science and from Michel Foucault in philosophy.

Lévi-Strauss revived interest in classification in his studies of totemism and more generally of what he called 'wild thought' (*la pensée sauvage*), defined as concrete rather than abstract. Where westerners distinguish 'nature' and 'culture', for example, Amerindian myths, according to Lévi-Strauss, are built around the opposition between the 'raw' and the 'cooked'.[22] Foucault, who was trained in the history of medicine as well as in philosophy, gradually widened his interests. He invented a whole vocabulary – 'archaeology', 'genealogy', 'regime', and so on – for discussing the relation between knowledge and power at different levels, from the microlevel of the family to the macrolevel of the state, as well as analysing the various spaces

---

[19] Foucault (1980), 112; Shapin (1994).
[20] Merton (1938, 1941, 1945, 1957, 1968); Luhmann (1990).
[21] Berger and Luckmann (1966); Gurvitch (1966).
[22] Lévi-Strauss (1962, 1964).

or 'sites' of knowledge – clinics, schools and so on.[23] As for Kuhn, he shocked or stimulated his colleagues by his claim that scientific revolutions recur in history and that they have a similar 'structure' or cycle of development, originating in dissatisfaction with an ortho- dox theory or 'paradigm' and ending by the invention of a new para- digm which comes to be viewed as 'normal science' until another generation of researchers in its turn becomes dissatisfied with this conventional wisdom.[24]

The subject of knowledge has engaged the atttention of some of the leading social and cultural theorists of the last generation. Towards the end of his career, Norbert Elias, a former assistant of Mannheim's, studied the process of intellectual detachment as well as putting forward what he called 'a theory of scientific establishments'.[25] Jürgen Habermas has discussed the relation between knowledge, human interests and the public sphere.[26] Pierre Bourdieu has put knowledge back on the map of sociology in a series of studies about 'theoretical practice', 'cultural capital', and the power of institutions such as universities to define what counts as legitimate knowledge and what does not.[27]

Bourdieu was trained as an anthropologist, and other anthropo- logists have made important contributions to this field. Clifford Geertz, for instance, has devoted several of his essays to problems of local knowledge, information, and common sense, placing them under the microscope in the sense of examining them in the context of the face- to-face communities which he studied in the field.[28] Jack Goody has examined alternative paths to knowledge in oral and literate cultures, while his colleague the late Ernest Gellner analysed the changing rela- tions between the economic, political and intellectual spheres, which he described as systems of production, coercion and cognition.[29] It would be easy to add other names to this list, and other disciplines as well, from geography to economics.[30]

As is commonly the case with revivals, the participants in the 'new sociology of knowledge', as it has been called, sometimes exaggerate their distance from their predecessors.[31] Foucault, Bourdieu and Lévi- Strauss all owe a considerable debt to Durkheim and his concern with

[23] Foucault (1966, 1980).
[24] Kuhn (1962).
[25] Elias (1982); cf. Wilterdink (1977).
[26] Habermas (1962).
[27] Bourdieu (1972, 1984, 1989).
[28] Geertz (1975, 1979, 1983).
[29] Goody (1978); Gellner (1988).
[30] Pred (1973); Thrift (1985); Machlup (1962, 1980–4); Schiller (1986, 1996).
[31] Law (1986); Woolgar (1988).

categories and classification, even though, like most creative thinkers, they work within more than one tradition and distance themselves from their masters. The debate on the relation between knowledge and interests rumbles on.[32] The 'microscopic' approach, however new it may seem, was already preached by Karl Mannheim and practised by Ludwik Fleck before the Second World War.[33] As for the power to define what kind of knowledge is legitimate, emphasized in the work of Bourdieu, its importance was already obvious to the Victorian satirist who put into the mouth of Benjamin Jowett (below, 18), the claim that 'What I don't know isn't knowledge.'

In spite of these qualifications, the second wave of the sociology of knowledge still looks differerent from the first wave in its emphases, four in particular. In the first place, the stress has shifted from the acquisition and transmission of knowledge to its 'construction', 'production', or even 'manufacture', a shift which forms part of a general post-structuralist or postmodern turn in sociology and other disciplines.[34] There is less stress on social structure and more stress on individuals, on language, and on practices such as classification and experiment. There is less stress on the economics and more on the politics of knowledge and the 'knowledge-holders'.[35]

In the second place, these knowledge-holders are viewed as a larger and a more varied group than used to be the case. Practical, local or 'everyday' knowledge, as well as the activities of intellectuals, is now taken seriously by sociologists, notably those of the so-called 'ethnomethodological' school.[36]

A third way in which the new sociology of knowledge differs from the old one is in its greater concern with microsociology, with the everyday intellectual life of small groups, circles, networks or 'epistemological communities', viewed as the fundamental units which construct knowledge and direct its diffusion through certain channels.[37] Following the lead of Foucault, these epistemological communities are often studied through the micro-spaces in which they work, from laboratories to libraries.[38] In these ways the new approach is close to anthropology, and the phrase 'the anthropology of knowledge' has come into regular use.[39]

---

[32] Barnes (1977); Woolgar (1988).
[33] Mannheim (1936), 46n; Fleck (1935); cf. Baldamus (1977).
[34] Mendelsohn (1977); Knorr-Cetina (1981).
[35] Pels (1996, 1997).
[36] Berger and Luckmann (1966); Bourdieu (1972); Turner (1974).
[37] Crane (1972); Latour (1986); Brown (1989); Potter (1993); Alexandrov (1995).
[38] Foucault (1961); Shapin (1988); Ophir and Shapin (1991).
[39] Elkanah (1981); Crick (1982).

In the fourth place, when the German school of sociologists asserted that knowledge was socially situated, they were thinking above
all of social class (though Mannheim, at least, also took generations
into account).[40] In the current phase, on the other hand, more attention is being paid to gender and to geography.

In the case of gender, there has been a series of studies of the
'obstacle race' faced by women scholars, whether their ambition
was to be humanists or scientists, although there remains a need for
a comparative study of the extent to which women were excluded
from intellectual life in different places, moments and disciplines.[41] On
the positive side, feminists have claimed that gender helps constitute
experience, so that there are specific 'women's ways of knowing'.[42]

Geographers have become interested in the spatial distribution of
knowledge, and, no less important, its failure to be distributed, its
restriction to certain groups in certain places.[43] Curiously enough,
the most famous contribution to the geography of knowledge has
been made by a literary critic. In a study which has provoked considerable debate, Edward Said, following the lead of Foucault, has
analysed 'orientalism', in other words western knowledge of the
Middle East, as an institution in the service of imperialism.[44]

Although the author is a cultural and socal historian, this book
will draw on many of these approaches in order to try to correct the
specialization and consequent fragmentation so characteristic of our
own world of knowledge.

THE SOCIAL HISTORY OF KNOWLEDGE

So far, relatively few historians have taken the sociology of knowledge seriously. One of the exceptions was James Harvey Robinson,
a leader of the American 'new history' movement at the beginning of
the twentieth century. Robinson was a friend of Thorstein Veblen's.
His encouragement of a doctoral dissertation by Martha Ornstein on
the role of scientific societies in the seventeenth century (below, 39)
was a result of his asking himself 'what part the ancient and honorable
centers of learning – the universities – had had in the advancement of
knowledge. There may have been a trace of malice aforethought in

---

[40] Mannheim (1952); Fleck (1935).
[41] King (1976); Jardine (1983, 1985); Schiebinger (1989); Phillips (1990); Shteir
(1996).
[42] Belenky et al. (1986); Haraway (1988); Durán (1991); Alcoff and Potter (1993).
[43] Pred (1973); Thrift (1985).
[44] Said (1978).

the query – some foresight of that long withheld work on *The Higher Learning* by his friend Veblen' (the book had been written around 1908 but it was only published ten years later).[45]

However, Robinson had no more followers in this direction. Between the 1920s and the 1950s, a few Marxist scholars, from the Russian Boris Hessen to the Englishman Joseph Needham, attempted to write social histories of scientific research, but they were more or less shunned by mainstream historians of science. Only from the 1960s onwards did it become normal to examine science from a social point of view. Much less has been written on the social sciences, and still less on the humanities, from this perspective, and what has been written concentrates on the nineteenth and twentieth centuries rather than the early modern period.[46]

A consciousness of this lacuna in the scholarly literature was one reason for my choice of this topic. It is an essay, or series of essays, on a subject so large that any survey which did not take a consciously provisional form would be not only immodest to attempt but impossible to carry out. I must confess to a predilection for short studies of large subjects, which attempt to make connections between different places, topics, periods or individuals, to assemble small fragments into a big picture. However, the need for such a book is particularly obvious in an area which is not normally viewed as a field at all but rather as a collection of disciplines or subdisciplines such as bibliography, the history of science, the history of reading, intellectual history, the history of cartography and the history of historiography (my original topic of research).

Anyone who argues that knowledge is socially situated is surely obliged to situate him- or herself. Some of my biases, the result of class, gender, nation and generation, will doubtless become apparent soon enough. Here I shall simply confess that the title of this book was chosen in homage to Mannheim, whose work aroused my interest in the subject forty years ago, even if I have gradually distanced myself from his approach. The book attempts a social history informed by theory, the 'classical' theories of Emile Durkheim and Max Weber no less than the more recent formulations of Foucault and Bourdieu. Chapters 2 and 3 offer a kind of retrospective sociology of knowledge, chapter 4 offers a geography of knowledge, chapter 5 an anthropology. The sixth chapter discusses the politics of knowledge, the seventh its economics, the eighth adopts a more literary approach, and the coda raises some philosophical questions.

---

[45] Ornstein (1913), ix–x; cf. Lux (1991a, 1991b).
[46] Ringer (1990, 1992).

Despite this trespassing into other disciplines, it will be clear enough to readers of this study that it is the work of a historian, essentially a historian of early modern Europe. The chronological limits of this book are the Renaissance and the Enlightenment. Both spatial and temporal boundaries will be transgressed from time to time in order to make comparisons and contrasts, but the book remains a history of knowledge in 'early modern' Europe.

The early modern period will be defined here as the centuries from Gutenberg to Diderot, in other words from the invention of printing with movable type in Germany around the year 1450 to the publication of the *Encyclopédie* from the 1750s onwards. The *Encyclopédie* was a summa of the information available in its time, as well as a vivid illustration of both the politics and the economics of knowledge. As for the links between knowledge and print, they will be discussed more than once in the following pages. Here it may suffice to say that the importance of the new medium was not limited to spreading knowledge more widely and taking relatively private or even secret knowledges (from technical secrets to secrets of state) into the public domain. Print also facilitated the interaction between different knowledges, a recurrent theme in this study. It standardized knowledge by allowing people in different places to read identical texts or examine identical images. It also encouraged scepticism, as chapter 9 will suggest, by allowing the same person to compare and contrast rival and incompatible accounts of the same phenomenon or event.[47]

WHAT IS KNOWLEDGE?

The question, What is knowledge? is almost as difficult to answer as the even more famous question, What is truth? Mannheim has often been criticized for describing categories, values and observations as socially determined without making distinctions between them. We also need to distinguish knowledge from information, 'knowing how' from 'knowing that', and what is explicit from what is taken for granted. For convenience this book will use the term 'information' to refer to what is relatively 'raw', specific and practical, while 'knowledge' denotes what has been 'cooked', processed or systematized by thought. Needless to say, the distinction is only a relative one, since our brains process everything we perceive, but the importance of the elaboration and classification of knowledge is a theme which will recur below (especially in chapter 5).

---

[47] Eisenstein (1979); Giesecke (1991); Eamon (1994).

What will be discussed in the pages which follow is what early modern people – rather than the present author or his readers – considered to be knowledge. Knowledge of magic, witchcraft, angels and demons is therefore included. Early modern conceptions of knowledge are obviously central to the social history of knowledge and they will be discussed in more detail below. At this point it may be sufficient to note the awareness of different kinds of knowledge enshrined in the distinction between *ars* and *scientia*, for example (closer to 'practice' and 'theory' than to our 'art' and 'science'), or in the use of terms such as 'learning', 'philosophy', 'curiosity' and their equivalents in different European languages. Enthusiasts for new kinds of knowledge, which they described on occasion as 'real knowledge', sometimes dismissed traditional knowledge as empty 'jargon' or useless 'pedantry'. A history of concepts, *Begriffsgeschichte* as it is called in German, is an indispensable part of this enterprise. This history is concerned not only with the rise of new words as an indicator of new interests and attitudes, but also with changes in the meaning of older terms, replacing them in their linguistic fields, examining the social contexts in which they were used and recovering their original associations.[48]

A traditional assumption which I shall try to avoid in what follows is that of intellectual progress, or as it is sometimes called, 'cognitive growth'. Such a concept may be useful insofar as it refers to a whole society, to what different people – the contributors to an encyclopaedia, for instance – know between them. It would be difficult to deny a cumulative element in the history of knowledge in early modern Europe. Reference books multiplied, libraries and encyclopaedias expanded, and more resources were available in each successive century to someone seeking knowledge on a particular topic (chapter 8).

Wisdom, on the other hand, is not cumulative but has to be learned more or less painfully by each individual. Even in the case of knowledge, there was and still is regress as well as progress at the individual level. Increasing specialization in schools and universities over the last century or so in particular has produced students with a much more limited knowledge than before (whether or not decreasing breadth has been compensated by increasing depth). Today, alternative knowledges compete for our attention and each choice has its price. When encyclopaedias are updated, information drops out of them to make room for other things, so that for some purposes it is better to consult the eleventh edition of the *Encyclopaedia Britannica*

---

[48] Koselleck (1972); Kenny (1998).

(1910–11) rather than the current one. In early modern Europe, a 'knowledge explosion' followed the invention of printing, the great discoveries, the so-called 'Scientific Revolution' and so on. However, this accumulation of knowledge created problems as well as solving problems, another theme which will recur in the pages which follow.

Needless to say, my own knowledge of knowledge is incomplete and it will be necessary to limit this enterprise not only chronologically and geographically but socially as well. The book originated as a series of lectures and it is intended as a reconnaissance of a vast intellectual terrain, an essay rather than an encyclopaedia. The virtual restriction of this book to dominant forms of knowledge deserves a little more in the way of explanation.

THE PLURALITY OF KNOWLEDGES

This book is based for the most part on texts which were published in the sixteenth, seventeenth and eighteenth centuries. It will attempt to avoid graphocentrism, by discussing oral knowledge, and even logocentrism, by treating images (including maps) as ways of communicating knowledge and by including illustrations. Material objects, from shells to coins and from stuffed alligators to statues, will also be mentioned from time to time, since they were collected with enthusiasm in this period, classified, and displayed in cabinets or museums.[49] Non-verbal practices – building, cooking, weaving, healing, hunting, cultivating the soil and so on – will also be included in the definition of knowledge. Yet a large question remains. Whose knowledge is the subject of this study?

In early modern Europe, elites often identified knowledge with their knowledge, and they sometimes argued, like Cardinal Richelieu in his *Political Testament*, that knowledge should not be communicated to the people, lest they become discontented with their station in life. The Spanish humanist Luis Vives was relatively unusual in his admission that 'peasants and artisans know nature better than so many philosophers' (*melius agricolae et fabri norunt quam ipsi tanti philosophi*).[50]

Today, following what might be called the 'rehabilitation' of local knowledge and everyday knowledge, it should be obvious that there are 'knowledges' in the plural in every culture and that social history,

---

[49] Lugli (1983); Impey and Macgregor (1985); Pomian (1987); Findlen (1989, 1994).
[50] Rossi (1962), 15; cf. Roche (1981), part 3; Böhme (1984); Worsley (1997).

like sociology, must be concerned 'with everything that passes for knowledge in society'.[51] One way of distinguishing between knowledges is according to their functions or uses. The sociologist Georges Gurvitch, for example, distinguished seven types of knowledge: perceptual, social, everyday, technical, political, scientific and philosophical.[52]

Another approach, closer to social history, might distinguish between the knowledges produced and transmitted by different social groups. Intellectuals are masters of some kinds of knowledge, but other fields of expertise or 'know-how' are cultivated by such groups as bureaucrats, artisans, peasants, midwives and popular healers. These fields of implicit knowledge have recently attracted some attention from historians, especially in the context of imperialism and the contribution made by indigenous inhabitants to the knowledges which European rulers, cartographers and physicians were claiming as their own.[53]

Most studies of knowledge deal with the knowledge of elites, while studies of popular culture (including my own, dating from 1978) have relatively little to say about its cognitive element, popular or everyday knowledge.[54] In this book too the emphasis, following the sources, will fall on dominant or even 'academic' forms of knowledge, on 'learning' as it was often called in the early modern period. All the same, a serious attempt will be made to place academic knowledge in a wider framework. The competition, conflict and exchange between the intellectual systems of academic elites and what might be called 'alternative knowledges' will be a recurrent theme in this study.[55] The conflicts are particularly clear in the case of medicine, as practised by the 'cunning folk', itinerant healers, Moriscos or women.[56] For a concrete example one might turn to the *Observations diverses* published in 1609 by the Parisian midwife Louise Bourgeois, who described herself as 'the first woman of my trade who has taken pen in hand to describe the knowledge that God has given me'.

If I wanted to cause a sensation, I would claim at this point that the so-called intellectual revolutions of early modern Europe – the Renaissance, the Scientific Revolution and the Enlightenment – were no more than the surfacing into visibility (and more especially into print), of certain kinds of popular or practical knowledge and

[51] Berger and Luckmann (1966), 26.
[52] Gurvitch (1966).
[53] Figueiredo (1984); Bayly (1996); Grove (1996); Mundy (1996); Edney (1997), 68, 76, 81, 98, 125.
[54] Roche (1981).
[55] Potter (1993).
[56] Ballester (1977, 1993); Huisman (1989).

their legitimation by some academic establishments. Such a claim, however exaggerated, would be no more one-sided than the more conventional assumption identifying knowledge with the learning of scholars. The knowledge gathered by Europeans in other continents, for example, was not always the result of the direct observation of nature and society, but depended on local informants (below, chapter 4).

For an example of interactions between scholars and craftsmen one might turn to Renaissance Italy. In early fifteenth-century Florence, for example, the humanist Leonbattista Alberti had frequent conversations with the sculptor Donatello and the engineer Filippo Brunelleschi. Without the help of such experts it would have been difficult for him to write his treatises on painting and architecture. Specialists in the architecture of the Renaissance have discussed the interaction between the craft traditions of master masons and the humanist knowledge of the patrons, who sometimes commissioned their houses with copies of Vitruvius in their hands. Indeed, it is hard to imagine how the text of this ancient Roman treatise on architecture could have been edited and illustrated, as it was in Renaissance Italy, without collaboration of some kind between experts on classical Latin and experts on building. When the text was edited and translated by a Venetian patrician, Daniele Barbaro, in 1556, it was with the help of the architect Palladio, who had been trained as a mason.[57]

In a number of fields, practical men or women as well as scholars had something to contribute to printed knowledge.[58] The humanist Georg Agricola's book on mining (1556) obviously owed a good deal to the oral knowledge of the miners of Joachimsthal, where he made his living as a physician. Montaigne went so far as to argue in his famous essay on cannibals that a simple man, *homme simple et grossier*, might offer a more reliable testimony of his experiences in the New World than *les fines gens*, with their biases and prejudices.

Turning to the humanities, the rise of the discipline of economics (discussed below, 101) was not an invention out of nothing. It involved not only the elaboration of new theories but also the conferring of academic respectability on the practical knowledge of merchants, an originally oral knowledge which came to circulate more and more widely in print in the sixteenth and seventeenth centuries, in treatises such as Sir Josiah Child's *Discourse of Trade* (1665), written by a

---

[57] Burke (1998c), 34, 175.
[58] Zilsel (1941); Panofsky (1953); Hall (1962); Rossi (1962); Eisenstein (1979).

London merchant who was to become the chairman of the East India Company.

There were similar exchanges between political theory and political practice, even if crossing the boundaries exacted a price. Machiavelli caused an uproar by stating in explicit and theoretical form some rules which men of affairs had sometimes discussed in meetings and rulers had often followed in practice. *The Prince*, a confidential document which Machiavelli had presented to a member of the Medici family in the hope of furthering his career, was published in 1532, a few years after the author's death.[59] Francis Bacon was making a perceptive general point in his *Advancement of Learning* (1605), though he was a little unfair to his predecessor Machiavelli, when he claimed that 'The wisdom touching negotiation or business hath not been hitherto collected into writing.'

Again, the knowledge of painting and its techniques, which came to be known as 'connoisseurship', was an orally transmitted knowledge which began to appear in print in the sixteenth century, notably in Giorgio Vasari's *Lives* of artists, first published in 1550. A reminder of the interactions between theory and practice in this period is preserved in the vocabulary of philosophy. 'Empiricism' is derived from 'empiric', a traditional English term for practitioners of alternative medicine, men and women innocent of theory. In his *Advancement of Learning*, Francis Bacon condemned 'empiric physicians' who knew neither the true causes of an illness nor the true method of curing it, but he was an equally severe critic of scholastic philosophers who deduced their conclusions without paying attention to the everyday world. 'The true way, as yet untried', according to Bacon's *New Organon* (1620), was to follow neither the empiric ant, mindlessly collecting data, nor the scholastic spider, spinning a web from inside itself, but the bee, who both collects and digests. The point was to begin 'from the senses and particulars' and then to rise by stages to general conclusions (Aphorisms xix, xcv). This middle way, discussed in chapter 9 below, is what we now call 'empiricism' and the French *empirisme*, a term coined in 1736 and discussed in the article on the subject in that Baconian enterprise the *Encyclopédie*.

There is a link between Bacon's empiricist epistemology and his belief – shared with Luis Vives, who tried to reform the system of knowledge a century earlier – that even the learned might have something to learn from ordinary people. The Royal Society of London carried on the Baconian tradition and published accounts of the specialized knowledges or secrets of different trades and crafts. The point

---

[59] Albertini (1955); Gilbert (1965).

was, as the polymath Gottfried Leibniz put it, in a characteristic mixture of German and Latin, 'to join theorists and empirics in a happy marriage' (*Theoricos Empiricis felici connubio zu conjungiren*).

Denis Diderot was another admirer of Bacon in this respect. His concern with the knowledge of artisans as well as *philosophes* is apparent in the *Encyclopédie*, in the article on 'Art' for instance, in which the distinction between the liberal and mechanical arts (below, chapter 5), is described as an unfortunate one because it lowers the status of estimable and useful people. Like the Royal Society, Diderot and his collaborators made craft knowledges public in the *Encyclo-pédie*, a book which was apparently of use in some practical situations. For example, the article on cannon-founding ('Alésoir') was used by a military adviser to the Ottoman sultan, when manufacturing artillery in the 1770s.[60]

Within the context of exchanges of this kind, this study will concentrate on dominant forms of knowledge, particularly the know-ledge possessed by European intellectuals. But who were the intellectuals in early modern Europe? This problem will be discussed in the following chapter.

---

[60] Proust (1962), 177–232; Wilson (1972), 136.

2

Professing Knowledge:
The European Clerisy

> Learning . . . a calling . . . endowing us with light to
> see farther than other men.
>
> Barrow

> First come I; my name is Jowett.
> There's no knowledge but I know it.
> I am Master of this college.
> What I don't know isn't knowledge.
>
> H. C. Beeching

THIS chapter is concerned with the main discoverers, producers and disseminators of knowledge in early modern Europe. These discoverers, producers and disseminators are often known as 'intellectuals'. Karl Mannheim described them as the social groups in every society 'whose special task it is to provide an interpretation of the world for that society'. In a famous phrase, already quoted (5), he called them the 'free-floating intelligentsia', an 'unanchored, relatively classless stratum'.[1]

CONTINUITIES AND DISCONTINUITIES

It is often claimed that the intellectual emerged only in mid-nineteenth-century Russia, when the word 'intelligentsia' was coined to refer to the men of letters who were unwilling or unable to find posts in the bureaucracy. Alternatively, the emergence of the group is dated to the end of the nineteenth century, in the course of the French debate over the guilt or innocence of Captain Dreyfus, with the *Manifeste des intellectuels* in the captain's favour.[2] Other historians, notably Jacques Le Goff, speak about intellectuals in the Middle

---

[1] Mannheim (1936), 137–8.
[2] Pipes (1960); Charle (1990).

Ages, at least in the context of universities.[3] These disagreements are partly over definitions but they also reveal a major difference of opinion over the relative importance of change and continuity in European cultural history.

A common view of modern intellectuals is that they are the descendants of the radical intelligentsia of the nineteenth century, who are the descendants of the *philosophes* of the Enlightenment, who are either a secular version of the Protestant clergy, or the descendants of the humanists of the Renaissance. Such a view is too 'present-minded', in the sense of scanning the past only for people more or less like ourselves. Michel Foucault was not the first person to see present-mindedness and continuity as problematic, but he remains the most radical critic of these common assumptions.

A Foucauldian history of intellectuals might discuss the discontinuity between the nineteenth-century *intelligentsia*, who wanted to overthrow their old regime, and the eighteenth-century *philosophes*, who wanted to reform theirs. Again, it might note the gap between the anticlerical *philosophes* and the English puritan clergy of the seventeenth century, who have been described as the first example in history of 'radical intellectuals' in a traditional society, 'freed from feudal connections'.[4] However, in the eyes of these puritans, their true or general vocation or 'calling' was neither learning nor political activity, which were simply different means to a higher end, religion. Their ideal was that of the 'saint', and this aim led some of them to express anti-intellectual attitudes.[5] Another discontinuity separates the Protestant clergy from their predecessors the Renaissance humanists, and yet another divides the humanists from the scholastic philosophers they so often denounced, Le Goff's medieval intellectuals.

To avoid confusion, it might be a good idea to follow the lead of Samuel Coleridge and Ernest Gellner and to describe the specialists in knowledge as a 'clerisy'.[6] The term will be employed below from time to time to describe social groups whose members variously thought of themselves as 'men of learning' (*docti, eruditi, savants, Gelehrten*), or 'men of letters' (*literati, hommes de lettres*). In this context *lettres* meant learning rather than literature (hence the need for the adjective in *belles-lettres*).

From the fifteenth century to the eighteenth, scholars regularly referred to themselves as citizens of the 'Republic of Letters' (*Respublica*

---

[3] Le Goff (1957).
[4] Walzer (1965).
[5] Solt (1956).
[6] Gellner (1988), 70–1, 79.

litteraria), a phrase which expressed their sense of belonging to a community which transcended national frontiers. It was essentially an imagined community, but one which developed customs of its own such as the exchange of letters, books and visits, not to mention the ritualized ways in which younger scholars paid their respects to senior colleagues who might help launch their careers.[7]

The aim of this chapter is to discuss what a famous sociological essay of 1940 described as 'the social role of the man of knowledge'.[8] Today, that phrase irresistibly prompts a question about the women of knowledge at this time. They were more or less 'excluded' from the pursuit of learning, as the seventeenth-century French philosopher Poulain de la Barre pointed out in his treatise *The Equality of the Two Sexes* (1673).

It is true that women of letters or 'learned ladies' existed throughout the period, although the term 'bluestocking' was not coined until the late eighteenth century. Among the most famous of these were Christine de Pisan, the fifteenth-century author of *The City of Women*; Marie Le Jars de Gournay, who edited Montaigne's *Essays*, studied alchemy and wrote a treatise on the equality of men and women; the universal scholar Anne-Marie Schuurman, who lived in the Dutch Republic, attended lectures at the University of Utrecht and wrote a treatise on the aptitude of women for study; and Queen Kristina of Sweden, who summoned René Descartes, Hugo Grotius and other scholars to her court in Stockholm, and after her abdication founded the Academia Fisico-Matematica in Rome.

All the same, women were unable to participate in the republic of letters on the same terms as men. It was extremely rare for them to study at a university. They might learn Latin from relatives or from a private tutor, but if they attempted to enter the circle of the humanists, for example, they might be rebuffed, as in the case of the fifteenth-century Italian learned ladies Isotta Nogarola and Cassandra Fedele. Isotta entered a convent following the public ridicule of what men saw as her intellectual pretensions.[9]

Women were also involved in the Scientific Revolution and the Enlightenment. Margaret Cavendish, Duchess of Newcastle, attended meetings of the Royal Society and published her philosophical opinions. Voltaire wrote his *Essay on Manners* for the marquise du Châtelet in order to persuade her that history was as worthy of study as the natural philosophy she favoured. In these areas too the position

---

[7] Goldgar (1995); Bots and Waquet (1997); Burke (1999a).
[8] Znaniecki (1940).
[9] King (1976); Jardine (1983, 1985).

of women was a marginal one. Bernard de Fontenelle wrote his dialogues on the plurality of worlds for a female audience, and Francesco Algarotti published a treatise called *Newtonianism for Ladies*, on the somewhat patronizing assumption that intelligent women could understand the new science if it was explained to them in simple terms.[10]

THE MIDDLE AGES

The example of Héloïse, who was Abelard's pupil before she became his lover, reminds us that women of knowledge could already be found in the twelfth century. It was at that time that a European clerisy became visible in the world outside the monasteries for the first time since late antiquity. This development, like that of the universities, was a result of the increasing division of labour associated with the rise of towns.

The clerisy included a group of learned laymen, usually either physicians or lawyers. Law and medicine were the two secular learned professions, with their place within the medieval university as well as status in the world outside it.[11] They were corporate groups, sometimes organized in colleges (like the London College of Physicians, founded in 1518), concerned to maintain a monopoly of knowledge and practice against unofficial competitors.

However, in the Middle Ages the majority of university teachers and students were members of the clergy, often members of religious orders, above all the Dominicans, who included the most famous medieval teacher of all, Thomas Aquinas. Even academic investigators of nature such as Albert the Great and Roger Bacon were friars. The students often wandered from university to university, so they were an international group, conscious – as their Latin songs show – of their difference from the normal inhabitants of the city in which they happened to live. As for the teachers, they were mainly what we describe as 'scholastic' philosophers and theologians, although they did not use this term but referred to themselves as 'men of letters' (*viri litterati*), 'clerks' (*clerici*), 'masters' (*magistri*) or 'philosophers' (*philosophi*). Some of these men of letters, like the twelfth-century Englishman John of Salisbury, could also be found at courts.[12]

---

[10] Schiebinger (1989); Goodman (1994); Shteir (1996).
[11] Bouwsma (1973).
[12] Le Goff (1957); cf. Murray (1978), 227–33, 263–5, Brocchieri (1987), Verger (1997).

As for the word 'schoolmen' (*scholastici*), it was a term of contempt invented by the supporters of a new-style university curriculum, the 'humanities' (below, chapter 5). Teachers of this new curriculum were nicknamed the 'humanists' (*humanistae*) and the term spread, first in Italy and then through other parts of Europe. These humanists were a new form of clerisy. Some were in holy orders but many were laymen, teaching in schools or universities or as private tutors or depending on the largesse of patrons. For some of them at least, teaching was a fate rather than a vocation, and one Italian humanist wrote sadly to another in the later fifteenth century that 'I, who have until recently enjoyed the friendship of princes, have now, because of my evil star, opened a school.' The generally low rate of remuneration for teachers in schools and universities, apart from some stars, mainly in law faculties, makes his reaction all too easy to understand. Teaching offered a way of making a living from knowledge, but not a very good living.[13]

The emergence of the word 'humanist' suggests that in universities at least, teaching the humanities encouraged a sense of a common identity among the teachers. The societies or academies founded by these humanists (institutions which will be discussed in chapter 3 below), also suggest the emergence of a collective identity.[14]

THE CONSEQUENCES OF PRINTING

One major consequence of the invention of printing was to widen the career opportunities open to the clerisy. Some of them became scholar-printers, like Aldus Manutius in Venice.[15] Others worked for the press, correcting proofs for example, making indexes, translating or even writing new books on commission from printer-publishers. It became easier, although it was still difficult, to follow the career of a 'man of letters'. Erasmus, at least, was successful enough with his books to free himself from dependence on patrons. Indeed, Norbert Elias portrayed the humanists in general and Erasmus in particular in the manner of Mannheim as examples of the free-floating intellectual, their detachment linked to their opportunity of 'distancing themselves' from all the social groups in their world.[16]

In Venice in particular a group of writers with a humanist education managed to make a living from their pens in mid-sixteenth-century

---

[13] Kristeller (1955); Dionisotti (1967); Romano and Tenenti (1967); Burke (1986).
[14] Benzoni (1978), 159ff.
[15] Schottenloher (1935).
[16] Elias (1939), 1, 73.

Venice, writing so much and on such a variety of topics that they were known as *poligrafi* (below, chapter 7). Similar figures can be found in Paris, London and other cities in the later sixteenth century, producing among other publications chronologies, cosmographies, dictionaries and other guides to knowledge.

OPPORTUNITIES IN CHURCHES AND STATES

The groups mentioned so far did not exhaust the opportunities open to the learned in the sixteenth century. The Reformation added another. Martin Luther's idea of the priesthood of all believers had originally seemed to make the clergy superfluous. His even more radical colleague at the university of Wittenberg, Andreas Karlstadt, went so far as to suggest the abolition of academic degrees. However, Luther came in time to support the idea of a learned clergy who would preach the Gospel to the people, and Jean Calvin and other Protestant reformers followed him in this respect. On the Catholic side the foundation of seminaries from the mid-sixteenth century onwards showed a similar concern for the education of parish priests.[17] Some of the clergy educated in these institutions appear to have taken scholarship as their vocation, while continuing to serve their parishes, as in the case of the Lutheran pastor Paul Bolduan, a pioneer compiler of subject bibliographies. In this way the churches may be described as having funded scholarship unintentionally.

The rise in the number of students in the sixteenth and early seventeenth centuries was in part the result of the new function of the university as a training institution for the parish clergy, as well as of the increasing demand by governments for officials with degrees in law. By the middle of the seventeenth century, the supply of students was coming to exceed the demand for their services, and a substantial proportion of graduates were becoming frustrated in their aspirations. In Naples, students took part in the famous revolt against Spain in 1647–8. On one occasion, 300 armed students marched through the streets in protest against a rise in the expense of doctorates. In the case of England, it has even been suggested that these 'alienated intellectuals' were in part responsible for the English Revolution.[18]

Some university-trained men of letters found employment as secretaries to rulers, aristocrats or men of learning. A succession of leading Italian humanists, including Leonardo Bruni, Poggio Braccriolini and

---

[17] Burke (1988); Prosperi (1981).
[18] Curtis (1962); cf. Chartier (1982), Roche (1982).

Lorenzo Valla, were secretaries to the popes. The occupation was not a new one, but the number of treatises, especially Italian treatises explaining how to do the job, suggests that it increased in importance in this period, as paper-work increased for rulers and nobles alike (below, chapter 6).[19] In Sweden, the later sixteenth century has gone down in history as the age of the 'rule of the secretaries', men of low birth such as the clergyman's son Jöran Persson. Persson, who was more of an adviser than a clerk, was the right-hand man of King Erik XIV until his enemies the aristocrats had him put to death. In Spain, where the rule of secretaries was even more obvious at this time, the age of Philip II, the term *letrado* (derived from *litteratus*) came into use to describe the lawyers in royal service, men of letters as opposed to the men of arms who had traditionally surrounded the king. Their role was to give good counsel, a major political function of the clerisy in many cultures.[20]

Scholars too might take a secretary or amanuensis into their service. Erasmus, for example, employed Gilbert Cousin, himself a scholar, while the secretaries of Francis Bacon included the young Thomas Hobbes. Ambassadors too had their assistants, sometimes men of letters like Amelot de la Houssaie, secretary to the French ambassador to Venice, who used his position to acquire a knowledge of the hidden workings of the Venetian state, knowledge which he subsequently published (below, 147). By the seventeenth century, the function of secretary to a learned society had come into existence. Bernard de Fontenelle was secretary to the French Académie des Sciences, Henry Oldenburg to the Royal Society, Formey to the Berlin Academy and Per Wilhelm Warentin to the Swedish Academy. The post sometimes carried a salary, as it did in Oldenburg's case.

By the mid-seventeenth century, it was becoming increasingly possible, though still risky, for writers and scholars to support themselves from a mixture of patronage and publishing. An analysis of 559 French writers active between 1643 and 1665 suggests that, given the right strategies, it had become possible to make a career from literature – in a wide sense of that term, including dictionaries and works of history as well as the plays of Racine and the poems of Boileau.[21]

The break with tradition must not be exaggerated. Royal pensions remained an important source of income. For example, Louis XIV granted generous pensions not only to Boileau, Racine and other poets

---

[19] Nigro (1991).
[20] Stehr (1992).
[21] Viala (1985).

but to the astronomer Gian-Domenico Cassini and the philologist Charles Du Cange. Lawyers such as Nicholas de Peiresc and John Selden and physicians such as Theodor Zwinger and Ole Worm continued to make important contributions to scholarship in their spare time. The number of writers who were clerics or at least existed on the margin of the clergy remained significant. Indeed, they may still have been in a majority in the age of Louis XIV.[22] Until the end of our period, and even beyond, a substantial proportion of the learned works published were still being written by members of the clergy.

STRUCTURAL DIFFERENTIATION

By 1600 or thereabouts a process of social differentiation within the European clerisy had become apparent. Writers were one semi-independent group, their increasing self-consciousness marked, as in seventeenth-century France, by the increasing use of terms such as *auteur* and *écrivain*.[23] A small but influential group might be described in the language of our own day as 'information brokers', because they put scholars in different places in touch with one another, or as 'knowledge managers', because they tried to organize as well as to collect material. Some of their names will recur in these pages, among them Francis Bacon, Jean-Baptiste Colbert, Denis Diderot, Samuel Hartlib, Gottfried Wilhelm Leibniz, Marin Mersenne, Gabriel Naudé, Henry Oldenburg, Théophraste Renaudot.[24]

University professors were also becoming a distinct group, especially in the German-speaking world – in which there were more than forty universities by the later eighteenth century, not counting other institutions of higher education. They were often laymen, not infrequently the sons or sons-in-law of other professors. Their sense of a separate identity is revealed by an increasing concern with academic dress and titles as well as by the rise of galleries displaying portraits of professors at the University of Uppsala and elsewhere. Like Benjamin Jowett in nineteenth-century Oxford, Master of Balliol College from 1870 to 1893 (and the target of the verses printed in the epigraph to this chapter), the early modern professorate embodied intellectual authority.

Early modern scholars were coming to view their work as a vocation. In late seventeenth-century England, more than two centuries

---

[22] Viala (1985), 247.
[23] Viala (1985), 270–80; Vandermeersch (1996), 223–4, 246–8.
[24] Hall (1965); Rochot (1966); Solomon (1972); Webster (1975); Revel (1996).

before Max Weber's famous reflections on the topic, Isaac Barrow, Master of Trinity College Cambridge, discussed scholarship as a vocation or 'calling' in his treatise *Of Industry*, arguing that the 'business' of academics was 'to find truth' and to 'attain knowledge'. By 'knowledge', Barrow meant not information about 'obvious and vulgar matters' but 'sublime, abstruse, intricate and knotty subjects, remote from common observation and sense'. Members of specific learned professions sometimes regarded their work as a calling, including the German historian Johann Sleidan and the French historian Henri de La Popelinière.[25]

With this social differentiation in the world of learning came conflicts between the different groups. For example, there were increasingly forceful attacks, from the middle of the seventeenth century onwards, on what the English called 'priestcraft', in other words an attack on the authority of one group of men of knowledge on the grounds that they were deceiving ordinary people.[26] Such attacks would have been unnecessary if the clergy had not remained a powerful force in the world of learning, but they would have been impossible without the existence of a substantial body of lay scholars, committed to a new ideal, that of detachment, or as they said at the time 'impartiality', in the sense of a critical distance from parties in Church and state alike (only at the end of the eighteenth century did people begin to speak about knowledge as 'objective'). Lawyers and physicians also came under attack as secular versions of the clergy, defending their monopolies with the help of languages which were unintelligible to their clients.[27]

Again, the French emphasis on *lettres* and the vernacular, from the middle of the sixteenth century onwards, contrasted with the German interest in Latin culture and *Gelehrtheit*. The Germans thought the French superficial, the French thought the Germans pedantic. Noble amateurs, or *virtuosi* as they were called in Italy (and in England too in the later seventeenth century, whether they studied art, antiquities or the works of nature), sometimes looked down on professional teachers and writers. In a phrase reminiscent of Mannheim's (but written nearly 300 years earlier), the historian of the newly founded Royal Society, Thomas Sprat, argued the importance of the role of gentlemen in research in natural philosophy precisely because they were 'free and unconfined'. The descriptions of some French scholars as *curieux* gave the impression, and were doubtless designed

---

[25] Kelley (1971, 1980).
[26] Goldie (1987).
[27] Hill (1972); Webster (1975), 250–64.

to give the impression, that what drove them was disinterested intellectual curiosity.[28]

From 1700 or thereabouts it became possible to pursue an intellectual career not only as a teacher or writer but also as a salaried member of certain organizations dedicated to the accumulation of knowledge, notably the Academies of Science founded and funded in Paris, Berlin, Stockholm and St Petersburg, even if the limited funds available generally compelled the recipients to supplement their salaries with other forms of employment. Whether or not we call such men 'scientists' (a term which was only coined in the nineteenth century), the emergence of this group was surely a significant moment in the history of the European clerisy. Some members of the group chose their occupation in conscious preference to a traditional university career.[29]

Individuals of the stature of Gottfried Leibniz and Isaac Newton headed learned societies, combining these posts with other occupations. Leibniz, for example was active as a librarian, another career which was growing in importance in the early modern period. Scholar-librarians included Bartolommeo Platina at the Vatican in the fifteenth century, Hugo Blotius in sixteenth-century Vienna, Gabriel Naudé in seventeenth-century Rome and Paris, Daniel Morhof in seventeenth-century Kiel, Burkhard Struve in eighteenth-century Jena and the historian Ludovico Muratori in eighteenth-century Modena. Librarians of this period have been described as crucial 'mediators' in the Republic of Letters. Often scholars themselves, they brought information to the notice of their colleagues and were slower than most of these colleagues to abandon the ideal of universal knowledge.[30]

Another alternative to work in universities was to serve a ruler as a counsellor or as an official historian. Appointments of this kind were already made in the Middle Ages, but their numbers rose in time with the rise of more centralized states in the early modern period, and included such well-known scholars and writers as Jean Racine (historian to Louis XIV), John Dryden (to Charles II), Samuel Pufendorf (to the rulers of Prussia and Sweden), and even Voltaire (to Louis XV). To this group one might add a smaller number of men of letters who made a career out of advising governments on what we might call 'cultural affairs' or 'propaganda'. In Louis XIV's France, for example, the poet and critic Jean Chapelain, Charles Perrault (better know today as a writer of fairy tales) and others formed a 'little

[28] Houghton (1942); Kenny (1998).
[29] Hahn (1971, 1975); McClellan (1985), xxiv–xxv, 233–51.
[30] Clarke (1966); Rosa (1994).

academy' which considered how best to present the public image
of the monarch.[31] Some German scholars, such as Herman Conring
(below, 91) and Burkhard Struve doubled as university professors
and as counsellors to the local prince. Like Chinese officials, they
were given power on the basis of intellectual distinction. The rise of
the German mandarins had already begun.[32]

GROUP IDENTITIES

That the group identity of the clerisy was becoming stronger, despite
differentiation and conflicts, is suggested by the publication of books
on the man of letters, like the Italian Jesuit Daniele Bartoli's *The Man
of Letters* (1645, much reprinted and translated), or the marquis
d'Alembert's 'essay' on the same subject (1752). The *Encyclopédie*
carried an entry on 'Gens de lettres' which stressed the point that
they were not narrow specialists but 'capable of entering these different fields even if they could not cultivate them all' (*en état de porter
leurs pas dans ces différentes terrains, s'ils ne peuvent les cultiver
tous*). The eighteenth-century Swiss physician Simon Tissot even wrote
a book about the health hazards specific to the profession of letters
(1766).

For their part, the German mandarins preferred the title of 'man
of learning' (*Gelehrte*), or 'polymath' (*Polyhistor*). In seventeenth-
century Germany, these people were sometimes described as a social
class or order (*der Gelehrten Stand*). One sign of their collective self-
consciousness was the publication of Daniel Morhof's *Polyhistor*
(1688), a guide to the scholarship of the time, which went through
many editions, like its rival Burkhard Struve's *Introduction to
the Knowledge of Learning* (1704). Another was the appearance of
collections of biographies such as the 'Dictionary of the Learned'
(*Gelehrten-Lexicon*, 1715), edited by Professor Johann Burchard
Mencke, and the 'Temple of Honour of German Scholarship'
(*Ehrentempel der Deutsche Gelehrsamkeit*, 1747) edited by the philosopher Jakob Brucker. Yet another sign of self-consciousness was
the claim of the critic Johann Christoph Gottsched that scholars in
action were as free as rulers, 'recognizing no one as their superior but
reason and a more powerful pen' (*die Vernunft und eine mächtigere
Feder*).[33] At the end of our period, the young Goethe, a student at

---

[31] Burke (1992).
[32] Ringer (1969).
[33] Quoted in Dülmen (1978), 257.

the university of Leipzig, was impressed by the high status of the professors there.

The European clerisy also defined themselves as citizens of the Republic of Letters, a phrase which goes back to the fifteenth century but was employed with increasing frequency from the mid-seventeenth century onwards. *Nouvelles de la République des Lettres* was the title of of a journal founded in 1684, one of an increasing number of learned or cultural reviews which were published from the 1660s onwards and helped create a new identity for their readers: the *Journal des Savants* (1665), The Royal Society's *Philosophical Transactions* (1665), the *Giornale de' letterati* of Rome (1668), the *Acta Eruditorum* of Leipzig (1682) and many others.[34]

The *Nouvelles* was edited by Pierre Bayle, who has been described as an archetypical intellectual of the period. Bayle was a French Calvinist professor who emigrated to the Dutch Republic to escape the persecution of the Protestants by the regime of Louis XIV. He taught at Rotterdam for a time but then turned to writing for a living. Thanks to his place in the history of dictionaries and the history of the footnote as well as in the history of scepticism, Bayle's name will recur in the course of this study.[35]

Like Bayle, a number of Calvinist pastors also emigrated from France at this point, following the revocation in 1685 of the royal edict which had allowed Protestants freedom of worship. Discovering that the supply of Calvinist clergy exceeded the demand for pastors and preachers, some of them turned to the profession of letters and in particular to the periodical press (below, chapter 7). These ex-pastors were among the first 'journalists', a term which was just coming into use in French, English and Italian around 1700 to refer to writers in the learned or literary journals, as opposed to the lower-status *gazetiers* who reported the news on a daily or weekly basis. Printing was thus continuing to generate new professions.[36]

In the eighteenth century, journalists became increasingly influential as periodicals proliferated. The rewards to leading men of letters, including historians, were rising (below, chapter 8). In England, Alexander Pope has been described as the first independent man of letters, soon followed by Samuel Johnson.[37] In France, *philosophes* such as Diderot and other contributors to the *Encylopédie* followed

---

[34] Morgan (1929); Gardair (1984); Laeven (1986).
[35] Labrousse (1963–4, 1983); Bost (1994).
[36] Haase (1959), 404–17; Labrousse (1963–4); Yardeni (1973, 1985); Martens (1974); Gibbs (1975); Bost (1994), 232–9.
[37] Beljame (1881).

the example of Bayle and Johnson in producing a reference book in order to make a living from their pens, although the use of an encyclopaedia to support a political project was a major novelty.

The well-known examples of literary success should not allow us to forget the 'literary underground', or 'Grub Street', as it was called in eighteenth-century England, in other words the world of the unsuccessful and impoverished writers, described by Voltaire as *la canaille de la littérature*.[38] All the same, from a comparative point of view, what is striking is the emergence in most parts of Europe by the middle of the eighteenth century of a group of more or less independent men of letters with political views of their own, concentrated in a few major cities, notably Paris, London, Amsterdam and Berlin, and in regular contact with one another. The reference to 'most parts' of Europe is intended as a reminder of the fact that in the world of Orthodox or Eastern Christendom, the clerisy was still almost entirely clerical, with the exception of a tiny group of 'westernized' men of learning such as Dimitri Cantemir (prince of Moldavia and a member of the Berlin Academy), or Mikhail Lomonosov, the great Russian polymath, who began his education in a seminary but was transferred to the college of the Academy of Sciences in St Petersburg in 1736.

ISLAM AND CHINA

The western clerisy was not of course unique. In Islam, for example, the *'ulama* (in other words the specialists in *'ilm*, 'knowledge') had long had an honourable position in society, whether as teachers in the schools attached to mosques (the *madrasas*), as judges or as the counsellors of rulers. As in the medieval West, this clerisy was associated with religion (including the sacred law). They were not clergy in the Christian sense because Muslims deny the possibility of mediation between the individual and God.[39] Some scholars acquired an international reputation, as in the case of Ibn Sina ('Avicenna') and Ibn Rushd ('Averroes'), both of whom were known in the West in the Middle Ages.

In the early modern Ottoman Empire, as in western Europe, students were coming to expect employment in the *'ulama* or 'learned hierarchy' after their studies were finished, and the frustration of these expectations in the middle of the seventeenth century led to discontent in Istanbul as it did in Oxford or Naples.[40] The great contrast between Muslim scholars and their counterparts in early

---

[38] Darnton (1982); Masseau (1994).
[39] Repp (1972; 1986); Fleischer (1986); Zilfi (1988).
[40] Itzkowitz (1972).

modern Europe was a contrast between media of communication. As we have seen, the printing press offered a variety of opportunities to European men of letters. The world of Islam, on the other hand, rejected the printing press and remained until 1800 or thereabouts a world of oral and manuscript communication.[41]

In China the position of the *shen-shih* or 'scholar-gentry' was even more honourable, since it was this group which (with some competition from eunuchs and others) managed the state for the emperor for some 2,000 years. For much of this time the political elite, magistrates or mandarins, were chosen on the basis of the results of competitive examinations at different levels (the district, the prefecture, the province and finally the metropolis). The candidates were isolated from one another in individual cubicles in the examination compound. Their answers, usually commentaries on the Confucian classics, were marked by examiners who did not know the identity of the candidates. The system was closer to a 'meritocracy' than any other in the early modern world.[42]

The increasing western interest in China (to be discussed below, 193), included a lively curiosity about its clerisy (known in Europe as *literati*), not to mention some envy. In his famous *Anatomy of Melancholy* (1621), Robert Burton, an Oxford don, offered what he called 'an Utopia of mine own'. In this ideal commonwealth, magistrates would be chosen by examination, 'as the *literati* in China'. A writer in the Royal Society's *Philosophical Transactions* (July 1666) raised the same fundamental issues in the course of reviewing a new description of China, when he noted that 'their Nobility is raised from Learning and Knowledge, without regard to blood or parentage.' It was for this reason that the eighteenth-century French reformer François Quesnay wanted to imitate the Chinese examination system, while Voltaire was among those who admired the mandarins, *fonctionnaires lettrés* as he called them. The Chinese system may well have inspired the introduction of examinations for candidates for the civil service in France, Prussia and Britain in the nineteenth century.[43]

This brief discussion of the clerisy in early modern Europe – a topic which surely deserves a book-length study – may at least be sufficient to indicate the difficulty of defining their identity without taking into account the different kinds of institution in which they pursued their careers. To examine these institutions and their contributions to knowledge is the purpose of the following chapter.

---

[41] Messick (1993); Robinson (1993).
[42] Marsh (1961); Miyazaki (1963); Chaffee (1985).
[43] Teng (1942–3).

3

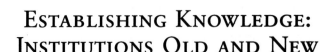

Establishing Knowledge: Institutions Old and New

> In the customs and institutions of schools, academies, colleges and similar bodies destined for the abode of learned men and the cultivation of learning, everything is found adverse to the progress of knowledge.
>
> Bacon

> Gutenberg war nicht Privatdozent, Columbus nicht ordinarius.
> (Gutenberg was not a university teacher, or Columbus a professor.)
>
> Schöffler

ACCORDING to Karl Mannheim, as we have seen (above, 5), the beliefs of the 'free-floating intelligentsia' (*freischwebende Intelligenz*) are less subject to social pressures than the beliefs of other groups. This statement provoked the reply from the economist Josef Schumpeter that Mannheim's intellectual was just 'a bundle of prejudices'.[1] Whether or not this is the case, we certainly need to take note of the fact that most of the early modern clerisy, like modern intellectuals, did not float completely freely but were attached to institutions, such as universities. The institutional context of knowledge is an essential part of its history.[2] Institutions develop social impulses of their own as well as being subject to pressures from outside. The drive to innovate and the opposite drive to resist innovation are of particular relevance to this study of the social history of knowledge.

Before turning to early modern Europe, it may be illuminating to introduce two general theories into the discussion, concerned respectively with the sociology of intellectual innovation and of cultural reproduction. The first, associated with Thorstein Veblen (above, 3), focuses on outsiders, on individuals and groups at the margin of society. In his essay on 'the intellectual pre-eminence of Jews in modern Europe', Veblen explained this pre-eminence, as we have seen, by the position of Jewish intellectuals on the border of two cultural

---

[1] Schumpeter (1942).
[2] Lemaine et al. (1976), 8–9.

worlds, a position which encouraged scepticism and detachment and so fitted them to become what another sociologist, the Italian Vilfredo Pareto, called intellectual 'speculators'.[3]

Pareto contrasted these speculators with the opposite social type, the intellectual 'rentiers' who work within the framework of a tradition. The second theory, associated with Pierre Bourdieu, is concerned with the production of rentiers of this kind by academic institutions and with the tendency of these institutions to reproduce themselves, building up and transmitting what he calls 'cultural capital'. In other words, they develop 'vested interests'. A similar point was made by Norbert Elias in terms of 'establishments'. In a short but penetrating essay, Elias described academic departments as having 'some of the characteristics of sovereign states', and went on to analyse their competition for resources and their attempts to set up monopolies and to exclude outsiders.[4] Similar strategies of monopolization and exclusion can be seen in the history of the professions – the clergy, lawyers and physicians, joined in the nineteenth century by engineers, architects, accountants and so on.

It would of course be unwise to assume that these two theories, which appear to fit together rather neatly, are universally applicable without qualification. All the same, it may be useful to keep them in mind in the course of this brief examination of the organization of learning between 1450 and 1750.

For the later Middle Ages, the theory of Bourdieu and Elias seems to work quite well. As we have seen, the rise of cities and the rise of universities occurred together in Europe from the twelfth century onwards. The model institutions of Bologna and Paris were followed by Oxford, Salamanca (1219), Naples (1224), Prague (1347), Pavia (1361), Cracow (1364), Leuven (1425) and many more. By 1451, when Glasgow was founded, about fifty universities were in operation. These universities were corporations. They had legal privileges, including independence and the monopoly of higher education in their region, and they recognized one another's degrees.[5]

At this time it was assumed rather than argued that universities ought to concentrate on transmitting knowledge as opposed to discovering it. In similar fashion, it was assumed that the opinions and interpretations of the great scholars and philosophers of the past could not be equalled or refuted by posterity, so that the task of the teacher was to expound the views of the authorities (Aristotle,

---

[3] Pareto (1916), section 2233.
[4] Bourdieu (1989); Elias (1982).
[5] Le Goff (1957), 80ff; Ridder-Symoens (1992, 1996).

Hippocrates, Aquinas and so on). The disciplines which could be studied, officially at least, were fixed: the seven liberal arts and the three postgraduate courses in theology, law and medicine.

Despite these assumptions, debate was encouraged, especially the formal 'disputation', an adversarial system like a court of law in which different individuals defended or opposed a particular 'thesis'. The example of Thomas Aquinas is a reminder that it was possible for 'moderns' to become authorities in their turn, even if Aquinas did this by producing a synthesis of elements from different traditions rather than by offering something completely new. The strength of the opposition to Aquinas's use of the pagan thinker Aristotle in his discussion of theology shows how mistaken it would be to describe these institutions purely in terms of intellectual consensus. So do the controversies between different philosophical schools in later medieval universities, notably the conflicts between 'realists' and 'nominalists'. Indeed, in the early modern period medieval universities were criticized not as too consensual but as too disputatious. All the same, the protagonists in these debates shared so many assumptions that their controversies were generally limited to a few precise topics such as the logical status of general statements or 'universals'.[6]

As we have seen in chapter 2, in medieval Europe university teachers were almost all clerics. The relatively new institution of the university, which developed in the twelfth century, was embedded in a much older institution, the Church. No wonder that it is common to describe the medieval Church as having exercised a monopoly of knowledge.[7] All the same, as was noted in chapter 1, we should not forget the plurality of knowledges, in this case the different knowledges of medieval artisans (who had their own training institutions, their workshops and guilds), of knights, of peasants, of midwives, housewives and so on. All these knowledges were transmitted mainly by word of mouth. However, by the time of the invention of printing, lay literacy already had a long history in western Europe (in eastern Europe, by contrast, where the religion was Orthodox Christian and the script Cyrillic, lay literacy was relatively rare). Heretics, who multiplied at about the same time as the universities, have been described as 'textual communities', held together by their discussions of ideas written down in books.[8]

The diversity of knowledges, sometimes in competition and conflict, helps to explain intellectual change. However, important questions

---

[6] Ridder-Symoens (1992); Verger (1997).
[7] Innis (1950).
[8] Stock (1983).

remain open. Did heretics and other outsiders ever enter the intellectual establishment? If so, how did this happen? Were the changes
which were made in the system official or unofficial? Were they the
result of intellectual persuasion or political alliances? Did intellectual
innovation lead to the reform of institutions, or did new institutions have to be founded to provide ecological niches in which such
innovation could flourish?[9] These questions were sometimes discussed in the period itself, notably by Francis Bacon. Like Louis XIV's
minister Jean-Baptiste Colbert a generation later (below, 129), Bacon
was extremely conscious of the importance in the history of learning
of material factors such as buildings, foundations and endowments.
So were his English followers in the middle of the seventeenth century,
who were fertile in projects for what they called the 'reformation of
learning'.[10]

The following sections will examine three centuries of intellectual
change, focusing on three of the major cultural movements of the
period – the Renaissance, the Scientific Revolution and the Enlightenment – paying particular attention to the place of institutions in the
process of intellectual innovation, whether they are to be viewed as
helps or as hindrances. The invention and establishment of new disciplines will be discussed in more detail in chapter 5 (below, 99) as
part of a later reclassification of knowledge.

THE RENAISSANCE

The humanist movement associated with the Renaissance was at least
in intention a movement not of innovation but of revival, the revival
of the classical tradition. Nonetheless this movement was innovative,
and self-consciously so, in the sense of opposing much of the conventional wisdom of the 'scholastics', in other words the philosophers
and theologians who dominated the universities of the 'Middle Ages'.
The very terms 'scholastics' and 'Middle Ages' were inventions of the
humanists of this time, in order to define themselves more clearly by
contrast to the past.

The majority of the humanists had studied at the universities they
criticized. All the same, it is noticeable that some of the most creative
individuals spent much of their lives outside the system. Petrarch, for
instance, was a wandering man of letters. Lorenzo Valla left the

---

[9] McClellan (1985).
[10] Webster (1975).

University of Pavia under a cloud after criticizing the intellectual 'authorities', and entered the service of the king of Naples and later of the pope. Leonardo Bruni was the chancellor of Florence, writing letters on behalf of the republic. Marsilio Ficino was a physician in the service of the Medici. Even more creative and even more marginal was Leonardo da Vinci, who had been trained as a painter and became a self-taught universal man. Outside Italy, the most famous humanist of all, Erasmus, refused to stay very long at any university, despite many offers of permanent employment from Paris to Poland.

The humanists developed their ideas in discussion, but their debates took place not so much in the environment of universities, where longer-established groups were often hostile to new subjects, as in a new kind of institution they created for themselves, the 'academy'. Inspired by Plato, the academy was closer to the ancient symposium (drinking included) than to the modern seminar. More formal and longer-lasting than a circle (Petrarch's disciples, for example), but less formal than a university faculty, the academy was an ideal social form in which to explore innovation. Little by little these groups turned into institutions, with fixed memberships, statutes and regular times of meeting. By the year 1600 nearly 400 academies had been founded in Italy alone, while they could also be found in other parts of Europe, from Portugal to Poland.[11]

Discussions of ideas were no monopoly of academics. In early fifteenth-century Florence, as we have seen (above, 15) the humanist Leonbattista Alberti had frequent conversations with the sculptor Donatello and the engineer Filippo Brunelleschi. Another member of Alberti's circle was the mathematician Paolo Toscanelli, whose interests included geography, especially routes to the Indies. Toscanelli obtained information on this subject from questioning travellers who passed through Florence after their return to Europe, and he may have been in touch with Columbus.[12]

What Toscanelli was doing informally was done more officially in Portugal and Spain. In fifteenth-century Portugal, information as well as goods coming from Asia found its way to 'India House' in Lisbon (A Casa da India). In Seville, the 'House of Trade' (La Casa de Contratación), founded in 1503, was a similar store of knowledge about the New World. It was also a training school for pilots, under the direction of the *piloto mayor* (at one time Amerigo Vespucci, and later Sebastian Cabot). Instruction was sometimes given in the pilot's home, sometimes in the chapel of the Casa. The first school of naviga-

---

[11] Field (1988); Hankins (1991).
[12] Garin (1961); cf. Goldstein (1965).

tion in Europe, it soon acquired an international reputation (as an English visitor in 1558, the pilot Stephen Borough, bears witness).[13]

Royal support was crucial in the establishment of the Houses of India and of Trade, and of other institutions as well. In Paris in the early sixteenth century, the humanists, opposed by the Faculty of Theology, appealed to King François I, who founded the Collège des Lecteurs Royaux to encourage the study of Greek and Hebrew. Later in the century, King Henri III was the patron of a palace academy in which lectures were given on the ideas of Plato (a link with the so-called 'Platonic Academy' of Florence).[14]

Royal support was also important to humanists because they met with opposition in some intellectual circles. The strength of the opposition varied from university to university. It was strong in early sixteenth-century Leipzig, for instance, and also in Oxford, where a group hostile to the study of Greek became known as the 'Trojans'. That opposition to humanism was less vigorous in newer institutions, which were free, for a time at least, from the pressure to do what had 'always' been done in the past, is suggested by the cases of the new universities of Wittenberg, Alcalà and Leiden.[15]

Wittenberg, which was founded in 1502, was originally organized on fairly traditional lines by scholars who had themselves been trained at Leipzig and Tübingen. However, within five or six years the humanists had come to play an unusually important role in the university. It is probably easier for would-be innovators to take over new institutions than old ones, so it may be no accident that the Reformation was launched by Professor Luther at a time when his university was only fifteen years old. A year later, Philip Melanchthon was appointed professor of Greek, with the approval of Luther and other members of faculty, as part of a programme of reform. His reform of the arts curriculum was taken as a model by teachers in the Protestant universities of the later sixteenth century, such as Marburg (founded 1527), Koenigsberg (1544), Jena (1558) and Helmstedt (1576), new institutions in which there were fewer traditions and less hostility to humanism than elsewhere.[16]

Alcalà opened six years later than Wittenberg, in 1508. Its foundation cannot be interpreted as a triumph of humanism, since the university was consciously modelled on Paris and staffed by old Paris men or Salamanca men.[17] However, as at Wittenberg, the balance

[13] Stevenson (1927); Pulido Rubio (1950), 65, 68, 255–90; Goodman (1988), 72–81.
[14] Yates (1947); Sealy (1981); Hankins (1990).
[15] Burke (1983).
[16] Grossmann (1975).
[17] Codina Mir (1968), 18–49.

between humanism and scholasticism had shifted to the advantage of the former. A 'trilingual' college was founded at Alcalà to encourage the study of the three biblical languages, Latin, Greek and Hebrew, a few years before the foundation of a similar college in the older university of Leuven in 1517. It was at Alcalà that the famous polyglot edition of the Bible was edited and printed between 1514 and 1517, the work of a team of scholars including the famous humanist Antonio de Nebrija.[18]

Unlike Wittenberg and Alcalà, Leiden was founded (in 1575) for essentially ideological reasons, as a Calvinist university. The first president of the board of governors, Janus Dousa, built up the university by methods which have become familiar in our own century, making offers of high salaries and low teaching loads in order to attract distinguished scholars, including the botanists Rembert Dodoens and Charles de l'Ecluse and the classicist Joseph Scaliger. Leiden was not new in its formal structure, but two relatively new arts subjects, history and politics, quickly acquired an unusually important position there. History was taught by a leading humanist, Justus Lipsius. Quantitatively speaking, politics was an even greater success; there were 762 students of politics at Leiden between 1613 and 1697.[19]

The point of these examples is not to argue that all teachers in new universities are innovators, and still less that new ideas are a monopoly of new institutions. It was not the universities but certain groups within certain universities who were hostile to humanism. The foundation of chairs of rhetoric in Leuven (in 1477) and Salamanca (in 1484) indicates sympathy with the *studia humanitatis*, like the lectureships in history founded in Oxford and Cambridge in the early seventeenth century. The ideas of the humanists gradually infiltrated the universities, especially in the sense of influencing the unofficial curricula rather than the official regulations.[20] By the time this happened, however, the most creative phase of the humanist movement was over. The challenge to the establishment now came from 'the new philosophy', in other words from what we call 'science'.

THE SCIENTIFIC REVOLUTION

The so-called 'new philosophy', 'natural philosophy' or 'mechanical philosophy' of the seventeenth century was an even more self-

---

[18] Bentley (1983), 70–111.
[19] Lunsingh Scheurleer and Posthumus Meyes (1975); Wansink (1975).
[20] Fletcher (1981); Giard (1983–5); Rüegg (1992), 456–9; Pedersen (1996).

conscious process of intellectual innovation than the Renaissance, since it involved the rejection of classical as well as medieval traditions, including a world-view based on the ideas of Aristotle and Ptolemy. The new ideas were associated with a movement generally known (despite growing doubts about the appropriateness of this label), as the Scientific Revolution.[21] Like the humanists, but on a grander scale, the supporters of this movement tried to incorporate alternative knowledges into learning. Chemistry, for instance, owed a good deal to the craft tradition of metallurgy. Botany developed out of the knowledge of gardeners and folk healers.[22]

Although some leading figures in this movement worked in universities – Galileo and Newton among them – there was considerable opposition to the new philosophy in academic circles (a major exception, but one which fits the general argument, is that of the new university of Leiden, which became a major centre of innovation in medicine in the seventeenth century).[23] In reaction to the opposition, supporters of the new approach founded their own organizations, societies such as the Accademia del Cimento in Florence (1657), the Royal Society of London (1660), the Académie Royale des Sciences in Paris (1666), and so on, organizations reminiscent in many ways of the humanist academies but placing more emphasis on the study of nature.

The argument that the hostility of the universities to the new philosophy led to the creation of 'scientific societies' as an alternative institutional framework was put forward by Martha Ornstein in a book published in 1913 (above, 9). According to Ornstein, 'with the exception of the medical faculties, universities contributed little to the advancement of science' in the seventeenth century. The claim has often been reiterated.[24] In the case of England, for example, historians have linked the foundation of the Royal Society to the criticisms of Oxford and Cambridge put forward in the middle of the seventeenth century by William Dell, John Webster and others.[25] Webster, for example, who was active as a surgeon and an alchemist as well as as a clergyman, criticized the universities in his *Examination of Academies* (1654) as strongholds of a scholastic philosophy concerned with 'idle and fruitless speculations', and suggested that students should spend more time on the study of nature and 'put their hands

---

[21] Shapin (1996).
[22] Hall (1962); Rossi (1962).
[23] Ruestow (1973), esp. 1–13.
[24] Ornstein (1913), 257. Cf. Brown (1934), Middleton (1971).
[25] Hill (1965), Webster (1975), 185–202.

to the coals and furnace'. It has often been pointed out that there was no chair of mathematics at Cambridge until 1663.

The traditional view that universities opposed the 'new philosophy' or at least did little to further it is one which has come under fire in a series of studies published from the late 1970s onwards. Their authors argue that the study of mathematics and natural philosophy had an important place in universities and that contemporary criticisms of universities were either ill-informed or deliberately misleading. In the case of Oxford, the foundation of chairs of astronomy and geometry in 1597 and 1619 has often been noted. The interest in new ideas in university circles has been emphasized. The views of Descartes were sometimes discussed at the university of Paris, for example, those of Copernicus at Oxford and those of Newton at the university of Leiden. As for the critique of the universities by contemporaries, it has been pointed out that the Royal Society was concerned to make publicity and to generate support for itself, while Dell and Webster, both of whom were radical Protestants, also had their own agenda, so that their remarks cannot be taken at face value.[26]

As the dust settles on the controversy, it is becoming increasingly clear that any simple opposition between progressive academies and reactionary universities is misleading. It is difficult to measure the relative importance of universities and other institutions, since a number of scholars belonged to both. As so often in this kind of debate, what are needed are distinctions – between different universities, different moments, different disciplines, and, not least, between different questions – whether the universities failed to originate the new ideas, or were slow to disseminate them, or actively opposed them.[27] Despite these problems, it seems possible to reach a few provisional conclusions.

In the first place, as in the case of the humanist movement, the proliferation of new forms of institution gives the impression that a considerable number of supporters of the movement to reform natural philosophy themselves perceived the universities as obstacles to reform, at least in that movement's early stages. These locales offered appropriate micro-environments or material bases for the new networks, small groups or 'epistemological communities' which have so often proved to play an important role in the history of knowledge (above, chapter 1).

In the second place, distinctions between these new forms of institution are in order. Some of them were founded within the universities

---

[26] Ruestow (1973); Tyacke (1978); Feingold (1984, 1989, 1991, 1997); Brockliss (1987); Lux (1991a, 1991b); Porter (1996).
[27] Cohen (1989).

themselves, botanical gardens for example, anatomy theatres, laboratories and observatories, all of which were islands of innovation within more traditional structures. The new university of Leiden had a botanical garden by 1587, an anatomy theatre by 1597, an observatory by 1633 and a laboratory by 1669. The relatively new university of Altdorf acquired its garden in 1626, its anatomy theatre in 1650, its observatory in 1657 and its laboratory in 1682.

Some institutions were founded from below, by a group of like-minded people who formed a society, like the natural philosophers or 'Lynxes' (Lincei) in seventeenth-century Rome, or an individual who turned part of his house into a museum or 'cabinet of curiosities' which might display stones or shells or exotic animals (alligators, for example) or 'sports of nature'. The rise of museums of this kind in the seventeenth century is a clear indication of the spread of a less logocentric conception of knowledge, a concern with things as well as words of the kind recommended by the Czech educational reformer Jan Amos Comenius (below, 85).[28]

Other institutions were called into existence from above, by governments, whose resources were necessary for large-scale projects and expensive equipment. The astronomer Tycho Brahe's famous observatory on the island of Hveen (figure 1) was founded (in 1576) and funded by the king of Denmark. The French Academy of Sciences was another royal foundation. The Paris Observatory (1667) was funded by Louis XIV, and the Royal Observatory at Greenwich (1676) by Charles II, to compete with his powerful rival.

The courts of princes themselves offered some opportunities for the practice of natural philosophy, as in the case of Prague in the time of the Emperor Rudolf II (himself fascinated by these studies), or Florence in the age of Grand Duke Cosimo II. An innovative projector such as Johann Joachim Becher, whose interests included alchemy, mechanics, medicine and political economy, was more at home in the world of the court of Vienna in the mid-seventeenth century than he would have been in any university of the time.[29] Yet these opportunities sometimes had their price. Galileo had to play the courtier in Florence, while the French Academy of Sciences was encouraged by the government to turn away from 'curious' research, dismissed as a 'game', to 'useful research which has some connection with the service of the king and of the state'.[30]

Again, some new institutions were exclusive, like the Academy of Sciences and to a lesser degree the Royal Society, while others had

---

[28] Impey and Macgregor (1985); Pomian (1987); Findlen (1994).
[29] Evans (1973), 196–242; Moran (1991), 169ff; Smith (1994), 56–92.
[30] Biagioli (1993); Stroup (1990), esp. 108.

1   ENGRAVING, *THE OBSERVATORY AT HVEEN*, FROM TYCHO BRAHE,
ASTRONOMIAE INSTAURATAE MECHANICA (1598)

the function of widening the public for the new ideas. In London,
for example, the lectures at Gresham College, which began in the
early seventeenth century, were open to all, and most of them were
delivered in English, not the Latin customary at the universities. In

Paris, Théophraste Renaudot organized lectures on a wide variety of subjects for a wide public at his Bureau d'Adresse from 1633 onwards. The Royal Garden in Paris, which opened to the public in 1640, offered them lectures on anatomy, botany and chemistry.[31]

The interest in the so-called 'mechanical philosophy' shown by the groups and organizations discussed in the last few paragraphs, and the success of this philosophy in the eighteenth century, should not lead us to forget the rival, 'occult philosophy'. An increasing concern with the occult was another form of innovation in the early modern period, a concern visible at some courts (notably that of Rudolf II) but one which also generated its own institutions, asociations like the Rosicrucians, a secret society concerned with secret knowledge.

The new institutions discussed in the preceding paragraphs were not limited to the domain of natural philosophy. The Royal Society, for example, in their instructions for travellers (below, 202) were concerned not only with the fauna and flora of different parts of the world but with the customs of the inhabitants. When Leibniz planned a German learned society around 1670, he referred to the Royal Society and the Academy of Sciences as models but placed more emphasis than they did on what he called *res litteraria*, in other words the humanities. Museums and cabinets of curiosities generally contained not only shells and stuffed animals but Roman coins or objects from distant places such as China or Mexico. A number of the most famous learned societies of the seventeenth century were concerned with language, notably the Crusca of Florence (which brought out a dictionary in 1612), the German Fruchtbringende Gesellschaft (founded in 1617) and the Académie Française (1635). So were the more informal salons which flourished in Paris from about 1610 to 1665 under the patronage of aristocratic intellectual ladies at the Hôtel de Rambouillet and elsewhere.[32]

Other societies were concerned with history, like the Society of Antiquaries (founded in the 1580s) in London or the Antikvitetskollegiet at Uppsala (1666). Libraries as well as laboratories sometimes became meeting-places for scholars. The convents of religious orders sometimes became the setting for collective scholarly projects, such as the lives of the saints written by the Bollandists in the Jesuit house in Antwerp or the ambitious historical works produced by the Maurists in the Benedictine monastery of Saint-Germain-des-Prés, the setting for weekly discussions sometimes described as an 'academy'.[33]

---

[31] Hill (1965), 37–61; Mazauric (1997); Ames-Lewis (1999).
[32] Picard (1943); Lougee (1976); Viala (1985), 132–7.
[33] Knowles (1958, 1959).

What was common to these new 'seats and places of learning', as Bacon called them (or 'seats of knowledge', in the words of the Baconian Thomas Sprat, the historian of the Royal Society), was the fact that they provided opportunities for innovation – for new ideas, new approaches, new topics – and also for innovators, whether or not they were academically respectable. The encouragement of discussion in these places also deserves to be emphasized. Intellectual debates owe a good deal to the forms of sociability and so to the social frameworks in which they take place, from the seminar room to the café. In early modern Europe, learned societies helped create a collective identity for the clerisy and encouraged the development of intellectual communities, both the smaller and more intimate face-to-face groups and the wider community of the Republic of Letters (above, 19), linked by visits and especially by correspondence. In short, what has been called 'the importance of being institutionalized' should not be forgotten.[34]

THE ENLIGHTENMENT

From an institutional point of view, the eighteenth century marks a turning-point in the history of European knowledge in a number of respects. In the first place, the virtual monopoly of higher education enjoyed by the universities was challenged at this time. In the second place, we see the rise of the research institute, the professional researcher and indeed of the very idea of 'research'. In the third place, the clerisy, especially in France, were more deeply involved than ever before with projects for economic, social and political reform – in other words, with the Enlightenment. These three points need to be discussed in more detail, one by one.

Some alternative institutions for higher education already existed in 1700. Although artists continued to receive much of their training in workshops, the instruction they provided was increasingly supplemented by attendance at academies in Florence, Bologna, Paris and elsewhere. Academies for noble boys to learn mathematics, fortification, modern languages and other skills considered useful for their future careers in the army or in diplomacy had been founded in Sorø (1586), Tübingen (1589), Madrid (1629) and elsewhere. Academies or quasi-universities for French Calvinists had been founded in Sedan and Saumur around 1600 and played an important part in intellectual life until their suppression in 1685. In Amsterdam the

---

[34] Hunter (1989), 1–14.

Athenaeum (founded in 1632) emphasized new subjects such as his-tory and botany.

It was in the eighteenth century, however, that these initiatives multiplied. Academies for the arts were founded in Brussels (1711), Madrid (1744), Venice (1756) and London (1768). New noble academies were founded in Berlin (1705) and in many other places. Between 1663 and 1750 nearly sixty academies for 'Dissenters' from the Church of England, who were excluded from Oxford and Cambridge, were founded in or near London and in a number of provincial towns such as Warrington in Lancashire (where one of the teachers was the natural philosopher Joseph Priestley).

The Dissenting academies taught a less traditional curriculum than the universities, designed for future businessmen rather than gentle-men, paying attention to modern philosophy (the ideas of Locke, for example), natural philosophy and modern history (a common textbook was the political history of Europe by the German lawyer Samuel Pufendorf). Teaching sometimes took place in English rather than Latin.[35] In central Europe, colleges such as the Karlschule at Stuttgart were founded to teach the art of government to future officials. New institutions, the equivalent of later colleges of techno-logy, were also founded to teach engineering, mining, metallurgy and forestry; the Collegium Carolinum in Kassel, for example, founded in 1709, the engineering academies of Vienna (1717) and Prague (1718), the forestry school founded in the Harz mountains in 1763 and the mining academies of Selmecbánya in Hungary and Freiberg in Saxony (1765).

The second important development in the eighteenth century was the founding of organizations to foster research. The word 'research' (*recherche, ricerca*, etc), is of course derived from 'search' and it can already be found in book titles in the sixteenth century, including Etienne Pasquier's *Recherches de la France* (1560). The term was used more in the plural than the singular and it became more com-mon from the end of the seventeenth century, and more common still at the end of the eighteenth, whether to refer to the arts or the sci-ences, historical or medical studies. Together with the word 'research', other terms came into more regular use, notably 'investigation' (and its Italian equivalent *indagine*), which widened out from its original legal context, and 'experiment' (in Italian *cimento*), which narrowed down from tests in general to the testing of laws of nature in particu-lar. Galileo's famous pamphlet *Il Saggiatore* used the metaphor of 'assaying' in a similar sense.

---

[35] Parker (1914).

Taken together, this cluster of terms suggests an increasing aware-ness in some circles of the need for searches for knowledge to be systematic, professional, useful and co-operative. The Florentine Accademia del Cimento published anonymous accounts of its experi-ments, as if concerned with what the sociologist Auguste Comte would later call 'history without names' (above, 3). For all these reasons one might speak of a shift around the year 1700 from 'curiosity' to 'research', summed up in a memorandum of Leibniz, recommending the establishment of an Academy in Berlin but defining its purpose in contrast to mere curiosity (*Appetit zur Curiosität*). This sense of research was connected with the idea that the stock of knowledge was not constant in quality or quantity but could be 'advanced' or 'improved', an idea discussed in more detail below.

There is an obvious link between this awareness and the develop-ment of organizations to foster research. Bacon's famous vision of 'Solomon's House' in his philosophical romance *New Atlantis* (1626), described a research institute with a staff of thirty-three (not count-ing assistants), divided into 'merchants of light' (who travelled in order to bring back knowledge), observers, experimenters, compilers, interpreters and so on. Something like this, on a more modest scale, already existed in a few places in Europe. Bacon's vision may owe more than is generally recognized to the Academy of the Lincei in Rome, of which Galileo was a member; to Tycho Brahe's observat-ory at Uraniborg, with its complex of buildings and assistants; or to the House of Trade in Seville (above, 36), where data were collected and charts updated.

In turn, Bacon's description probably stimulated change in institu-tions. The Royal Society, full of admirers of Bacon, hoped to estab-lish a laboratory, an observatory and a museum. It also funded the research of Robert Hooke and Nehemiah Grew by collecting subscriptions. On a grander scale, Louis XIV's minister Colbert spent 240,000 livres on research within the framework of the Academy of Sciences, partly in the form of salaries to certain scholars, the *pensionnaires*, to allow them to carry out collective projects such as a natural history of plants.[36]

These initiatives of the 1660s were taken further in the eighteenth century, the age of academies, generally supported by rulers, which paid salaries to savants to conduct their investigations, allowing them to pursue at least part-time careers outside the universities. The professional scientist of the nineteenth century emerged from a

---

[36] Hunter (1989), 1, 188, 261, 264–5; Stroup (1990), 51; Christianson (2000).

semi-professional tradition. Some seventy learned societies concerned wholly or partly with natural philosophy were founded in the eighteenth century, of which the Academies of Berlin, St Petersburg and Stockholm (Kungliga Svenska Vetenskapsakademie) were the most famous, while the French Academy of Sciences was reorganized in 1699. With a vigorous president (such as Banks in London or Maupertuis in Berlin), or an active secretary (such as Formey in Berlin or Wargentin in Stockholm), there was much that these societies could achieve. They organized knowledge-gathering expeditions (below, 129), offered prizes, and increasingly formed an international network, exchanging visits, letters and publications and on occasion carrying out common projects, thus participating in the 'trade' in learning recommended by Leibniz, *einen Handel und Commercium mit Wissenschaften*.[37]

This increasingly formal organization of knowledge was not confined to the study of nature. Monasteries, especially Benedictine monasteries, following the example of the late seventeenth-century Maurists but placing greater stress on collective research, became important seats of historical learning in France and in the German-speaking parts of Europe in the eighteenth century.[38] Leibniz suggested that one of the tasks of the new Academy of Berlin should be historical research. Research of this kind was taken seriously in a number of French provincial academies as well as in German ones. It was also funded by the government in the form of salaries for members of the Paris Academy of Inscriptions, reorganized in 1701 according to the model of the Academy of Sciences.[39] Academies for the study of politics were founded in Paris by the foreign minister, the marquis de Torcy (1712) and in Strasbourg by a professor, Johann Daniel Schöpflin (c.1757).[40] Research, including historical research, was important in the new university of Göttingen, founded in the 1730s.

The eighteenth century was a great age for voluntary associations of many kinds, many of them devoted to the exchange of information and ideas, often in the service of reform. Three examples from the British Isles may serve to exemplify the rising interest in useful knowledge: the Dublin Society for the Improvement of Husbandry (1731); the London Society of Arts (1754), founded to encourage trade and manufactures; and the Lunar Society of Birmingham (1775), which exchanged scientific and technical information.[41] The rise of

---

[37] Hahn (1975); Gillispie (1980); McClellan (1985); Lux (1991).
[38] Voss (1972), 220–9; Gasnault (1976); Hammermeyer (1976); Ziegler (1981).
[39] Voss (1972), 230–3; Roche (1976, 1978); Voss (1980).
[40] Klaits (1971); Keens-Soper (1972); Voss (1979).
[41] Im Hoff (1982; 1994, 105–54); Dülmen (1986).

masonic lodges in London, Paris and elsewhere in the early eighteenth century illustrates this new trend as well as an older tradition of secret knowledge.

Even less formal organizations such as the salon and the coffee-house had a part to play in the communication of ideas during the Enlightenment. In Paris, the salons have been described as the 'working spaces of the project of Enlightenment'. Under the direction of Madame de Tencin, for example, Fontenelle, Montesquieu, Mably and Helvétius met for regular discussions, while Mme de L'Espinasse played hostess to d'Alembert, Turgot and other members of the group which produced the *Encyclopédie*.[42] Coffee-houses played an important role in Italian, French and British intellectual life from the late seventeenth century onwards. Lectures on mathematics were given at Douglas's and the Marine Coffee-House in London, while Child's was for booksellers and writers, Will's for the poet John Dryden and his friends, and French Protestant refugees congregated in the Rainbow. In Paris, Procope's, founded in 1689, served as a meeting-place for Diderot and his friends. The proprietors of coffee-houses often displayed newspapers and journals as a way of attracting clients, and thus encouraged public discussion of the news, the rise of what is often called 'public opinion' or 'the public sphere'. These institutions facilitated encounters between ideas as well as between individuals.[43]

The press, especially the periodical press, may also be regarded as an institution, and one which made an increasingly important contribution to intellectual life in the eighteenth century, contributing to the spread, the cohesion and the power of the imagined community of the Republic of Letters. No fewer than 1,267 journals in French are known to have been founded between 1600 and 1789, 176 of them between 1600 and 1699 and the rest thereafter.[44]

To sum up so far, the example of the institutions of learning in early modern Europe appears to confirm both the ideas of Bourdieu on cultural reproduction and those of Veblen on the link between marginality and innovation. The universities may have continued to perform their traditional function of teaching effectively, but they were not, generally speaking, the locales in which new ideas developed. They suffered from what has been called 'institutional inertia', maintaining their corporate traditions at the price of isolation from new trends.[45]

---

[42] Goodman (1994), 53, 73–89; Im Hoff (1994), 113–17.
[43] Habermas (1962); Stewart (1992); Johns (1998), 553–6.
[44] Calculated from Sgard (1991).
[45] Julia (1986), 194.

Over the long term, what we see are cycles of innovation followed by what Max Weber used to call 'routinization' (*Veralltäglichung*) and Thomas Kuhn described as 'normal science'. In Europe, these cycles are visible from the twelfth century, when new institutions called universities replaced monasteries as centres of learning, to the present. The creative, marginal and informal groups of one period regularly turn into the formal, mainstream and conservative organizations of the next generation or the next-but-one. This is not to say that the reform or renewal of traditional organizations is impossible. The new role played by a very old institution, the Benedictine monastery, in the organization of research in the eighteenth century (above, 43, 47) is proof to the contrary. In similar fashion, in the reorganization of research in the nineteenth century, it would be the universities, especially in Germany, which would recover the initiative and leap ahead of the academies.

CONCLUSIONS AND COMPARISONS

Are these cycles of creativity and routinization a universal phenomenon, or are they confined to some periods in the history of the West? An obvious comparison is that between the early modern European system and the system of *madrasas* in the Muslim world, especially in Baghdad, Damascus and Cairo in what westerners call the 'Middle Ages' and in the Ottoman Empire in the sixteenth and seventeenth centuries.

Although there are no clergy in Islam, the *madrasas*, teaching institutions attached to mosques, look remarkably like the Church-dominated educational institutions of Europe. The main subjects studied were the Quran, the Hadith (the sayings of the Prophet) and the law of Islam. The *khans* in which the students lived, the salaries of professors, the stipends of students and the tax-exempt foundations or *wakfs* which supported the system are all reminiscent of the college system which still exists in Oxford and Cambridge, and they may have influenced that system in the twelfth century. The formal organization of argument in the *munazara* resembled the western disputation, while the *ijaza* or licence to teach which a master gave his students resembled the medieval European *licentia docendi*.[46]

The historian who drew these parallels and raised the possibility of conscious western borrowing from the Muslims did not deny the existence of major differences between the two systems. However,

---

[46] Pedersen and Makdisi (1979); Makdisi (1981).

more recent research suggests that he overemphasized the formal organization of knowledge and education in the Middle East, and that the 'system' – if one should call it that – was a fluid one. The *ijaza* was a personal licence, not a degree from an institution. What mattered in the career of a teacher was not where one had studied, but with whom. The central place of learning was an informal study circle (*halqa*), actually a semicircle at a respectful distance from the master (*shaykh*), whether in his house or in a mosque. There was no fixed curriculum. The students moved from master to master as they pleased. Indeed, even the term 'student' is not always appropriate since some members of study-circles attended part-time, including women. No wonder that a recent historian of the *madrasa* speaks of 'persistent informality'.[47]

The contrast between the Christian and Muslim educational worlds must not be drawn too sharply. Western universities were less formal in early modern times than they became after 1800.[48] All the same, the protracted Islamic resistance to institutional congealment is impressive. There remains the question whether institutional fluidity was associated with a more open intellectual system. Apparently not. A student might move from one master to another, but he was expected to follow the ideas of a senior scholar, rather than engaging in private reading and putting forward personal views.[49]

The Ottoman *medrese* (the Turkish form of the word *madrasa*) followed a similar pattern. The mosque which Sultan Mehmed II founded in Istanbul soon after conquering the city had eight colleges attached to it. By the seventeenth century there were ninety-five colleges in the city, rising to 200 in the eighteenth century. The lectures were open, but for the students who wanted to attain high office in the *ulema* (above) as judge, counsellor or teacher (*müderris*), the support of a particular master was essential. By 1550, to have studied in certain prestigious colleges, the so-called 'inner' group, was a virtual prerequisite for high office. Diplomas and examinations were introduced, so many signs that the system was becoming more formal.[50]

In this system, in both its Arab and Ottoman forms, the study of nature was marginal. It was carried on for the most part outside the colleges. Medical teaching took place in hospitals, foundations with a long history in the Muslim world, while astronomy was studied in specialized observatories. The first known observatory was founded

---

[47] Berkey (1992), 20, 30; Chamberlain (1994).
[48] Curtis (1959); Stichweh (1991), 56.
[49] Berkey (1992), 30; Chamberlain (1994), 141.
[50] Repp (1972; 1986, 27–72); Fleischer (1986); Zilfi (1988).

in 1259, while a new one was founded at Galata in 1577 – the year after Uraniborg – by a scholar, Takiyyüddin, with the support of Sultan Murad III. It was destroyed by soldiers in 1580, a sign that the knowledge of nature was not only institutionally marginal but considered by some as irreligious.[51] However, marginality, as we have already seen, can sometimes be an advantage. At any rate, medicine and astronomy were at once marginal areas and seats of innovation in the world of Islam.

The example of the Muslim world, more especially that of the Ottoman Empire, appears to confirm the theories of Veblen and Bourdieu in some respects, although the persistence of an informal system over the long term shows that institutionalization cannot be taken for granted. A comparison and contrast between the worlds of Islam and Christendom (Catholic and more especially Protestant Christendom, rather than the world of Orthodoxy), highlights the relative strength of opposition to intellectual innovation in Islam, including opposition to the new technology of the intellect, the printing press. The hypothesis that printing, which made intellectual conflicts more widely known, also encouraged critical detachment, receives some support from comparative historical analysis.[52]

Generally speaking, it seems that the marginal individual finds it easier to produce brilliant new ideas. On the other hand, to put these ideas into practice it is necessary to found institutions. In the case of what we call 'science', for example, the institutional innovations of the eighteenth century seem to have had important effects on the practice of the disciplines.[53] Yet it is virtually inevitable that institutions will sooner or later congeal and become obstacles to further innovation. They become the seats of vested interests, populated by groups who have invested in the system and fear to lose their intellectual capital. There are social as well as intellectual reasons for the dominance of what Kuhn calls 'normal science'.

Thus the social history of knowledge, like the social history of religion, is the story of the shift from spontaneous sects to established churches, a shift which has been repeated many times over. It is a history of the interaction between outsiders and establishments, between amateurs and professionals, intellectual entrepreneurs and intellectual rentiers. There is also interplay between innovation and routine, fluidity and fixity, 'thawing and freezing trends', official and unofficial knowledge. On one side we see open circles or

[51] Huff (1993), 71–83, 151–60, 170–86.
[52] Eisenstein (1979).
[53] Gillispie (1980), 75; Lux (1991a), 194.

networks, on the other institutions with fixed membership and officially defined spheres of competence, constructing and maintaining
barriers which separate them from their rivals and also from laymen
and laywomen.[54] The reader is probably tempted to side with the
innovators against the supporters of tradition, but it is likely that in
the long history of knowledge the two groups have played equally
important roles.

---

[54] Kuhn (1962); Shapin (1982); Elias (1982), 50.

4

LOCATING KNOWLEDGE: CENTRES AND PERIPHERIES

Vérité au deçà des Pyrénées, erreur au delà.

Pascal

So it is in travelling: a man must carry knowledge with him if he would
bring home knowledge.

Dr Johnson

IN Leiden in 1654, an Italian Catholic Sinologist met a Dutch
Protestant Arabist. The encounter was an unlikely but also a
fruitful one. Both men – like a number of their contemporaries –
were interested in problems of comparative chronology, more exactly
in synchronism. Jacob Golius, professor of Arabic in Leiden, knew
no Chinese but suspected the dependence of the chronology of the
fifteenth-century Muslim scholar Ulugh Beg on Chinese sources.
Martino Martini, the Italian Jesuit who spent much of his life as a
missionary in China and had studied some of these Chinese sources,
knew no Arabic. However, when the two men translated their texts
into their common language, Latin, the links between Islam and China
became apparent.

The story reveals a number of features of the Republic of Letters
at this time. For example, it confirms the idea that scholarly co-
operation transcended religious differences, at least on occasion.
It also tells us about the importance of location in the history of
knowledge.

In the first place, the importance of personal encounters, an importance which is not confined to the transfer of technology, though it
may be even more important in that domain of knowledge than in
others.[1] Personal encounters were more effective than exchanges of
letters, as in the case of Golius and Martini. They also had a more
profound effect. Lorenzo Magalotti wrote about China after meeting
a German missionary, Johan Greuber, in Florence, while Leibniz owed

---

[1] Cipolla (1972); Schilling (1983).

2   MAP OF NANKING PROVINCE IN M. MARTINI, *NOVUS ATLAS SINENSIS*
(AMSTERDAM C.1655), BETWEEN pp. 96 AND 97: COPY IN CAMBRIDGE
UNIVERSITY LIBRARY (ATLAS 3.65.12)

his passion for Chinese studies to a meeting in Rome with another
missionary, C. F. Grimaldi.

In the second place, the story of the meeting in Leiden reminds us
of the function of cities as cross-roads and meeting-places. It was as
difficult to synchronize the lives of Golius and Martini as to synchronize their chronologies. Martini was returning from China to Rome to
report on his mission. On the way he was captured by the Dutch, but
was allowed to board a ship bound for Amsterdam, where he planned
to hand over his atlas of China to the famous printing firm of the
Blaeus, which specialized in maps (figure 2).[2] When his ship put in at
Bergen in December 1653, news of Martini's intentions reached the
scholar Ole Worm in Copenhagen. Worm, whose manifold interests
extended to China, wrote to his son, who was living in Leiden, and
asked him to tell Golius that Martini was coming. Golius then wrote

---

[2] Koeman (1970).

to Martini in Amsterdam and asked him to take the barge to Leiden. The two men met again in Antwerp a few weeks later, after Golius had obtained permission from his university to be absent for a few days.[3]

Scholars needed to go to all this trouble to meet because knowledge was not spread evenly over early modern Europe. This chapter will examine its geography. The idea of a geography of truth is as shocking as the idea of its social history (above, 5). Indeed, the idea was already exploited for this purpose by Montaigne, who wrote in his *Essais* (Book 2, no. 12) about 'the truth which is bounded by these mountains, which is falsehood in the world on the other side' (*quelle vérité que ces montagnes bornent, qui est mensonge au monde qui se tient au delà*). Pascal was still more laconic in his reference in his *Thoughts* (no. 60) to 'Truth on this side of the Pyrenees, error on the other' (*Vérité au deçà des Pyrénées, erreur au delà*).

The subject of this chapter – following recent work in geography and in the history of science – is essentially the 'spatial distribution' of knowledge, the places in which knowledge was discovered, stored or elaborated as well as those to which it was diffused.[4]

What people knew was closely related to where they lived. For example the monk Maxim Grek, who had spent some years in Italy, was apparently the first to inform the Russians, around 1518, about Columbus's discoveries. By contrast, the map made by the Turkish admiral Piri Reis in 1513 already showed America (it derived from a copy of a map made by Columbus on his third voyage, acquired from a Spanish captive).[5]

In using the phrase 'the geography of knowledge', it is important to distinguish two levels. At the microlevel, there were the 'seats of knowledge', some of them discussed in the previous chapter. Traditional locales such as the monastery, the university, the library and the hospital (and for news, the tavern and the barber's shop), were joined by new ones – the laboratory, the art gallery, the bookshop, the library, the anatomy theatre, the office and the coffee-house.[6] The printing-house bookshop, for instance, was a place to meet and converse as well as to look at new publications. Erasmus used to frequent the printing-house of the scholar-printer Aldus Manutius in Venice. Paolo Sarpi and his friends met in a shop called 'the Ship' in

---

[3] Duyvendak (1936).
[4] Thrift (1985); Thrift, Driver and Livingstone (1995); cf. Livingstone (1995), Harris (1998, 1999) and Jacob (1999).
[5] Hess (1974); Soucek (1992), 269.
[6] Heckscher (1958); Foucault (1961); Habermas (1962); Hannaway (1986); Shapin (1988), etc.

early seventeenth-century Venice, while Galileo's enemy Orazio Grassi frequented 'the Sun' in Rome, and James Boswell first met Samuel Johnson in the back parlour of Tom Davies's bookshop in London.

The library increased in importance as well as in size after the invention of printing. Within the university, it became a rival to the lecture-room, at least in some places. The university of Leuven still claimed in 1639 that it was unnecessary to have a library 'because the professors are walking libraries', but at Leiden, by contrast, the library opened twice a week and the professors sometimes lent their keys to the students.[7] Outside the university, certain private or public libraries, discussed below, became centres of scholarship, locales of learned sociability and the exchange of information and ideas as well as for reading books. The enforcement of silence in libraries would have been impossible and may have been unimaginable at this time. Like the bookshop and the coffee-house, the library encouraged the combination of oral with printed communication. No wonder then that the reform of libraries had a place in the Baconian reformation of learning planned in England in the mid-seventeenth century. Librarians, according to one reformer, John Durie, should be 'agents for the advancement of universal learning'. What this meant in practice might have become clearer if Durie's friend Samuel Hartlib (below, 74) had been appointed Bodleian Librarian in the 1650s, as some reformers had hoped.[8]

Seats of knowledge multiplied and became more specialized in relatively large cities such as Venice, Rome, Paris, Amsterdam and London, cities which will therefore receive a good deal of attention in the pages which follow. The public spaces of cities facilitated inter-action between men of affairs and men of learning, between gentlemen and craftsmen, between the field and the study, in short between different knowledges (above, 13). Forms of sociability had – and still have – their influence on the distribution and even the production of knowledge.

At the macrolevel too, cities played an important role as staging-posts in the 'long-distance networks' which linked Europe to China or the Americas: Asian cities such as Goa, Macau and Nagasaki, American cities such as Lima and Mexico, and European cities such as Seville, Rome, Amsterdam and London.[9] No wonder then that the 'memorial for universal learning' which called in the mid-seventeenth century for professional 'intelligencers' to send information to England

---

[7] Aubert et al. (1976), 80; Hulshoff Pol (1975).
[8] Webster (1975), 193–4.
[9] Harris (1996); Miller (1996).

from foreign parts, specified that these intelligencers should reside in 'the best and most central places'.[10]

At this macrolevel, the history of knowledge in the early modern world is sometimes viewed in simple diffusionist terms as the spread of information, and in particular of scientific information, from Europe to other parts of the globe. This centre–periphery model has been criticized on a number of grounds, for leaving out the politics of imperialism, for example, and for failing to take sufficient account of flows of knowledge from periphery to centre as well as in the opposite direction.[11]

It is actually with the movement from the periphery of Europe to its centres that this chapter is most concerned, leaving the politics of knowledge for chapter 6. Other kinds of knowledge will not be forgotten but the emphasis will fall on the increasing awareness on the part of Europeans of the world beyond Europe. This awareness was often fuelled by religious, economic and political interests, but it also included knowledge for its own sake. The contrast between instrumental knowledge and disinterested curiosity must not be made too sharp.[12] Nevertheless, the distinction remains a useful one.

In what follows the main theme will be the increasing centralization of knowledge, linked to improvements in physical communication and also to the rise of the printed book. These developments are linked in turn to the rise of a world-economy (below, 157), to the rise of a few great cities (often the homes of major libraries), and above all to the centralization of power (below, 101). However, the centralization of knowledge was partly autonomous, the result of the intellectual exchanges associated with the Republic of Letters.

THE REPUBLIC OF LETTERS

The Republic of Letters or 'Commonwealth of Learning' (*Respublica Literaria*) was a phrase which came into increasingly frequent use in early modern Europe to refer to the international community of scholars.[13] The geography of this republic was itself changing during the period. Sweden, for example, despite the foundation of Uppsala University in 1477, effectively entered only in the seventeenth century, when Queen Kristina invited Descartes and other scholars to Stockholm, and the nobleman and soldier Carl Gustaf Wrangel, in

---

[10] Webster (1975), 552.
[11] Basalla (1987); Macleod (1987).
[12] Schaffer (1996).
[13] Fumaroli (1988); Bots and Waquet (1997).

his country house at Skokloster near Uppsala, kept in touch with recent developments in natural philosophy through a network of correspondents in Hamburg, Amsterdam, London, Warsaw, Vienna and elsewhere. North America entered in the eighteenth century, when men of letters such as Cotton Mather and Jonathan Edwards may be found trying to keep in touch with what was happening on the European cultural scene by subscribing to English journals such as the *History of the Works of the Learned*.[14]

Russia entered the European community of scholars a little later than Sweden and a little earlier than North America, towards the end of the reign of Tsar Peter the Great. A Russian nobleman, Alexandr Menshikov, was elected a Fellow of the Royal Society in 1714, a year also marked by the opening of the first public library in Russia. Leibniz, who was concerned with what he called the 'transplantation' of the arts and sciences to Russia, met the tsar on more than one occasion to explain his ideas. Peter appears to have been impressed by his arguments, for he paid him a salary as an adviser, and when the tsar founded the Academy of Sciences in St Petersburg in 1724 it followed the model of the Academy of Berlin, planned by Leibniz a few years earlier. In the year of the tsar's death, 1725, the French astronomer Joseph-Nicholas Delisle arrived in St Petersburg, where he would spend the next twenty years training Russian astronomers. In the next generation, Mikhail Lomonosov would study chemistry in Marburg, correspond with Voltaire and help found Moscow University.[15]

What has been called the 'Russian discovery of Europe' coincided with the European discovery of Russia. Before 1550, little information about 'Muscovy', as it was known at the time, was available in print. The situation changed slowly after 1550 and rapidly after 1697, the date of Peter the Great's 'Great Embassy' to the West, in which some 250 Russians, including the tsar himself, went to study in the Dutch Republic, England, France, Italy and elsewhere, and in the process made western Europeans more aware of Russia. Among the books which introduced western European readers to Russian culture were J. Crull's *Present Condition of the Muscovite Empire* (1699), E. Y. Ides's *Three Years' Travels* (1704), J. Perry's *State of Russia* (1716), and F. C. Weber's *The New Russia* (1721), which was soon translated from German into French and English.[16]

---

[14] Fiering (1976); Losman (1983), 195–8; Åkerman (1991).
[15] Richter (1946), 44; Vucinich (1963); Sazonova (1996).
[16] Anderson (1978).

The knowledge of geography is far from identical with the geography of knowledge. Nevertheless there is a cross-roads where the two topics meet, in other words the geography of geography.[17] As a case-study, it may be illuminating to examine knowledge of the world beyond Europe in the Republic of Letters at a time when important new channels of information were becoming available.[18]

NAGASAKI AND DESHIMA

For a case-study within this case-study let us take the example of Japan. Europeans knew little about Japan before 1550 or thereabouts. The thirteenth-century traveller Marco Polo had mentioned 'Cipangu' but he gave few details about it. The Jesuit missionary Francis Xavier arrived in 1549 in a land which was almost entirely unfamiliar to him and his compatriots. From the late sixteenth century onwards, the route by which knowledge of Japan travelled to the West went through the port of Nagasaki. In 1580 a powerful convert to Christianity donated the city to the Jesuits. They lost control of Nagasaki in 1587, but the mission remained, and a press was set up there.

The Christian mission to Japan was a success. Indeed, it was too successful for its own good, since the spread of Christianity alarmed the rulers of Japan and led not only to the persecution of missionaries and their converts but also to a policy of 'national seclusion' (*sakoku*), which lasted from the 1630s to the 1850s. The country was not completely closed to foreigners, but relations with foreign countries, including commercial relations, were reduced to a minimum and strictly controlled. In this period, Dutch merchants took over from Portuguese Jesuits as the main channel of communication between Japan and the West, while Nagasaki was replaced by the neighbouring island of Deshima.

Deshima was an artificial island, extending for only a few hundred feet in each direction, which was built in the harbour of Nagasaki precisely in order to keep the dangerous westerners under control. The Dutch traders, members of the United East India Company (the VOC) were confined to this microspace of exchange. All the trade between Japan and the West went through Deshima from 1641 until the 1850s, when Japan was forced by an American fleet to open its

---

[17] Livingstone (1995); Withers (1998).
[18] Lach (1965).

ports to the West.[19] Deshima was also a micro-environment for the exchange of knowledge, despite official obstacles. The government of Japan forbade the export of maps of the country, as well as discouraging foreigners from learning Japanese. These obstacles could be surmounted, however, and among the westerners who spent some time in Deshima were three who wrote descriptions of Japan which became well known in Europe. The first was François Caron, who headed the VOC establishment there in 1639–40.[20] The second was Engelbert Kaempfer, a German who worked in Deshima in the service of the VOC between 1690 and 1692. The third, at the very end of our period, was Carl Peter Thunberg, a Swedish botanist who served the VOC as a physician and lived in Deshima in 1775–6.

THE FIELD AND THE STUDY

Nagasaki was a major city, and so – from the European point of view – the centre of a periphery. The mediating function of presses in cities elsewhere on the distant periphery of Europe should not be forgotten: Goa, for example, Macau, Batavia, Mexico City and Lima.

Some major European cities were still more important in the process of transmitting knowledge about other parts of the world to the West. Different kinds of city – ports, capitals and university cities – had different functions in this respect, and the differences will be discussed in due course. However, the stress in what follows will fall on the interaction between peripheries and centres, or more concretely between the field and the study. The twin themes will be the 'import' of knowledge into Europe and its subsequent 'processing' – compilation, calculation, classification and criticism.

Famous European collectors of exotic knowledge in the field included Pierre Belon, who explored the Middle East between 1546 and 1550, looking for new species of birds and fish, and Francisco Hernández, who spent the years 1570–7 in Mexico on a mission from the Spanish king to study the local animals, plants and minerals.[21] The vast amount of information about the natural history of other parts of the world which flowed into Europe in the early modern period must not be forgotten. In what follows, however, I shall privilege knowledge of other cultures and their religions, languages and customs, Thunberg's descriptions of Japanese people, for instance, rather than his descriptions of Japanese flowers.

---

[19] Boxer (1936), especially 58–66; Keene (1952); Goodman (1967), 18–24, 32–42.
[20] Lach and Kley (1993), 1855.
[21] Bustamante García (1997); Brentjes (1999).

IMPORTING KNOWLEDGE

The phrase 'importing knowledge' is intended as a reminder of the importance of trade and more particularly of ports in the spread of information, as in the case of Nagasaki. The inhabitants of ports regularly went down to the water's edge to speak to sailors on newly arrived ships. Ports were centres of the trade in astrolabes, charts, maps and globes. They were also the main locales for encounters between different kinds of knowledge as well as between different kinds of people. These encounters will be illustrated by examples from the history of the leading European ports of the period: Lisbon, Seville, Venice and Amsterdam.

The importance of Lisbon in the history of knowledge, especially in the fifteenth and sixteenth centuries, derived from its position as the capital of the Portuguese seaborne empire. 'India House' (Casa da India) and the 'Warehouse of Guinea' (Armazém de Guiné) received information as well as goods from Goa, Macau, Salvador, West Africa and elsewhere. Thus the historian João de Barros, who worked for much of his life in India House, had unrivalled opportunities to collect information about Asia. In the case of India, he consulted soldiers and administrators as well as merchants who had returned from Goa. For information about Persia, he could speak to men who had traded in Ormuz. For Japan and Siam, he could learn from the travellers Mendes Pinto and Domingo de Seixas. As for China, Barros bought a slave to translate texts for him.[22]

The advantage of Seville as a centre of information, especially in the boom years of the sixteenth century, was that it was the only official place of entry for the silver imported into Spain from Mexico and Peru. The annual arrival of the silver fleet brought information about the New World. That the physician Nicolás Monardes was able to write his famous books about the drugs of the Americas without leaving his native Seville is some testimony to the information opportunities provided in that city.

As chapter 3 noted, the Casa de Contratación or 'House of Trade' in Seville was a store of knowledge, especially knowledge of sea routes, the site of a model chart (known as the *padrón real*) which was regularly updated when pilots returned from their voyages with new information. 'Cosmographers' (combining knowledge of geography and astronomy) were attached to the Casa. The colonies of foreign merchants, notably the Genoese, were well-informed about the other

---

[22] Boxer (1948).

parts of the world where their relatives and compatriots were trading.[23] The city was also an important printing centre, and at least 300 books were published there between 1500 and 1520, a number of them by German immigrants. It was mainly through Seville that foreign books were imported into Spain at this time. The importance of the city as a centre of knowledge was enhanced by the library of Fernando Colón (the son of Columbus), which was reputed to contain 20,000 volumes, and also by a number of learned academies which flourished in the sixteenth and early seventeenth centuries.[24]

As for Venice, it was described by a French historian half a century ago as 'the most important information agency of the early modern world'.[25] The advantage of Venice, in the fifteenth and sixteenth centuries, was its position as a broker between East and West. The Venetian maritime empire included Dalmatia, Cyprus (until 1570), and Crete. The Ottoman Empire was a powerful neighbour, so that knowledge of the character and policies of sultans and grand viziers and the movement of Turkish troops and galleys was necessary to Venetian political survival. The Venetian official known as the *bailo* was posted to Istanbul not only to look after the interests of the colony of Venetian merchants established there but also to send political news (often acquired from the sultan's interpreters and physicians) to the doge and his councillors.

The latest 'news on the Rialto' was equally necessary to the economic survival of many Venetians. The letters home written by merchants stationed abroad functioned as a kind of 'data bank' for family businesses. Information arrived regularly from Aleppo, Alexandria and Damascus, where Venetian merchants were also established, and irregularly from places further east. Three Venetians in particular contributed to western knowledge of Burma: Nicolo Conti in the fifteenth century, Cesare Federici and Gasparo Balbi in the sixteenth.[26] When rumours about spices from India arriving in Lisbon reached Venice in 1501, the reaction of the government was to send a secret agent to Portugal to discover what was happening and report back to them. His report still survives. News of the discovery of America reached Venice later than Rome, Paris and Florence, but Venetians took a great interest in the New World throughout the sixteenth century.[27]

[23] Stevenson (1927); Pulido Rubio (1950), 65, 68, 255–90; Lamb (1969, 1976); Goodman (1988), 72–81.
[24] Brown (1978), 21–43.
[25] Sardella (1948).
[26] Doria (1986); Burke (2000a).
[27] Ambrosini (1982); Caracciolo Aricò (1990).

By the seventeenth century, the commercial centres of Lisbon, Seville and Venice were no longer as important as they had once been. They had been overtaken by the ports of Antwerp (for a brief period in the mid-sixteenth century), Amsterdam and London. Antwerp was a centre of trade in knowledge as well as in other commodities, a centre of map-making, especially in the age of Abraham Ortelius, and of the publication of accounts of distant lands, from the account of Mexico by Hernán Cortés (1522) to the Jesuit letters from Japan (from 1611 to 1632).

In Amsterdam, West India House (figure 3) and East India House took the places as well as following the model of earlier houses of trade. East India House was the destination of the annual reports from the Batavia office of the VOC, which covered the whole of the East Indies operation (below, 157). The Amsterdam Stock Exchange (figure 4), extremely sensitive to news about supplies of spices and other commodities, was another centre of information from overseas.[28] Ethnic minorities (including Spanish and Portuguese Jews, Scandinavian sailors, and English and French religious refugees), were an important source of information in Amsterdam, just as Greeks, Slavs, Spaniards and Turks had been in Venice, Spaniards and Italians in Antwerp and Genoese in Seville. The information which came into the city through all these channels went out again with considerable speed via newspapers (below, 168) and other means of communication. In this way Amsterdam became 'a central information exchange for all of Europe'.[29]

CAPITALS OF KNOWLEDGE

Ports had no monopoly of information opportunities. Capital cities, especially Rome, Paris and London, were among their most important competitors, especially but not exclusively in the realm of political news.

Rome had long rivalled Venice as a centre of information.[30] In the first place, the Vatican was the headquarters of the Catholic world, the centre to which ambassadors came from Japan, Ethiopia and Tibet as well as from European countries, and to which regular reports were sent by the pope's ambassadors, the nuncios. In the second place, Rome was the headquarters of missionary orders such as the

---

[28] Barbour (1950), 74–84.
[29] Smith (1984), 987.
[30] Burke (2001).

HET WEST INDISCH HUYS.

3 ENGRAVING, *WEST INDISCH HUIS*, FROM P. ZESEN, *BESCHREIBUNG VON AMSTERDAM* (AMSTERDAM, 1664): COPY IN BRITISH LIBRARY (1300 D.7)

4 E. DE WITTE, PAINTING, *AMSTERDAM STOCK EXCHANGE* (1653):
ROTTERDAM, BOYMANS-VAN BEUNINGEN MUSEUM

Dominicans, the Franciscans and above all the Jesuits, who adopted a system of regular reports or 'annual letters' to the general in Rome from all the Jesuit houses and colleges in the world. The seventeenth-century Congregation for the Propagation of the Faith (near the Spanish Steps) was another centre of information from the mission field.

Giovanni Botero's 'Descriptions of the World' (*Relazioni universali*), compiled in Rome in the 1590s, depended on his access to the Jesuit network. For example, he cited Possevino on Russia, Gonzalvo de Silva on Monomotapa in Africa, and the recently returned Michele Ruggiero on China. Although he chose to present his material in the form of a treatise, Botero sometimes transmitted relatively hot news, interrupting an account of China to tell his readers that 'while I was writing this, news came that two fathers who had remained in that kingdom had suffered various persecutions.'[31]

Rome was also a centre of learned information. Its educational institutions, famous throughout Europe, included the Sapienza, the Collegio Romano, and the colleges founded to train foreign students as missionaries, the German college (1552), the Greek College (1577), the English College (1578), the Maronite College (1584), and the Irish College (1628). The city was also the home of academies such as the Lincei and the Umoristi and of less formal networks such as the circles of the antiquary Fulvio Orsini, the connoisseur Cassiano del Pozzo and the polymath Athanasius Kircher. It attracted scholars from France, Spain, Germany and elsewhere.

Paris (together with its satellite Versailles, from the later seventeenth century onwards), was another centre of political information. The Turkish, Persian, Moroccan and Siamese embassies in the age of Louis XIV are a reminder that diplomatic exchanges were not confined to Europe. In the seventeenth century, the increasing centralization of the French state was accompanied by an increase in the flow of information to Paris (below).

Paris was also a centre of learned information, collected and discussed in official institutions such as the Royal Library, the Royal Garden, the Academy of Sciences, the Observatory and the Academy of Inscriptions. It was also a centre of unofficial societies or academies. Humanist scholars met in the house of the Dupuy brothers in rue des Poitevins, the site of the famous library of the historian Jacques-Auguste de Thou, which the Dupuys had inherited in 1617. Natural philosophers, including Descartes, Pascal and Gassendi, met in the convent of Marin Mersenne near the Place Royale (now Place des Vosges) between 1619 and 1648. Théophraste Renaudot organized lectures in French on a wide variety of topics for anyone who cared to listen at his Bureau d'Adresse located on rue de la Calandre near Notre-Dame and active between 1632 and 1642.[32]

As for London, its importance was that it combined the functions of a port and a capital. The city was the headquarters of the Russia Company (founded 1555), the Levant Company (founded 1581), the East India Company (founded 1599), and the Africa Company (founded 1672). Much information from abroad was sent to individual merchants in London, but it was also collected at company headquarters,

[31] Chabod (1934); Albònico (1992); John Headley is preparing a study of Botero from this perspective.
[32] Rochot (1966); Solomon (1972), 60–99; Mazauric (1997).

Muscovy House for example, where scholars such as John Dee and Richard Hakluyt met merchants in order to discuss maps and routes. East India House in Leadenhall Street performed some of the functions of its Dutch rival. Maps, charts and ships' logs were stored there, while the letters arriving at that address provided detailed information about the prices of goods in India and many other matters.

The information which came into London in this way was not purely commercial. In his preface to the third year of the *Philosophical Transactions*, the secretary to the Royal Society, Henry Oldenburg, noted the information arriving in 'this famous Metropolis' from the 'American colonies' and many other places, thanks to trade.[33] In similar fashion, the historian of the Royal Society, Thomas Sprat, considered London, 'the head of a mighty empire', as 'the most proper seat for the advancement of knowledge', the 'place of residence so appropriate for that knowledge which is to be made up of the reports and intelligence of all countries'.

The Royal Society was an important locale for the exchange of information, but it had rivals. From the late sixteenth century onwards public lectures on natural philosophy and other subjects were given at Gresham College in Bishopsgate Street. Lectures were also given in the College of Physicians in Warwick Lane described by a physician writing in 1657 as a genuine Solomon's House. For the humanities there was the Society of Antiquaries, which met at the Herald's Office in Derby House near St Paul's from about 1586 to about 1608 to discuss the history of England. Officially speaking, London lacked a university, but it was the seat of the Inns of Court, training schools for lawyers sometimes described as a third university.[34]

Immigrants to London from other parts of Europe brought their knowledge with them and so increased what was available in the city. Oldenburg himself was originally from Bremen, and his acquaintance Hartlib from Elbing (now Elbląg in Poland). As in the case of Amsterdam, Protestant refugees from France, including a number of men of letters, settled in London in the later seventeenth century (above, 29).

THE GEOGRAPHY OF LIBRARIES

The predominance of certain European cities in the world of learning will be confirmed if we examine the geography of major libraries. It must be admitted that the correlation is not complete: the Bodleian Library in Oxford, for example, was a large library in a small university

[33] Hall (1965, 1975); Hunter (1989).
[34] Webster (1975), 51–7, 125.

town, while the Escorial library was situated far from any city. To explain their location would be impossible without discussing the interests of two wealthy individuals: King Philip II, who founded the Escorial, and Sir Thomas Bodley, who gave his collection of books to Oxford University.

In Italy and France, on the other hand, the best libraries were to be found in the largest cities. In Italy, the key cities were Florence (with the Laurenziana), Venice (with the Marciana), Milan (with the Ambrosiana) and above all Rome (with the Vatican, the university library at the Sapienza, the Jesuit library at the Collegio Romano and the Angelica, which opened in 1614, as well as important private libraries such as those of the Barberini, Cesi and Spada families and that of Queen Kristina). Guidebooks offered travellers information about these libraries, described most fully in a treatise by the Italian priest Carlo Piazza, *The Famous Libraries of Rome* (1698).

Naples was another Italian city with good libraries, including that of the lawyer Giuseppe Valletta, which contained some 10,000 volumes around the year 1700. As a centre of knowledge, however, the city was in decline by the later seventeenth century, as some of the local scholars explained to a British visitor, Gilbert Burnet, who recorded their complaints about the Inquisition and about the difficulty of obtaining books from England and the Dutch Republic.

To illustrate the problems of scholarship in Naples at the turn of the seventeenth and eighteenth centuries one might take the case of Giambattista Vico. The author of an ambitious work on comparative history obviously needed to be well-informed. Vico grew up in late seventeenth-century Naples, the centre of lively intellectual exchanges with access to new books in Latin. However, as he grew older, Vico and Naples alike became more isolated. French and English, languages which he had not mastered, were increasingly necessary for citizens of the Republic of Letters. One indicator among many of Vico's growing isolation is that in the final edition of his masterpiece the 'New Science' (*Scienza Nuova*), published in 1744, Japan was discussed without reference to the important study by Engelbert Kaempfer published nearly twenty years earlier (above, 60; below, 192).[35]

Parisians were more fortunate. As a city of libraries Paris surpassed even Rome, by the later seventeenth century if not before. Its resources included the twelfth-century library of Saint-Victor, catalogued around 1500 (below, 184) and officially open to the public in the seventeenth century; the university library; the library of the Jesuit college of Clermont (renamed Louis-le-Grand to honour Louis XIV);

[35] Burke (1985).

the library of Cardinal Mazarin, which became a public library after his death; and the royal library, which moved from Blois to Paris in the 1560s and became increasingly accessible to the public in the seventeenth and eighteenth centuries (chapter 8 below). A guide to Paris in 1692 listed no fewer than thirty-two libraries where readers were allowed to enter 'as a favour', as well as the three public libraries (the Mazarine, Saint-Victor, and that of the Royal Garden).

The cities mentioned so far were not distributed evenly over Europe, but clustered in the south and west. It is time to turn to the situation in the centre, north and east of the continent. Central Europe was relatively well off for universities, with a network dating from the fourteenth and fifteenth centuries, including Prague, Cracow, Vienna, Leipzig and Pozsony (now Bratislava). In the reign of the Emperor Rudolf II, from 1576 to 1612, his court in Prague was an intellectual centre which attracted the astronomers Tycho Brahe and Johann Kepler and the alchemists Michael Maier and Michael Sendivogius, as well as humanists such as the Hungarian Johannes Sambucus.[36] More important in the long term was Vienna, the seat not only of a university but also of the imperial library, the Hofbibliothek, which already possessed some 10,000 volumes by the year 1600, was described in detail in the 1660s by the librarian, Peter Lambeck, included 80,000 volumes by 1680, was rebuilt with great magnificence in the early eighteenth century and opened to the public soon after.

Northern and eastern Europe on the other hand were less densely populated, and their cities were generally both smaller (apart from Moscow), and further apart than was the case further south or west. Apart from Uppsala, founded in 1477, academic institutions arrived later – in Vilnius in 1578, for example, in Dorpat (Tartu) and Kiev in 1632, in Lund in 1668, in Lviv in 1661, in Moscow in 1687 (a theological academy) and in St Petersburg in 1724. There were fewer printers and bookshops in this large area, although a modest growth can be discerned in the later seventeenth century. The books printed in Amsterdam for the East European market (below, 164) were at once a boon to readers and an obstacle to the development of a local trade in knowledge.[37] Large libraries were a rarity in this large area, although the ducal library at Wolfenbüttel had 28,000 volumes in 1661, the university library at Göttingen 50,000 volumes in 1760 and the royal library at Berlin 80,000 volumes in 1786.

That access to knowledge was more difficult in these regions than it was in western Europe is suggested by two phenomena. In the first

---

[36] Evans (1973).
[37] Isaievych (1993).

place, the migration of scholars westwards, whether to use library facilities, like the Germans and Scandinavians who visited the Bodleian Library in the seventeenth century, or to live for years, like the Bohemian scholar Jan Amos Comenius in London or in Amsterdam. In the second place, the attempt by the Prussian and Russian governments in the early eighteenth century, following the advice of Leibniz, to make Berlin and St Petersburg centres of knowledge by importing foreign scholars, among them mathematicians such as Nicolas and Daniel Bernoulli, Leonhard Euler and Pierre Maupertuis.

It was possible to pursue a scholarly career in smaller towns in eastern or east-central Europe, subject to certain limitations. The historian Matthias Bél, for example, spent his life in Pozsony, but he worked on the history of his own region. Bartholomeus Keckermann spent most of his short life in Danzig (Gdańsk), yet published more than twenty-five books, but he was essentially a systematizer of academic disciplines who had little need for out-of-the-way information.

Even the acquisition of everyday scholarly knowledge required more effort for Europeans whose first language was not Italian, Spanish, French, German, Dutch or English. It was only very slowly that central and eastern Europe began to produce reference books in its own vernaculars: the *Hungarian Encyclopaedia* of Apáczai Csere János (1653), or the first encyclopaedia in Polish, Chmielowski's *Nowe Ateny*, published in the mid-eighteenth century.

For a vivid example of the problems faced by scholars still further from the centres of learning, one might take the case of Carlos de Sigüenza y Góngora in Mexico. He lived in a large city which posssessed a university, where he was professor of mathematics, as well as printing presses. All the same, writing about the history and antiquities of his own country, including the pictographic writing used before the Spanish conquest, Sigüenza was forced to refer to the books of Europeans such as Samuel Purchas and Athanasius Kircher. These foreign books offered the only printed illustrations of these pictograms available. To view the manuscripts themselves, which had been taken to Europe by the Spaniards and dispersed, Sigüenza would have had to visit cities as far away from him as Rome and Oxford.[38]

THE CITY AS A SOURCE OF INFORMATION ABOUT ITSELF

The growth of information services in early modern cities was in part an effect of the urban division of labour and in part a response to the

---

[38] Brading (1991), 366, 382; Burke (1995a).

increasing demand for information, itself a reaction to the sense of disorientation engendered by living in one of Europe's larger cities. These cities were coming to produce increasing amounts of information about themselves.

For example, the occupational structure of large cities increasingly included specialists in different kinds of oral communication. These specialists included the *corredors d'orella* at the Lonja in Barcelona, who listened to conversations and put merchants in touch with one another; the 'runners' who advertised clandestine marriage services in eighteenth-century London, or brought news of arriving ships to Lloyd's coffee-house; and the ballad-sellers who walked about the city or stationed themselves in particular locations like the Pont Neuf in Paris or the Puerta del Sol in Madrid, where blind singers, strategically located between the offices of the official *Gazette* and the terminus of the postal system, the *Correos*, sold almanacs, newspapers and official edicts.[39]

Official notices were multiplying on street corners or on church doors. In Florence in 1558, for example, the new Index of Prohibited Books was displayed on the church doors of the city. In London in the age of Charles II, placards posted in the street advertised plays. A Swiss visitor to London in 1782 was struck by the prevalence of shop names rather than signs. Street names were increasingly written on walls (in Paris, from 1728 onwards). House numbers were becoming increasingly common in the larger cities in the eighteenth century. An English visitor to Madrid in the 1770s observed that 'the names of the streets were painted on the corner-houses' and that 'the houses were all numbered.'

Every tourist knows that the larger the city, the greater the need for a guide, whether in the form of a person or a book. In early modern Europe there was a demand for professional guides or *ciceroni*, especially in Rome, Venice or Paris, to show the city to visitors. There was also a demand for guidebooks. Printed guides to Rome were particularly numerous, beginning with the so-called 'Marvels of the City of Rome', which already circulated in the Middle Ages. In successive printed editions this guide to relics, indulgences and popes came to include more secular information on the antiquities, the postal service, and painters. Francesco Sansovino's guide to Venice, first published in 1558, became a best-seller, replaced at the end of the seventeenth century by Vincenzo Coronelli's *Guide for Foreigners* and then by the *Foreigner Enlightened*, an eighteenth-century description of a six-day guided tour to the city and its environs.

---

[39] Kany (1932), 62–4.

These models were followed by later guides to Amsterdam, Paris, Naples and elsewhere. Amsterdam was described by Pontanus (1611), Dapper (1663), Zesen (1664), Commelin (1693) and the anonymous French-language *Guide to Amsterdam* (1701), several times reprinted and revised. Bacco's description of Naples was first published in 1616 and had eight editions by the end of the century, as well as rivals such as Mormile (1617), Sarnelli (1685), Celano (1692), and Sigismondo's *Description of the City of Naples* (1788), specifically addressed to foreigners. The *Description of Paris* (1684) by a professional guide, Germain Brice, reached its eighth edition in 1727. It was followed by the *Sojourn in Paris* (1727) by Neimetz, and by other competitors. The first guides to London date from 1681 (when rival accounts were published by Nathaniel Crouch and Thomas de Laure). In the eighteenth century, about a dozen more were published.

By the eighteenth century these guidebooks added to the descriptions of churches and works of art some practical information such as how to negotiate with cab-drivers or what streets to avoid at night. There was also a specialized literature about the confidence tricksters of the city and their repertoires: *The Frauds of London*, and so on. Practical information quickly went out of date, so that it is no surprise to find that a guide to Madrid for foreigners was published from 1722 onwards, the *Annual Calendar and Guide for Foreigners*.

Some cities even produced specialized guides to the world of prostitution. The 'Whores' Price List' (*Tariffa delle puttane*), published in Venice, *c*.1535, was a dialogue in verse with the names, addresses, attractions, criticisms and prices of 110 courtesans. It was followed by a catalogue of 1570, with 210 names, and later by imitations dealing with the attractions of Amsterdam (1630) and London – the *Commonwealth of Ladies* (1650) on those working at the New Exchange, and Harris's *List of Covent-Garden Ladies*, annually from 1760 onwards. It is not always clear whether these guides were intended for visitors or natives; how accurate they were; or indeed whether the intention of the authors was to offer practical information or pornography.

For even the natives of large cities were increasingly in need of orientation, for information about various forms of leisure, or where to find certain commodities and services. Posters were one solution to the problem. Take the playbill, for example. These advertisements pasted on walls go back to Spain in the late sixteenth century, the moment of the rise of the commercial theatre. The Spanish *cartel* was imitated by the Italian *manifesto*, the French *affiche*, the German *Plakat* and the English 'bill'. Pepys refers in 1662 to bills advertising plays and fixed to posts at the Temple and elsewhere. In Paris in the late eighteenth century, posters of this kind played an important role in urban life. They were strictly controlled, the forty official *afficheurs* or bill-posters wearing badges as evidence of their status. The information they posted ranged from advertisements concerning charlatans, lost dogs and preachers to decrees of the Paris Parlement.

To cater for some of these needs the so-called Bureau d'Adresse was established in Paris in the early seventeenth century (near the Pont Neuf, later at the Louvre) by Théophraste Renaudot, even better known as the editor of the official newspaper, the *Gazette*. The idea of the bureau was (for a fee) to put people in touch (servants and employers, for example), who had not known of one another's existence, thus combating the anonymity of the big city. As an English visitor to the Louvre reported, 'under the long gallery is a place called the *Bureau d'Addresse*. Here a man has a book of servants and lackey's names.' The bureau was well enough known to be the subject of court ballets in 1631 and 1640, one medium of communication thus giving publicity to another.[40]

This seventeenth-century version of the yellow pages did not last very long, but the idea was taken up again later in the century by an apothecary-physician called Nicolas de Blegny, who presented the material in printed form, this time under the title *The Convenient Book of Addresses in Paris* (1692), which included information about sales, vacant positions, libraries, public lectures, baths, music teachers, and the times and places of audiences with the archbishop of Paris or performances of the royal touch. He seems to have been wise to publish this work of reference under a pseudonym, 'Abraham du Pradel', for it was soon suppressed after complaints of invasion of privacy from some of the great and the good whose addresses he had listed.[41]

Yet the demand for this kind of information persisted, and in the eighteenth century the project was revived yet once more. The chevalier de Mouchy (better known for his organization of manuscript newsletters) also organized a *bureau d'adresse* on the rue Saint-Honoré around 1750. Information about leisure activities in Paris was available in the eighteenth century in journals such as *Affiches de Paris* (1716), *Journal des Spectacles de la Cour* (1764), later the *Journal des Théâtres* (1777), and *Calendrier des Loisirs* (1776). From 1751, the *Affiches* was published together with the *Gazette* at the 'bureau d'adresses et rencontres' in rue Baillette. It offered information about plays, sermons, decrees of the Parlement of Paris, the arrival of goods,

[40] Solomon (1972), 21–59.
[41] Solomon (1972), 217–18.

books recently printed, and so on. In similar fashion, the *Diario de Madrid* (1758–) included *noticias particulares de Madrid*, advertisements for someone to share a coach to Cadiz and a rubric 'Lost Things' (dogs, rosaries and so on).

In London, the idea of providing practical information for the inhabitants of the city was taken up towards the middle of the seventeenth century by Samuel Hartlib, whose Office of Address or Agency for Universal Learning tried to combine the practical services offered by Renaudot with a more ambitious project for the collection and the international diffusion of knowledge on all subjects.[42] A foreigner like Hartlib may have been particularly conscious of the need for orientation in a large city. His project, like Renaudot's, was short-lived, but – again like Renaudot's – it inspired imitators. For example the 'Office of Publick Advice' in London (1657) which published a weekly, the *Publick Adviser*, but also offered personal mediation; or the intelligence bureau set up by a certain T. Mayhew in London *c*.1680 at The Pea Hen, opposite Somerset House, which was concerned to register immigrants.

In eighteenth-century London, employment agencies or 'register offices' for servants were increasingly common. The novelist – and magistrate – Henry Fielding put forward a plan for a 'Universal Register-Office' in 1751, remarking that 'great and populous cities' require 'a method of communicating the various wants and talents of the members to each other', and proposing registers of estates to be sold, lodgings to let, lenders of money, positions vacant, travel services, and so on, in short what a playwright of the day called 'an Intelligence-Warehouse'. He was concerned that no servant be registered 'who cannot produce a real good character from the last place in which he or she actually lived'. It is no surprise to learn that Fielding was also responsible for the establishment of what has been called the 'first detective force in England', at the Bow Street Office in 1749. Fielding considered information a weapon against criminals and advocated a register of intelligence about robberies.

PROCESSING KNOWLEDGE

The systematization of knowledge in cities and elsewhere was part of a larger process of elaboration or 'processing' which included compiling, checking, editing, translating, commenting, criticizing, synthesizing and, as they said at the time, 'epitomizing and methodizing'.

---

[42] George (1926–9); Webster (1975), 67–77.

The process might be described in terms of an assembly-line. As items of information moved along the route from the field to the city, many different individuals added their contribution. By this means knowledge was 'produced', in the sense that new information was turned into what was regarded – by the clerisy, at least – as knowledge. It would be absurd to suggest that this new information arrived free from concepts or categories, so many 'raw materials' imported to the metropolis from the colonies. In the case of herbs and medicines from the East and West Indies, for example, it is clear that the knowledge had been elaborated locally by indigenous savants before its arrival in Europe.[43]

All the same, in order to be used effectively, this knowledge had to be assimilated or adapted to the categories of European culture. Despite famous examples to the contrary, such as the activities of Montaigne and Montesquieu on their country estates (discussed in chapter 8 below), this process of assimilation generally took place in urban environments. Cities have been described as 'centres of calculation', in other words places in which local information from different regions and concerning diverse topics is turned into general knowledge in the form of maps, statistics and so on. An early example is that of ancient Alexandria, with its famous library, in which scholars such as the geographer Eratosthenes turned local knowledge into general knowledge.[44]

Early modern cities might equally well be described as centres of calculation, criticism and synthesis. The atlases of this period clearly exemplify such syntheses; those of Mercator (produced in Antwerp), for example, or those of Blaeu (Amsterdam), Coronelli (Venice), Homann (Hamburg), or d'Anville (Paris). The papers of the cartographer Jean Baptiste d'Anville have survived and they frequently reveal him in the act of drawing on the oral and written reports of different kinds of traveller, such as merchants and diplomats, in order to make his synthesis.[45] The accommodation of local or even 'peripheral' knowledge to the concerns of the centre was assisted by the use of questionnaires (below, 126), which, like statistics, facilitated comparisons and contrasts.

Processing knowledge in these ways was a collective activity in which scholars participated alongside bureaucrats, artists and printers. This kind of collaboration was only possible in cities large enough to support a wide variety of specialist occupations. Different cities made

---

[43] Grove (1991); Edney (1997), 297.
[44] Latour (1983); cf. Jacob (1996), Miller (1996).
[45] Jacob (1999), 36–7.

distinctive contributions in an international division of labour. When Luther began to challenge the pope, the east German city of Wittenberg, where he taught in the new university, was on the margin of German culture (just as Calvin's Geneva was on the margin of French culture).[46] Thanks to these two reformers, however, Wittenberg and Geneva became holy cities, centres of religious knowledge, equivalents of Rome in the Lutheran and Calvinist worlds.

Again, Florence, Rome and Paris were all centres of connoisseurship. Again, thanks to their libraries and their professors, some university cities played a role in the elaboration of knowledge which was disproportionate to their size – sixteenth-century Padua and Montpellier in the case of medical knowledge, for instance, seventeenth-century Leiden for botany and Arabic studies and eighteenth-century Göttingen for history and Russian studies.

The linguistic minorities so prominent in certain European cities had an important role to play in the process of processing, thus linking the micro-geography of knowledge with its macro-geography. In Venice, for example, the Greeks and the 'Slavs' (*Schiavoni*, mainly from the Dalmatian coast) were involved in the production of books, classical Greek texts in the first case and liturgical texts in the second. Antwerp's Italians, Spaniards, English, French and other minorities were active in the editing, translating and printing of books in those languages. The same point might be made about Amsterdam, including its Russians and Armenians as well as larger minorities such as the French and the Spanish- or Portuguese-speaking Jews. The translation into Latin of vernacular accounts of Muscovy, China and Japan, which helped make these cultures more widely known to scholars elsewhere, often took place in cities with Jesuit colleges (among them Antwerp, Cologne, Mainz, Dillingen and Munich), thus combining the Jesuit interest in missions and in neo-Latin literature.

The rise of dictionaries of non-European languages may be a useful indicator of increasing European interest in and knowledge of other parts of the world. Spanish cities published the first dictionaries of Arabic (1505) and indigenous Amerindian languages such as Guarani (1639). Malay and Indonesian dictionaries were published in Amsterdam in 1603, 1623, 1640 and 1650, doubtless for the use of the VOC. Rome as a centre of missionary endeavour was the natural place of publication for dictionaries of Ethiopian, Turkish, Armenian, Georgian, Arabic, Persian and Vietnamese.

An important role in the processing of information was played by individuals, whether as writers or intellectual entrepreneurs (below,

---

[46] Schöffler (1936), 113.

160). Well-known examples include the Netherlander Johannes de Laet, the Frenchman Jean-Baptiste du Halde and the Germans Bernhard Varenius and Athanasius Kircher. These men never left Europe but all four published descriptions of Asia. De Laet wrote about the Ottoman and Mughal Empires, Varenius about Japan and Siam, and Kircher and du Halde about China.[47] Sedentary scholars of this kind, whose role was the complementary opposite of the itinerant collectors of knowledge such as Hernandez, Kaempfer or Martini, were usually to be found at work in major cities. De Laet worked in Leiden, with access to a major collection of oriental books and manuscripts which proved to be essential for his description of the Mughal Empire. Varenius worked in Amsterdam. Kircher spent forty years in Rome, which gave him access to information from returned missionaries such as Michael Boym and Martino Martini from China, Heinrich Roth from India, and Filippo Marini from Tonkin and Macau. In similar fashion du Halde, who lived in Paris, conversed with missionaries returning from China and edited their reports, published as a series of 'edifying letters' (*Lettres édifiantes*).

It does not detract from the achievements of these men or their colleagues (Giovanni Battista Ramusio in Venice, João Barros in Lisbon, Giovanni Botero in Rome, Richard Hakluyt in London, Jean Baptiste d'Anville and Denis Diderot in Paris or Caspar Barlaeus, Olfert Dapper and Jan Blaeu in Amsterdam) to say that they knew how to exploit the opportunities offered by their location in a major centre of information.

Workers in the 'field' such as the Italian Jesuit Martino Martini, with whom this chapter began, understood very well the need to keep in touch with these centres. Martini, for example, had regular contacts with Rome and visited Amsterdam, as we have seen, to hand over maps to the publisher Jan Blaeu. François Bernier, a physician who spent most of the period 1655–68 in India, sent information by letter to his friends in Paris as well as publishing a book about India on his return. The information garnered by Bernier would be used by John Locke and Charles de Montesquieu to furnish support for their general theories about topics as diverse as laws and ghosts.[48]

DISTRIBUTING KNOWLEDGE

After processing in the city, knowledge was distributed or re-exported through print, a medium which weakened geographical barriers,

---

[47] Bowen (1981), 77–90.
[48] Burke (1999b).

'dislocating' knowledges from their original milieux. The main European cities mentioned in this chapter were important printing centres. The importance of Venice, Amsterdam and London in this respect is well known and will be examined in more detail in an economic context (below). Rome was a major printing centre. So was Paris, its print-shops concentrated in the university quarter in the rue Saint-Jacques. Seville has been described as 'far and away the most important centre of news publishing' in Spain in the early seventeenth century.[49] The book distribution network tended to follow established trade routes, originally at least, but ended by creating some routes of its own.[50]

As a case-study of this process we might examine western knowledge of alternative medicines from other continents. Western physicians appear to have been more open to these alternatives in early modern times than they were in the following age of scientific and professional medicine. Two key texts about exotic herbs and drugs were published in the sixteenth century. One about India, by the Portuguese physician García d'Orta, was first published in Goa, and one about the Americas, by the Spanish physician Nicolás Monardes, was first published in Seville. That both texts became well known all over Europe is thanks in part to their translation into Latin. In the seventeenth century, knowledge of eastern medicine was supplemented by a series of texts published by employees of the VOC. Indian medicine was presented in Jacob de Bondt's *Medicine of the Indians* (1642), Hermann Grimm's *Compendium* (1679), and Hendrik van Rheede's twelve-volume herbal, the *Indian Garden of Malabar* (1678–1703), compiled in Goa but printed in Amsterdam. It is worth emphasizing that this compilation, far from exemplifying a western discovery of information which had previously been unknown to everyone, drew on indigenous Ayurvedic traditions. The manuscript was even revised by some Hindu physicians in Goa before being sent to Europe for publication.[51]

Still further east, Andreas Cleyer (drawing on the notes of a Jesuit missionary to China, Michael Boym), published a book on Chinese medicine, *Specimen of Chinese Medicine* (1682), discussing among other topics the Chinese manner of taking the pulse, while Willem ten Rhijne, in a book published in London in 1683, examined traditional Japanese medicine (acupuncture, moxibustion) and botany (especially the tea and camphor plants).

---

[49] Martin (1996); Ettinghausen (1984), 5.
[50] Raven (1993), 14.
[51] Boxer (1963); Figueiredo (1984); Grove (1996).

The work of Monardes was also supplemented in the seventeenth century, though less elaborately than the work of Orta. The information collected by the Spanish physician Francisco Hernández, who had been sent to Mexico by Philip II, was published in Rome, in Latin, in 1628, while a treatise on Amerindian medicine, *The Medicine of Brazil* (1648), was published by Willem Piso, physician to the Dutch expedition to Pernambuco in the 1630s. The debt of the taxonomies of exotic plants to non-western classifications, Orta to the Arabs, for instance, or Hernández to the Nahuatl system, has recently been recognized by European scholars.[52]

DISCOVERY IN GLOBAL CONTEXT

The European discovery of a wider world was itself part of a wider trend which included the Asian discovery of the Americas as well as the discovery of Europe. In the case of the Ottoman Empire, for example, the interest in America shown by Piri Reis has already been discussed (55). A history of the West Indies written for Sultan Murad III used the work of López de Gómara, Oviedo and Zárate. Mercator's *Atlas* was translated into Turkish in the middle of the seventeenth century, and Blaeu's *Atlas* (by order of Sultan Mehmed IV) in the 1670s.[53] These translations remained in manuscript, but one of the handful of books which came from the press briefly established in the Ottoman Empire in 1727 was a translation of López de Gómara.

Europe had of course already been discovered by the Arabs before 1450. For interest in a previously unknown Europe, it is necessary to look further East. In China, the Italian Jesuit missionary Matteo Ricci placed a map of the world, European-style, on display in his quarters in the late sixteenth century. It attracted some attention. The emperor owned a copy and the map was reproduced in Chinese treatises on geography – though without having much influence on the Chinese cartographical tradition.[54]

The mild interest in the West expressed by the Chinese contrasts with the situation in Japan. Despite – or because of – the government policy of 'seclusion' (above, 59), some Japanese developed a lively interest in foreign culture, especially from the later eighteenth century onwards. The Nagasaki interpreters were among the first to develop an interest in western knowledge, described at the time as

---

[52] Grove (1996): Bustamante García (1997).
[53] Karamustafa (1992), 218.
[54] Yee (1994b), 170, 174–5.

'Dutch knowledge' (*Rangaku*, from 'Oranda', the Japanese name for Holland). A Japanese screen made about 1625 shows a world map derived from Plancius's map of 1592, while a Blaeu world map of 1648 was soon in the possession of the shogun. Curiosity developed, and some Japanese scholars began to visit Nagasaki to learn more about the West. Arashiyama Hoan, for example, studied western medicine there and published a textbook on the subject in 1683. A section from the Dutch translation of Hübner's geography was published in Japanese in 1772. A group of Japanese physicians translated an anatomy textbook from Dutch and published it in 1774. Following his visit to Nagasaki, the scholar Otsuki Gentaku published an introduction to western knowledge in 1788. Only around the year 1800 did the specialists in Rangaku discover that Dutch was not necessarily the most useful western language to be learning.[55]

Like the Europeans, the Chinese and Japanese dealt with exotic knowledge by translating it into their own categories and finding a place for it in their own systems of classification. It is with the problems of classifying knowledge that the following chapter will be concerned.

---

[55] Unno (1994), fig. 11.22, 434.

5

CLASSIFYING KNOWLEDGE: CURRICULA, LIBRARIES AND ENCYCLOPAEDIAS

> The categories of human thought are never fixed in any one
> definite form; they are made, unmade and remade incessantly:
> they change with places and times.
>
> Durkheim

O NE of the most important elements in the elaboration of knowledge described in the last chapter was its classification. It is time to look at this topic in more detail, whether at attempts to fit new knowledge into traditional frameworks or at the opposite theme of the ways in which the frameworks changed over the long term in the course of attempts to accommodate novelties. As Durkheim pointed out, systems of classification 'are made, unmade and remade incessantly'.[1]

THE ANTHROPOLOGY OF KNOWLEDGE

Where the last chapter offered a geography of early modern knowledge, this chapter will sketch what might be called its 'anthropology', since from Durkheim onwards anthropologists have developed a tradition of taking other people's categories or classifications seriously and of investigating their social contexts. The tradition includes such classic studies as Marcel Granet's *Chinese Thought* (1934) and *The Savage Mind* (1962) by Claude Lévi-Strauss. Granet, for example, described Chinese categories such as Yin and Yang as examples of concrete or 'prelogical' thought. Lévi-Strauss rejected the idea of the pre-logical but he too stressed the concrete categories of so-called primitive peoples such as the American Indians, who make a distinction

---

[1] Durkheim (1912), 28; cf. Worsley (1956).

akin to our contrast between 'nature' and 'culture' via the categories of the 'raw' and the 'cooked'.[2]

Western category systems of the early modern period are so different from our own as to require an anthropological approach, as Michel Foucault realized in the 1960s. We have inherited some of the terminology, words like 'magic' or 'philosophy', for example, but these terms have changed their meaning as the intellectual system has changed. To avoid being deceived by these 'false friends', we need to defamiliarize ourselves with European categories, to learn to regard them as no less strange or constructed than those of (say) the Chinese. Foucault made this point with the aid of a fable borrowed from Jorge Luis Borges about the categories of animal to be found in a Chinese encyclopaedia – animals belonging to the emperor, those drawn with a fine camel-hair brush, those which from far off look like flies, and so on. The fable vividly illustrates the apparent arbitrariness of any system of categories when it is viewed from outside.[3]

In the last generation, a number of cultural historians, many of them working on the early modern period, have turned to the study of systems of classification.[4] Early modern Europe was itself a period of great interest in taxonomy on the part of scholars such as the Swiss Conrad Gesner in his natural history of animals (1551), and Ulisse Aldrovandi of Bologna. The Swedish botanist Carolus Linnaeus may have been the greatest and the most systematic of the intellectual taxonomists, but he was not alone in his interests.[5] It is the taxonomy of knowledge itself, however, which is the main theme of this chapter, the taxonomy of taxonomies, concentrating on academic knowledge but attempting to place it in the context of alternative knowledges.

VARIETIES OF KNOWLEDGE

In early modern Europe, knowledge was classified by different groups in a number of ways. This section will discuss a few of the most common distinctions, bearing in mind the fact that the categories changed over time, and also that they were often contested, implicitly or explicitly, with different individuals or groups drawing their distinctions in different places. The distinction between more or less certain knowledge will be discussed in chapter 9 below.

---

[2] Granet (1934); Lévi-Strauss (1962, 1964).
[3] Foucault (1966), 54–5; cf. Elkanah (1981), Crick (1982); Zhang (1998), 19–24.
[4] Kelley and Popkin (1991); Daston (1992); Zedelmaier (1992); Kusukawa (1996); Kelley (1997).
[5] Foucault (1966); Olmi (1992); Koerner (1996).

One recurrent distinction was between theoretical and practical knowledge, the knowledge of the philosophers and the knowledge of the empirics, or as some said, 'science' (*scientia*) and 'art' (*ars*). A vivid example of the employment of these categories in a practical context comes from the building of Milan cathedral around the year 1400. In the course of its construction a dispute developed between the French architect and the local master masons. A meeting of the masons argued that 'the science of geometry should not have a place in these matters since science is one thing and art another'. To this argument the architect in charge of the enterprise replied that 'art without science' (in other words, practice without theory) 'is worthless' (*ars sine scientia nihil est*).[6]

Another recurrent distinction was the one between public and 'private' knowledge (not so much in the sense of 'personal' knowledge as in the sense of information restricted to a particular elite group). In this sense, private knowledge included the secrets of state (*arcana imperii*), discussed in the following chapter, as well as the secrets of nature (*arcana naturae*), the study of which was sometimes known as the 'occult philosophy'. Alchemical secrets, for example, were transmitted, sometimes in cipher, via informal networks of friends and colleagues or within secret societies. Technical secrets were shared within guilds of craftsmen, but outsiders were excluded. The link between 'mysteries' and *métiers* was more than an etymological one.[7]

The question of what kinds of knowledge ought to be made public was a controversial one, answered in different ways in different generations and in different parts of Europe. The Reformation was among other things a debate over religious knowledge in which Luther and others argued that it should be shared with the laity. In Italy, England and elsewhere, reformers of the law argued in a similar manner that laws should be translated into the vernacular so as to free ordinary people from 'the tyranny of lawyers'.[8] Some learned societies were more or less secret societies, while others, like the Royal Society of London, were concerned to make knowledge public. Over the long term, the rise of the ideal of public knowledge is visible in the early modern period, linked with the rise of the printing-press.[9]

A similar distinction was made between legitimate and forbidden knowledge, the *arcana Dei*, knowledge which should be kept secret not only from the general public but from humanity. The extent to which

---

[6] Ackerman (1949).
[7] Principe (1992); Eamon (1994).
[8] Hill (1972), 269–76; Dooley (1999), 83.
[9] Yates (1979); Stolleis (1980); Eamon (1994).

intellectual curiosity was legitimate rather than a 'vanity' or a sin was a matter of debate. The reformer Jean Calvin, for example, followed St Augustine in condemning curiosity, but in the seventeenth century, as we have already seen (26), the word 'curious' was often used as a term of approval to refer to scholars, especially if they were gentlemen.[10]

The distinction between higher and lower knowledge (*scientia superior* and *inferior*) made by the Dominican Giovanni Maria Tolosani in the 1540s is a reminder of the importance of hierarchy in the intellectual organization of knowledge in this period.[11] Male knowledge, including knowledge of the public sphere, was regarded, by males at least, as superior to female knowledge, more or less limited to piety and the domestic realm.

The distinction between 'liberal' and 'useful' knowledge was an old one which continued to be drawn in the early modern period, although the relative evaluation of the two kinds of knowledge was in the process of reversal, at least in some circles. 'Liberal' knowledge, such as knowledge of the Greek and Latin classics, was high in status in 1450 or even 1550, while merely 'useful' knowledge, of trade for instance, or processes of production, was low in status, just like the tradesmen and craftsmen who possessed it. Following a medieval classification which was still in use at this time, craftsmen were viewed by the upper classes as practitioners of the seven 'mechanical arts', traditionally specified as cloth-making, shipbuilding, navigation, agriculture, hunting, healing and acting.[12]

For example, in his autobiography, the English mathematician John Wallis remembered that in the early seventeenth century, his subject was generally regarded not as 'academical studies, but rather mechanical', associated with 'merchants, seamen, carpenters, surveyors'. The assumption of the superiority of liberal to useful knowledge makes a vivid example of the intellectual consequences of the dominance of the old regime by what Veblen called a 'leisure class'. However, this superiority was undermined during the period, as we shall see.

Specialized knowledge was often contrasted with general or even universal knowledge. The ideal of the 'universal man' was taken seriously in some circles in fifteenth-century Italy, witness Matteo Palmieri's *Civil Life*, according to which 'a man is able to learn many things and make himself universal [*farsi universale*] in many excellent arts.' The Florentine poet and scholar Angelo Poliziano was a supporter of the ideal, as is shown by his little treatise on universal

---

[10] Blumenberg (1966); Ginzburg (1976); Kenny (1998).
[11] Feldhay (1995), 207.
[12] Kristeller (1951–2), 175; Rossi (1962).

knowledge, the *Panepistemon*. So was the humanist Giovanni Pico della Mirandola, as may be seen from the list of 900 theses which this bold young scholar proposed to defend in public debate in Rome in 1487. Pico was described by a character in Erasmus's dialogue the *Ciceronian* (1528) as an all-sided man (*ingenium ad omnia factum*).

To know everything, or at least to know something about everything, remained an ideal throughout our period, described as 'general learning', *polymathia* or *pansophia*, a key word in the writings of the Czech educational reformer Jan Amos Comenius and his followers. As the Cambridge don Isaac Barrow put it in his treatise *Of Industry*, 'he can hardly be a good scholar, who is not a general one.' General knowledge was made necessary by the 'connection of things, and dependence of notions', so that 'one part of learning doth confer light to another.' The ideal of generality was exemplified by a few remarkable individuals such as the French magistrate Nicolas de Peiresc, whose interests included law, history, mathematics and Egyptology; the Swedish academic Olaus Rudbeck, active in the fields of anatomy, botany and medicine as well as history; the German Jesuit Athanasius Kircher, who wrote (among other things) on magnetism, mathematics, mining, music and philology; and Daniel Morhof, whose book on the *Polyhistor* (1688) encouraged the use of that term to describe the ideal of general knowledge.[13]

All the same, this ideal was gradually abandoned. The religious writer Richard Baxter already noted with regret the growing fragmentation of knowledge in his *Holy Commonwealth* (1659). 'We parcel arts and sciences into fragments, according to the straitness of our capacities, and are not so pansophical as *uno intuitu* to see the whole.' The article on 'Gens de lettres' in the *Encyclopédie* was more resigned, declaring that 'Universal knowledge is no longer within the reach of man' (*la science universelle n'est plus à la portée de l'homme*). All that could be done was to try to avoid narrow specialism by encouraging a 'philosophical spirit'.

'Book-learning', as it was sometimes called, was distinguished on occasion, even by members of the clerisy, from the knowledge of things. Comenius, for example, emphasized the importance of studying things rather than words, and a similar distinction already underlay the humanist criticism of the wordiness and the hair-splitting of scholastic philosophers, the 'jargon of the schools'.[14] Quantitative knowledge was distinguished from qualitative knowledge and was taken increasingly seriously. As Galileo famously declared, the book

---

[13] Schmidt-Biggemann (1983), xiii–xiv, 141–54; Waquet (1993b); Serjeantson (1999).
[14] Burke (1995b).

of nature is written in the language of mathematics. From the middle of the seventeenth century onwards, information useful to the state was increasingly arranged in the form of 'statistics' (below, 135).

Central to this chapter, however, is academic knowledge and its various fields. 'Field' is a revealing metaphor for knowledge, which goes back a long way in western culture, at least as far as Cicero. In the article in the *Encyclopédie* already quoted, the *gens de lettres* are recommended to enter different 'fields', even if they cannot cultivate them all (above, 85). The term employed, *terrain*, calls up an image of scholar-peasants defending their intellectual turf against the encroachments of their disciplinary neighbours. The 'territorial imperative' was – and remains – important in the intellectual world as well as in the realms of politics and economics. The subject of this chapter might equally well be described as a historical geography of early modern academe and its various 'domains', or as Linnaeus would say, its 'kingdoms' (*regna*).[15]

Another key metaphor of the sixteenth century, as of the Middle Ages, for imagining the knowledge system was that of a tree and its branches. Besides trees of knowledge such as Ramon Lull's *Arbor Scientiae* (figure 5), written *c*.1300 but reprinted several times in the early modern period, there were trees of logic (the so-called 'Tree of Porphyry'), trees of consanguinity, trees of grammar, trees of love, trees of battles, and even a tree of Jesuits (on the analogy of the Tree of Jesse, with Ignatius at the root).[16] What we might call an 'organogram' of the French government was described in 1579 as 'the tree of French estates and offices' (figure 6), while in 1612, the German lawyer Ludwig Gilhausen published a treatise called *Arbor Judiciaria* ('The Tree of Judgments').

Thinking in terms of a tree suggested a distinction between dominant and subordinate, trunk and branches. Lull and Gilhausen followed the metaphor down into the roots and up into the twigs, flowers and fruits. The tree image illustrates a central phenomenon in cultural history, the naturalization of the conventional or the presentation of culture as if it were nature, invention as if it were discovery. This means denying that social groups are responsible for classifications, thus supporting cultural reproduction and resisting attempts at innovation.

In place of the 'tree', a more abstract term was coming into use in the seventeenth century to describe the organization of knowledge. This term (associated with the ancient Stoic philosophers) was 'system',

---

[15] Salmond (1982); Becher (1989).
[16] Rossi (1960), 47, 51–61; Ladner (1979); Tega (1984); Serrai (1988–92), vol. 2, 120–31.

5   *TREE OF KNOWLEDGE*, TITLE-PAGE OF R. LULL, *ARBOR SCIENTIAE*
(1515: RPR. 1635): COPY IN CAMBRIDGE UNIVERSITY LIBRARY (P*.3.52)

applied either to specific disciplines or to the whole of knowledge, as
in the case of the 'system of systems' offered by Bartholomaeus Keckermann and Johann Heinrich Alsted.[17] Three hundred and fifty years
before Foucault, in 1612, Alsted used the metaphor of 'archaeology'
to describe the analysis of the principles underlying the system of disciplines. To examine the ways in which the classification of academic
knowledge entered into everyday practice in European universities, it
may be useful to examine in turn three subsystems, a kind of intellectual tripod composed of curricula, libraries and encyclopaedias.

It should not be assumed that any of the three systems were
unproblematic reflections of general mental categories or ideas about

---

[17] Gilbert (1960), 214–20; Zedelmaier (1992), 125.

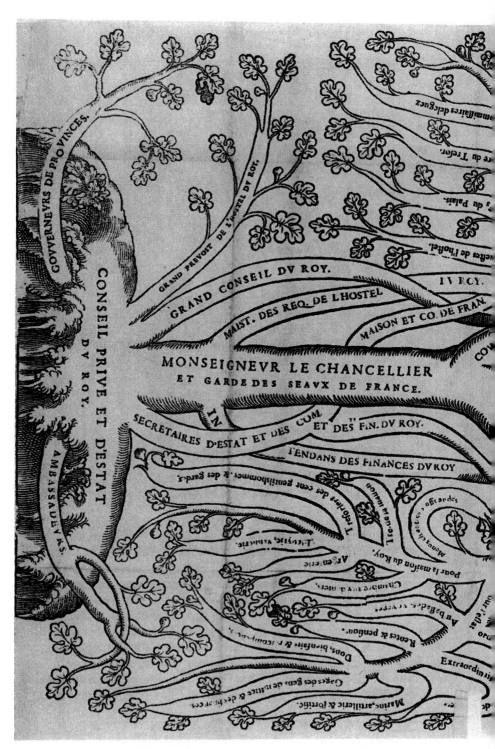

6   TREE OF FRENCH OFFICES, FROM CHARLES DE FIGON, *DISCOURS DES
ESTATS* (PARIS 1579): CAMBRIDGE UNIVERSITY LIBRARY
(PRYME D.I, FOLDING PLATE)

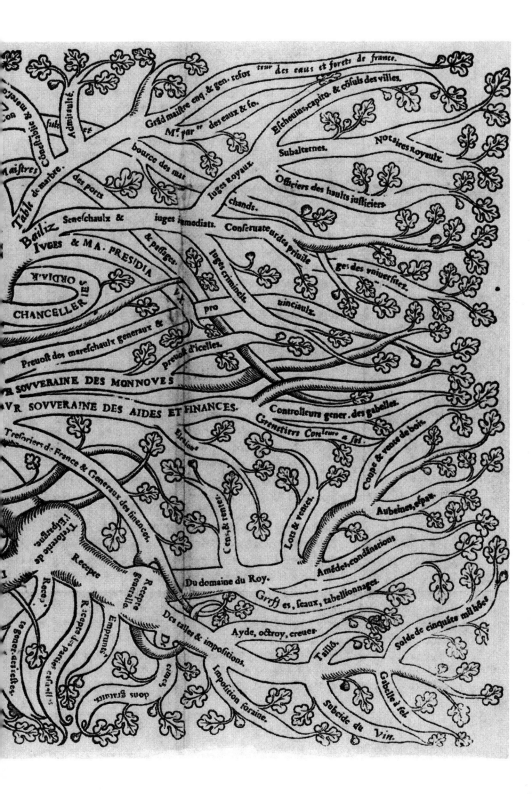

the organization of knowledge. It is certainly possible to offer intern-
alist or local explanations of developments in each area. The curriculum, for instance, is sometimes affected by the micropolitics of
universities: a new chair may be founded as the result of a successful
campaign. Alternatively the curriculum may change in response to
what are perceived as pedagogic needs, as was the case in eighteenth-
century Aberdeen, where logic was moved out of first-year courses
on the grounds that concrete knowledge (as Comenius had argued),
should come before abstractions.[18]

Again, the organization of libraries was obviously subject to both
financial and architectural constraints.[19] Encyclopaedias were products
sold on the open market and subject to its pressures, a point which
will be discussed in more detail below (172). However, where the three
systems overlap, the fundamental categories are likely to express the
assumptions of the university population if not the population in
general, or as the French historian Lucien Febvre used to say, their
'intellectual equipment' (*outillage mental*).

DISCIPLINE AND TEACHING

The curriculum is a metaphor from classical athletics. Like the 'course',
it is the route around which the students had to run. It was an order
or system of 'disciplines'. In ancient Rome the arts and the law were
already described – by Cicero and Varro, for example – as *disciplinae*,
a word derived from *discere*, 'to learn'. In the early modern period,
the word was used in an academic context by the Spanish humanist
Luis Vives, for example.[20] The term was not a neutral one. In the
classical world, discipline was associated with athletics, with the army,
and with the philosophy of the Stoics which emphasized self-control.
In the Middle Ages, discipline was associated with monasteries, with
penance and with scourging. In the sixteenth century, Calvinists in
particular spoke of Church discipline, while some secular writers,
notably Machiavelli, referred to military discipline, as in Roman times.
These associations are relevant to discussions of knowledge because
the sixteenth century saw a movement of 'disciplining' – *Disziplinierung*,
as the Germans say – in schools and universities as well as in churches.

Speaking about 'disciplines' in the plural runs the risk of projecting
the disciplinary conflicts of a later epoch onto the early modern period. Scientific disciplines in particular have been described as an

---

[18] Wood (1993).
[19] Zedelmaier (1992), 112ff.
[20] Kelley (1997), ix.

'invention' of the late eighteenth and early nineteenth centuries.[21] Anachronism is a constant danger. However, there is also an opposite danger, that of distinguishing too sharply – as in the case of the 'professionalization' debate – between early and late modern times. What was new around the year 1800 was not so much the idea of a discipline as its institutionalization in the form of academic 'departments' (a term first used in English in 1832, according to the *Oxford English Dictionary*). Even these departments were not so much a new invention as the elaboration of what the medieval university called 'faculties', a flexible term which referred at once to an ability, a branch of knowledge and a corporate group.

It would be easy to take the language of 'faculties' too literally and so to exaggerate the importance of the frontiers between subjects in early modern academe. A few talented men were willing and able to teach a variety of subjects, and the academic system allowed them to do so. The 'chemist' Andreas Libavius taught history and poetry at Jena, while the 'political scientist' Herman Conring taught medicine at Helmstedt. The Dutch natural philosopher Herman Boerhaave was a pluralist who occupied chairs in medicine, botany and chemistry at the same time at the university of Leiden. The problem of 'autonomy', another revealing metaphor which confirms Elias's analogies between university departments and nation-states (above, 33) had not yet arisen, at least not in acute form. Mathematics and astronomy, for example, have been described as 'semi-liberated' subjects at Oxford and Cambridge. In principle they remained part of philosophy yet in practice they possessed a certain measure of independence.[22]

THE ORGANIZATION OF CURRICULA

In 1450, the curriculum of the European universities, a network which extended from Coimbra to Cracow, was remarkably uniform, thus allowing students to move with relative ease from one institution to another (a practice known as the *peregrinatio academica*).[23] The first degree was the BA, and the arts of which the student became a bachelor were the seven 'liberal arts', divided into two parts, the more elementary *trivium*, concerned with language (grammar, logic and rhetoric), and the more advanced *quadrivium*, concerned with numbers (arithmetic, geometry, astronomy and music). In practice there was also a place for the 'three philosophies', ethics, metaphysics

[21] Stichweh (1991); cf. Lenoir (1997).
[22] Feingold (1984), 17.
[23] Costello (1958); Brockliss (1996).

and what was known as 'natural philosophy', the last of these subjects being studied with special reference to Aristotle's *Physics* and his treatise *On the Soul*.[24]

The first degree might be followed by a course in one of the three higher faculties, theology, law and medicine, a ternary scheme of a kind not uncommon in the Middle Ages, when society was divided into those who prayed, fought and ploughed, and the other world into heaven, hell and purgatory. Law meant the so-called 'two laws', civil and canon law. It was generally considered to have a higher status than medicine but lower than theology, known as the 'queen of the sciences'. The 'higher' faculties were considered more 'noble', another term which reveals the projection of the social hierarchy onto the world of the intellect. As we shall see, this medieval system was extended rather than reconstructed in early modern Europe, the basic ten elements (3+4+3) retaining their place but gradually coming to share it with an increasing number of newcomers such as history and chemistry.

Despite some obvious parallels evoked in chapter 3, the system differed in crucial respects from its equivalent in the world of Islam. In the Muslim system, there was a fundamental distinction between the 'foreign sciences' (essentially arithmetic and natural philosophy) and the 'Islamic sciences', which included not only the study of the Quran and the sayings of the prophet (*hadith*), but also Muslim law (*fiqh*), theology, poetry and the Arabic language. In Christendom, despite the high status of theology, a distinction between Christian and non-Christian disciplines was not built into the system. In similar fashion, the Christians used the word *scientia* for religious and secular knowledge alike, while Muslims distinguished religious knowledge (*'ilm*) from secular studies (*'ulum*, 'knowledges' in the plural, or *ma'rifa*).[25]

THE ORDER OF LIBRARIES

The 'natural' appearance of the traditional system of disciplines was reinforced by the second leg of the tripod, the arrangement of books in libraries. It was only to be expected that the 'order of books' (*ordo librorum*), as Gesner called it, would reproduce the order of the university curriculum.[26] It also supported this system of classification, as it still does, by making it material, physical and spatial. Surviving libraries allow us to study the 'archaeology of knowledge' in the literal sense of Foucault's famous phrase, examining the physical remains of

---

[24] Grant (1996), 42–9.
[25] Rosenthal (1970).
[26] Bouza (1988); Chartier (1992); Zedelmaier (1992), 112.

old classification systems. The catalogues of public and private libraries, and the organization of bibliographies (which were presented in the form of imaginary libraries, often using the title *Bibliotheca*), often followed the same order, with a few permutations and modifications.[27] The catalogue of the Bodleian Library, for example, published in 1605, divided books into four main groups – arts, theology, law and medicine, with a general index of authors and special indexes of commentators on Aristotle and the Bible.

The first printed bibliography (1545), an impressive scholarly achievement which took years of travel as well as study to compile, was the work of Conrad Gesner, who was as interested in classifying books as he was in classifying animals. It listed some 10,000 books by 3,000 authors. A second volume, the *Pandects* (1548), was concerned with subject classification or, as Gesner put it, 'general and particular arrangements' (*ordines universales et particulares*). The volume was divided into twenty-one sections. It began with the *trivium*, followed by poetry, the *quadrivium*, astrology; divination and magic; geography; history; mechanical arts; natural philosophy; metaphysics; moral philosophy; 'economic' philosophy; politics; and finally the three higher faculties, law, medicine and theology.[28]

Comparisons have the advantage of reminding us that this manner of ordering books was not the only one possible. In China, for example, the dominant classification of books from the seventh to the nineteenth centuries, to be found in the Emperor Qianlong's *Four Treasuries* and elsewhere, was a remarkably simple one, composed of no more than four groups: classics, history, philosophy and literature.[29] An Islamic jurist, Ibn Jama'a, recommended books to be arranged in a hierarchical order rather different from the Christian one. 'If there is a Quran among them, it should occupy the place of precedence ... then books of *hadith*, then interpretation of the Quran, then interpretation of *hadith*, then theology, then *fiqh*. If two books pertain to the same branch of knowledge, then the foremost should be the one containing the most quotations from the Quran and *hadith*.'[30]

THE ARRANGEMENT OF ENCYCLOPAEDIAS

The third leg of the tripod was the encyclopaedia.[31] The Greek term *encyclopaedia*, literally 'circle of learning', originally referred to the

[27] Besterman (1935); Pollard and Ehrman (1965); Serrai (1988–92); McKitterick (1992).
[28] Serrai (1990; 1988–92, vol. 2, 211–571); Zedelmaier (1992), 3–153.
[29] Drège (1991); Guy (1987).
[30] Chamberlain (1994), 161.
[31] Wells (1966); Dierse (1977); Kafker (1981); Eybl et al. (1995).

educational curriculum. The term came to be applied to certain books because they were organized in the same way as the system of education, whether in order to assist students in institutions of higher education or to offer a substitute for these institutions, a do-it-yourself course. It should not surprise us to find that in that age when the ideal of universal knowledge still appeared to be within reach, encyclopaedias were sometimes compiled by university teachers including Giorgio Valla, who taught at Pavia and in Venice, and Johann Heinrich Alsted, who taught at Herborn in Germany.

Encyclopaedias and their categories may be viewed as expressions or embodiments of a view of knowledge and indeed a view of the world (after all, from the Middle Ages onwards, the world was often described as a book).[32] Hence it is surely significant that medieval encyclopaedias continued to be used in the early modern period and were even reprinted on occasion. The *Speculum* or 'Mirror' of Vincent of Beauvais, for instance, was reprinted in Venice in 1590 and again in Douai in 1624. On the latter occasion, adapting the metaphor in the title to the age of print, the book was entitled 'the library of the world', *Bibliotheca Mundi*.

Vincent's encyclopaedia was divided into four parts, dealing in turn with the worlds of nature, doctrine, morality and history. Sixteenth-century encyclopaedias were also organized thematically, the main categories often corresponding to the ten disciplines of the medieval university. Gregor Reisch's encyclopaedia, for instance, first published in 1502 and much reprinted in the sixteenth century, was divided into twelve books summarizing the contents of the *trivium*, the *quadrivium* and natural and moral philosophy. On the other hand, Giorgio Valla, like a good humanist, combined the *trivium* with poetry, ethics and history in his encyclopaedia (1501).[33]

At this point it may be illuminating to return to the organization of Chinese encyclopaedias, as they appear in printed texts of the Ming and Qing dynasties rather than in the vivid imagination of Borges (above, 82). A typical arrangement was as follows: celestial phenomena; geography; emperors; human nature and conduct; government; rites; music; law; officialdom; ranks of nobility; military affairs; domestic economy; property; clothing; vehicles; tools; food; utensils; crafts; chess; Daoism; Buddhism; spirits; medicine; natural history. The contrast between the complexity of this system and the simple classification of Chinese libraries is worth noting.[34]

---

[32] Curtius (1948), 302–47; Gellrich (1985).
[33] Dierse (1977), 11ff; Schmidt-Biggemann (1983), 34–5.
[34] Teng and Biggerstaff (1936), 110.

COMMONPLACES

So far we have considered the intellectual organization of knowledge at what might be called the macrolevel. There is also something to say about the microlevel. In his *Organon* (literally 'instrument'), Aristotle had expounded a system of ten general categories (substance, quantity, quality, relation, place, time, position, condition, action and passion). These categories were widely known and used (indeed we still use them today, even if we no longer think of them as a closed system). In his treatise on logic, the fifteenth-century Dutch humanist Rudolf Agricola elaborated the categories into twenty-four topics which would allow arguments to be found more rapidly. Topics could be used as 'pigeonholes' (*niduli*), as Erasmus called them.[35]

Building on Agricola, Luther's friend and colleague Philipp Melanchthon published a highly successful textbook of theology known as the *Commonplaces* (1521), dividing his subject into its specific 'places' (*loci*) or 'heads' (*capita*), or as we would say, using the same metaphors, 'topics' and 'headings' such as God, creation, faith, hope, charity, sin, grace, sacraments and so on. For their part, Catholics could turn to the treatise on *Theological Topics* (1563) by the Spanish Dominican Melchor Cano. In similar fashion the Spanish Jesuit Francisco Labata's *Instrument of Preachers* (1614) provided an alphabetical list of moral or theological commonplaces such as the virtues, the seven deadly sins and the four last things (death, judgement, hell and heaven). Attempts were made to produce similar handbooks for other disciplines such as law and natural philosophy. Opposites such as industry and idleness were often juxtaposed, the dramatic contrast aiding the acquisition of knowledge discussed in more detail in chapter 8 (below, 181).[36]

These discipline-specific commonplaces, together with more general ones, were brought together in the Swiss physician Theodor Zwinger's ambitious encyclopaedia of topics, the *Theatre of Human Life* (1565) as he called it, based on the manuscripts – presumably commonplace books – bequeathed to him by another Swiss scholar, Conrad Lycosthenes but rearranged by Zwinger himself. The second edition, published in 1586–7, had expanded to four volumes. In the following century, the Protestant Zwinger's work was revised and enlarged and given a different religious tinge by the Flemish Catholic Laurentius Beyerlinck, in a book with the same title published in eight volumes in Leuven in 1656. That the tradition of commonplaces

---

[35] Schmidt-Biggemann (1983), 8–15.
[36] Gilbert (1960), 125–8; Schmidt-Biggemann (1983), 19–21; Moss (1996), 119–30.

was still active in the eighteenth century is clear from an inspection of Chambers's *Cyclopedia*.[37]

THE REORDERING OF THE SYSTEM

It is clear that the legs of the tripod supported one another, thus assisting cultural reproduction by making the categories appear to be natural, and alternatives unnatural or even absurd. The survival of traditional ideas of knowledge may be illustrated by juxtaposing two books discussing the conflicts for precedence between university faculties, one of them written by the Florentine humanist Coluccio Salutati at the beginning of the fifteenth century and the other by Immanuel Kant nearly 300 years later. Both focus on the conflicts between theology, law and medicine because these 'higher' disciplines retained their dominance throughout the early modern period. All the same, important changes did occur within the system of academic knowledge between the Renaissance and the Enlightenment, tendencies to 'remapping knowledge' as well as 'reshaping institutions'.[38]

The balance between continuity (or reproduction) and change gradually shifted in favour of the latter. At the level of theory, the shift is revealed by the number of schemes for reforming the classification of knowledge. Some of these schemes were put foward by famous philosophers such as Bacon, Descartes, Locke and Leibniz. Leibniz, for example, was interested in the reform of both libraries and encyclopaedias.[39] Other schemes were the work of men whom posterity has taken less seriously, professional 'systematizers' such as Ramus, Keckermann, Alsted and Kircher.

The French academic Petrus Ramus attacked the classifications used and recommended by Aristotle and Cicero, claiming that the latter was confused and had jumbled the arts. Ramus redrew the frontier between logic and rhetoric. In his own system, binary oppositions presented in tabular form played a major role.[40] These 'dichotomies' were adopted by his followers in encyclopaedias such as Zwinger's *Theatre* and also in textbooks. For example, Andreas Libavius – despite his opposition to Ramus in other respects – presented chemistry in this way (figure 7), while in the 1580s Thomas Frey (Freigius) and Abraham Fraunce offered Ramist analyses of the law, the civil law in

[37] Schmidt-Biggemann (1983), 59–66; Yeo (1991, 1996); Blair (1992); Goyet (1996), 441–3; Blair (1997), 46–8.
[38] Lemaine et al. (1976); Giard (1991).
[39] Flint (1904); Rossi (1960); Schulte-Albert (1971).
[40] Ong (1958); Gilbert (1960), 129–44.

7 *Tabula primi libri*, in Andreas Libavius, *Alchemia*
(Frankfurt, 1597), sig. b2, verso: copy in
Cambridge University Library (L.4.14)

the first case and the common law in the second. Even a description
of Tuscany published in 1605 by the Englishman Robert Dallington
included an 'analysis of the discourse' along these lines.

A more fluid or flexible classification of 'all the arts and sciences'
was presented by the Frenchman Christofle de Savigny in the form of
an oval diagram (figure 8). Around the edge runs a chain of eighteen
disciplines in which the trivium, quadrivium and the three higher
faculties have been joined by poetry, optics, geography, cosmography,
physics, metaphysics, ethics and chronology. In the centre float
seventy-five more ovals, attached by strings like so many balloons,
including subdivisions of the same eighteen disciplines. The diagram
offers a more flexible way of showing interdisciplinary links ('la suite
et liaison' as Savigny puts it), than the dichotomies of Ramus.

Ramus was not welcomed by everyone. His critique of Aristotle, for
example, seemed to some contemporaries to be a kind of *lèse-majesté*,

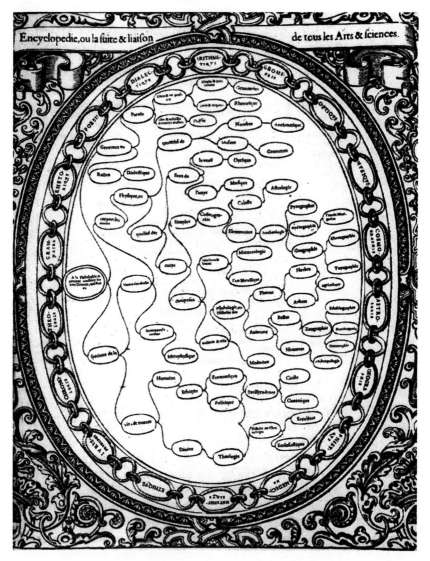

8 C. SAVIGNY, *TABLEAUX ACCOMPLIS*, 1587:
PARIS, BIBLIOTHÈQUE NATIONALE

a point dramatized by Christopher Marlowe in his play *The Massacre at Paris*, when the Duke of Guise, about to kill Ramus as a heretic, asks him: 'Was it not thou that scoff'dst the Organon / And said it was a heap of vanities?' Despite these reservations, some of Ramus's criticisms were widely accepted and attempts were made to incorporate them in eclectic solutions to the problem of classifying knowledge. Alsted, for example, tried to combine Aristotle with Ramus and also with Ramon Lull, whose tree of knowledge has already been mentioned. Kircher's *Great Art of Knowledge* was another attempt at a new synthesis, once again making use of Lull. Leibniz too discussed the work of Lull as well as that of Alsted.[41]

Francis Bacon's solution to the problem was an unusually bold one, appropriate to a man who announced his intention of replacing Aristotle by calling one of his books the *New Organon*. Bacon made the three faculties of the mind – memory, reason and imagination – the basis of his scheme, allocating history to the category 'memory', for instance, philosophy to 'reason', and poetry to 'imagination'.[42] An examination of the curriculum, the library and the encyclopaedia in the seventeenth and eighteenth centuries suggests that Bacon's reclassification was the most successful of the various attempts made at this time.

THE CURRICULUM REORGANIZED

The reorganization of curricula appears to follow certain patterns. There is a recurrent tendency towards differentiation, specialization, and even what might be called 'balkanization'.[43] New disciplines gain their autonomy only to fragment, like new nations in the later twentieth century. In his history of the French Academy of Sciences (1709), its secretary, Bernard de Fontenelle, compared the state of physics in 1650 to that of 'a great but dismembered kingdom' (*un grand royaume démembré*), in which provinces such as astronomy, optics and chemistry had become 'virtually independent'. We have returned to the problem of territoriality (above, 86).

The reorganization of the curriculum took different forms in different universities, but a few general trends are visible. In some places, such as the universities of Bologna or Rome, change was gradual, the balance between *trivium* and *quadrivium* gradually shifting to the advantage of the latter.[44] In many universities an alternative system to the *trivium* and the *quadrivium* invaded or infiltrated the curriculum. This was the system of the *studia humanitatis* consisting of five subjects: grammar and rhetoric (as in the *trivium*), plus poetry, history and ethics. Sometimes the new subjects entered quietly, but on occasion, as in the case of poetry at the University of Leipzig around 1500, bitter conflicts occurred.

---

[41] Rossi (1960), 179–84, 239; Schmidt-Biggemann (1983), 100–39.
[42] Kusukawa (1996), esp. 51–2.
[43] Lemaine et al. (1976), 1–23.
[44] Reiss (1997), 135–54.

The rise of history in particular was assisted by its links with law and with politics (in the sense of a career rather than a discipline). For example, by the eighteenth century, if not before, the study of international history was considered good training for diplomats at Paris. It was taught at the political academy founded in Paris by the foreign minister Torcy in 1712 and in Strasbourg in the 1750s. The foundation of the Regius chairs in History at Oxford and Cambridge in the early eighteenth century had similar origins.[45]

Geography, also known as cosmography, was another discipline which was becoming more prominent in the university in the early modern period, as well as in Jesuit colleges.[46] In Heidelberg in the 1520s, lectures on geography were given by Sebastian Münster, later the author of a famous treatise on cosmography (1544). In Oxford, they were given by Richard Hakluyt in the 1570s, before he became famous as an editor of travel books. The need for more knowledge of geography in an age of exploration and empire was obvious enough and as we have seen (above, 61), cosmography was taught to navigators at the House of Trade in Seville. The fact that ancient Greeks and Romans such as Ptolemy and Strabo had taken the subject seriously also helped to make geography respectable. So did the link between geography and astronomy, the terrestrial globe and the celestial. Geography was sometimes taught by the professor of astronomy, suggesting that the new subject entered the university more easily because it was clinging to the coat-tails of an established discipline. All the same, the fact that Philipp Cluverius was appointed to a paid research post in geography at the University of Leiden in 1616 may be a sign of the difficulty of fitting geography into the curriculum as well as of the university's concern with research, a concern unusual in the period.[47]

'Natural philosophy' gradually gained its independence from the quadrivium, only to split into virtually independent subjects such as physics, natural history, botany and chemistry. The first chair founded in natural history, for instance, was at Rome in 1513, followed by Ferrara and Pisa. Leiden had a chair of botany by 1593, Oxford by 1669 and Cambridge by 1724. Chemistry arrived a little later, in Cambridge in 1702, for example, in Uppsala in 1750 and in Lund in 1758. In the cases of botany and chemistry, the new subjects represent the conferring of a certain measure of academic respectability on certain traditional forms of alternative knowledge, that of the 'cunning folk' and the alchemists. The new university subjects of surgery and

---

[45] Hammerstein (1972), 216ff; Voss (1979).
[46] Dainville (1940); Brockliss (1987), 156.
[47] Baker (1935); Broc (1975, 1980); Cormack (1997), 14–15, 27–30; Jacob (1999).

pharmacy also represent some degree of recognition of alternative knowledges, for in seventeenth-century France apprentices in these 'arts' were allowed to attend lectures in some university faculties.[48]

What might be described as the 'coat-tails principle' was in operation here too, for both botany and chemistry gained a foothold in the university thanks to their association with the long-established faculty of medicine as 'ancillary' subjects, literally 'handmaids' to the master discipline, thanks to the healing power of certain herbs and chemical preparations. For example, Cesare Cesalpino did his botanical work while professor of medicine at Pisa, and Rembert Dodoens taught botany while occupying a chair in medicine at Leiden. A chair in medical chemistry was founded at the university of Marburg in 1609. Georg Stahl lectured on chemistry at the university of Halle although his appointment was in medicine, while Boerhaave's combination of medicine with botany and chemistry has already been mentioned.[49]

It is even possible that an association with medicine was of aid to another new discipline, politics. The images of the 'body politic', the 'physician of the state', 'political anatomy' and so on were more than mere metaphors, especially before 1700. When Conring lectured on medicine and politics in the university of Helmstedt in the middle of the seventeenth century, this combination of subjects may not have seemed as odd at the time as it does today. After all, the alchemist Johann Joachim Becher, who had been trained in medicine, claimed the right to speak on politics because the motto of both subjects was 'the welfare of the people is the supreme law' (*salus populi suprema lex*).[50]

In the case of politics and economics, however, it was the established discipline of philosophy which helped their entry to the academic curriculum. Keckermann reformed the curriculum at the gymnasium at Danzig by adding third-year courses on ethics, politics and 'economics' (*disciplina oeconomica*), in the ancient Greek sense of household management. At Halle, at the end of the seventeenth century, Christian Thomasius taught politics and economics as what he called 'practical philosophy' (*philosophia practica*).[51]

The rise of politics and, more slowly, of political economy was also assisted by the needs of the centralizing state. Politics was coming to be considered less of an 'art', to be learned by practice, and more of a science (*scientia, Wissenschaft*), which could be systematized and taught in an academic manner. Conring, for example, used the phrase *scientia politica*. A fashionable term in German-speaking lands from the late seventeenth century onwards was *Polizeywissenschaft*,

[48] Brockliss (1987), 393–4; Mandosio (1993).
[49] Hannaway (1975); Meinel (1988).
[50] Stolleis (1983); Seifert (1980, 1983); Smith (1994), 69.
[51] Hammerstein (1972), 62ff.

otherwise known as *Statsgelartheit* or *Staatswissenschaft*. The subject was taught outside universities, at special colleges for officials, before chairs in it were founded at the universities of Halle and Frankfurt-on-Oder in 1727.

As for 'political economy', it developed out of household management, the state being regarded as an enormous household. The phrase was apparently coined by the French Protestant playwright Antoine de Montchestien in his *Traité de l'économie politique* (1615). It was only in the eighteenth century, however, that we can observe the entry of the new discipline into the academic system, thus recognizing and theorizing the practical knowledge of merchants, bankers and speculators on the stock exchange. It was appropriate that Carl Ludovici, the author of an important encyclopaedia of commerce, should have held a chair in 'knowledge of the world' (*Weltweisheit*) at the university of Leipzig from 1733 onwards (that a chair could be founded with such a title gives the impression that the university was open to innovation at that point).

The entry of economics into the academic environment was not always simple or smooth. Adam Smith, who was employed at the university of Glasgow as a professor of moral philosophy, was unable to write the *Wealth of Nations* until he had resigned from his chair to become a travelling tutor to an aristocrat, although it is true that he had been able to try out his ideas on 'the general principles of law and government' in an informal manner in a so-called 'private' class at the university in 1762–4.

Smith might have found the academic environment more favourable to his ideas had he lived in the German-speaking world or in Naples. In Halle and Frankfurt-on-Oder, for instance, chairs in what was known as *Cameralia Oeconomica* were founded in 1727, followed by Rinteln (1730), Vienna (1751), Göttingen (1755), Prague (1763) and Leipzig (1764). In Naples, a chair of 'political economy' – the first in Europe with this name – was created in 1754 for Antonio Genovesi, while in Moscow University, founded a year later, economics (known as *kameralija* or *kameral'nykh nauk*) was taught virtually from the start.[52] By this time, the new discipline was well enough established to lend a helping hand to chemistry: it was in the faculty of *Kameralistik* that chairs of chemistry were located in German and Swedish universities. It had also begun to fragment into specialities such as forestry (*Forstwissenschaft*), which fortified its claims to scientific status by employing the latest quantitative methods.[53]

---

[52] Meier (1966), 214; Larrère (1992); Stichweh (1991), 4.
[53] Meinel (1988); Lowood (1990).

LIBRARIES REARRANGED

In libraries too there was a concern with reclassification, partly as a result of changes in the organization of universities, but also as a result of the multiplication of books which followed the invention of printing, an outpouring of books which alarmed some scholars. An Italian writer, Antonfrancesco Doni, was already complaining in 1550 that there were 'so many books that we do not even have time to read the titles'. Comenius referred to the 'vast quantities of books' (*granditas librorum*), and a French scholar of the later seventeenth century, Basnage, to the 'flood'.[54] Rather than an order of books, what some contemporaries perceived was a 'disorder of books' which needed to be brought under control. Even Gesner, who coined the phrase *ordo librorum*, also complained of 'that confused and irritating multitude of books' (*confusa et noxia illa librorum multitudo*).[55]

In this domain the intellectual frontier was necessarily more open than in the case of curricula, since books were material objects which had to be placed somewhere and might not fit any traditional category. Books on politics, for example, proliferated in the period, as is clear from subject bibliographies such as *De studio politico ordinando* (1621), by the German academic Christoph Colerus, or the *Bibliographia politica* (1633), by the French scholar-librarian Gabriel Naudé. Bibliographies, a form of reference book which became increasingly common in the period (below, 187) have been described as 'libraries without walls' which could travel all over Europe.[56]

Catalogues were indeed less resistant to novelty than were curricula. Gesner's general bibliography of 1548, for instance, already found a place for politics alongside subjects such as economic philosophy, geography, magic and the mechanical arts. His imaginary library became the basis of catalogues of actual libraries, such as the imperial library at Vienna at the time when the humanist Hugo Blotius was librarian. A new and complex system was proposed by the Spanish scholar Francisco de Aráoz in a treatise on *How to Arrange a Library* (1631). Aráoz divided books into fifteen 'predicaments' or categories. Five of these categories were religious: theology, biblical studies, ecclesiastical history, religious poetry and the works of the fathers of the Church. Ten were secular; dictionaries, books of commonplaces, rhetoric, secular history, secular poetry, mathematics, natural philosophy, moral philosophy, politics and law.

---

[54] Lieshout (1994), 134.
[55] Zedelmaier (1992), 19n.
[56] Stegmann (1988); Chartier (1992).

9 J. C. Woudanus, *Leiden University Library* (1610), engraved by W. Swanenburgh: Leiden University Library

A simpler solution to the problem of classification is recorded in an engraving of the interior of Leiden university library in 1610 (figure 9), showing books arranged in seven categories: the traditional faculties of theology, law and medicine together with mathematics, philosophy, literature and history. The catalogue of the same library, published in 1595, uses the same seven categories, while the 1674 catalogue added an eighth, 'oriental books' (by this time the university had become well known for its contribution to oriental studies).

Another simple solution was offered by Gabriel Naudé. In his *Advice on Building up a Library* (1627), which devoted its seventh chapter to the question of classification, Naudé declared that a pile of books was no more a library than a crowd of soldiers was an army, and criticized the famous Ambrosiana library in Milan for its lack of subject classification, its books 'heaped in confusion' (*peslemelez*). He also criticized 'capricious' schemes of classification on the grounds that the point of the scheme was simply to find books 'without labour, without trouble and without confusion'. For this reason he recommended following the order of the faculties of theology, medicine and law, together with 'history, philosophy, mathematics, humanities and others'.[57]

These solutions were pragmatic ones, shuffling the pack of disciplines but leaving more fundamental problems in suspense. Reformulating Plato, one might say that to introduce order into the realm of books, either librarian-philosophers or philosopher-librarians are required, combining the talents of John Dewey the pragmatist philosopher with those of Melvil Dewey, the originator of the famous Decimal System of Classification.[58] In the late seventeenth century, this ideal was briefly realized in the person of Leibniz, who was librarian of the duke's library at Wolfenbüttel. Thanks to this stimulus Leibniz, who wrote in a letter of 1679 that a library should be the equivalent of an encyclopaedia (*il faut qu'une Bibliothèque soit une Encyclopédie*), produced a 'Plan for Arranging a Library' (*Idea bibliothecae ordinandae*). This plan divided knowledge into nine parts, of which three corresponded to the traditional higher faculties of theology, law and medicine, joined by philosophy, mathematics, physics, philology, history and miscellaneous. In similar fashion the *Acta Eruditorum* of Leipzig, a journal which regularly reviewed new books, indexed them under seven categories: theology (including ecclesiastical history), law, medicine (including physics), mathematics,

---

[57] Blum (1963); Stenzel (1993); Revel (1996); Nelles (1997).
[58] Petrucci (1995), 350–1.

history (including geography), philosophy (including philology) and 'miscellaneous'.[59]

The category 'miscellaneous' deserves more attention than it has usually received. Indeed, it might be argued that a history of the different items which have been placed in this category over the centuries would make an illuminating contribution to intellectual history, focusing on whatever resisted successive modes of classification. Samuel Quiccheberg, the author of a guide to arranging collections (below, 109) used 'philology' as his miscellaneous category, including in it war and architecture. The French bibliographer La Croix used 'Mélanges' as one of his seven categories, including in it memoirs, recreational reading, paradise, purgatory, hell and the end of the world. Alsted included in his *Encyclopaedia* (1630), a large miscellaneous section (*farragines*) including history and the art of memory.

METHODIZING MUSEUMS

Problems of classification were even more acute in the case of museums than in that of libraries, since there was no medieval tradition for owners or curators of museums to follow or adapt. Museums or 'cabinets of curiosities' proliferated in the sixteenth, seventeenth and eighteenth centuries. Some of them were famous all over Europe: not only the cabinets of princes (Rudolf II in Prague, for example, or Louis XIV in Paris), but also of private individuals such as the cleric Manfredo Settala in Milan, the professor Ulisse Aldrovandi in Bologna, the apothecary Basilius Besler in Nuremberg, the physicians Pierre Borel in Castres and Ole Worm in Copenhagen or the virtuoso Hans Sloane in London (below, 110). No fewer than 723 collections are known to us from eighteenth-century Paris alone. Around the year 1700, medals were the most popular item, but the eighteenth century saw the rise of a competitor, shells, suggesting a shift from an amateur interest in classical erudition to an interest in natural philosophy.[60]

To reconstruct the organization of these collections, we have to rely on the evidence of images, while recognizing that the artist's intentions may have been to produce an allegorical rather than a realistic portrayal.[61] Seventeenth-century pictures are likely to give today's viewers an impression not only of abundance but also of heterogeneity. In the contemporary engraving of Worm's museum,

---

[59] Schulte-Albert (1971); Palumbo (1993a, 1993b).
[60] Pomian (1987), 121.
[61] Pomian (1987), 49–53.

for instance (figure 10), our attention is drawn by the statue of a man flanked by a jacket, boots and spurs, but also by the stuffed fish hanging from the ceiling (together with a small bear), and the deer's antlers displayed on a wall together with drinking-horns. The catalogue reveals an even wider range of objects, including an Egyptian mummy, an ancient Roman brooch, money from Java, manuscripts from Ethiopia and Japan and tobacco pipes from Brazil, as well as many Nordic antiquities – spears from Greenland, a bow from Lapland, skis from Finland and an ancient shield from Norway.

Looked at more carefully, however, the apparently heterogeneous display reveals the existence of a desire to classify. Worm's museum includes boxes labelled 'Metal', 'Stone', 'Wood', 'Shells', 'Herbs', 'Roots' and so on. The drinking-horns are displayed together with the deer's antlers because they are made from the same material. The description of the collection published by Worm's son is divided into four books, dealing respectively with stones and metals; plants; animals; and artifacts (*artificiosa*). In other words, the contents of the museum, whether natural objects or artifacts, are classified not by place or period but by the substances out of which they were made. Manfredo Settala of Milan adopted the same classification by raw material, thus encouraging the impression that the museum was a microcosm, a universe in miniature.

Again, Aldrovandi tried to impose order on his collection by dividing it into sixty-six chests (*cassette*), subdivided into no fewer than 7,000 compartments. An 'Index' in two large volumes assisted the task of finding a specific object. Catalogues of some collections, including those of Settala and Worm, were published in the seventeenth century and reveal the logic behind the arrangements.[62]

Similar problems of order arose in the case of collections of images. Aldrovandi, for example, commissioned painters to record the appearance of animals and birds. Another famous example is the 'paper museum' (*museo cartaceo*) of the Roman virtuoso Cassiano del Pozzo, featuring images of classical antiquity and much more. A third, in print this time, is the series of volumes *Antiquity Explained* (1719–) published by the Benedictine scholar Bernard de Montfaucon, with 1,120 plates illustrating different aspects of the ancient world – gods, cults, daily life, war, tombs and so on.[63]

The importance of the ordering of objects is also revealed by texts such as Samuel Quiccheberg's *Inscriptions* (1565), Jacques Oisel's *Treasury of Ancient Coins* (1677), and John Evelyn's *Discourse of*

---

[62] Olmi (1992), 195ff, 201ff, 274n, 285.
[63] Olmi (1992); Haskell (1993), 131–5; Cropper and Dempsey (1996), 110–13.

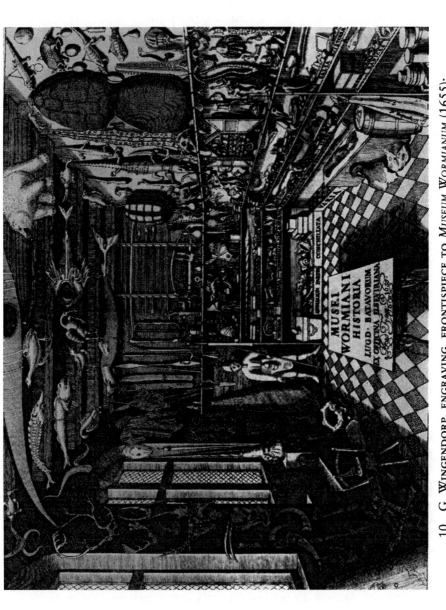

10 G. WINGENDORP, ENGRAVING, FRONTISPIECE TO *MUSEUM WORMIANUM* (1655): CAMBRIDGE UNIVERSITY LIBRARY (M.13.24)

Medals (1693). Quiccheberg, for example, recommended a division of museums into five categories, of which one was 'nature'. Oisel divided classical coins into ten classes, concerned respectively with emperors, provinces, gods, virtues, war, games, apotheoses, public buildings, priests and miscellaneous. Evelyn devoted some pages of his treatise, addressed to would-be collectors, to 'the method of ranging, marshalling and placing' medals, noting for example that the 20,000 medals in the cabinet of the king of France were 'ranked according to the dates'. Evelyn's concern with what he called 'methodizing' is reminiscent of Ramus and also of Gabriel Naudé, whose discussion of the ordering of books Evelyn translated into English.

No wonder then that the apparently irresistible rise of museums in this period has been explained not only as an indicator of the expansion of curiosity but as an attempt to manage a 'crisis of knowledge' following the flood of new objects into Europe from the New World and elsewhere – alligators, armadillos, feathered head-dresses, newly discovered Egyptian mummies, Chinese porcelain – objects which resisted attempts to fit them into traditional categories.[64]

ENCYCLOPAEDIAS ALPHABETIZED

In the case of encyclopaedias, the impetus to change was provided once again by the invention of printing. The rise of the printing industry had two important consequences in this domain. In the first place, it obviously made encyclopaedias more readily and more widely available. In the second place, it made them even more necessary than they had been before the invention of the press. To be more precise, one of their functions became increasingly necessary, that of guiding readers through the ever-growing forest – not to say jungle – of printed knowledge.

Compilers of encyclopaedias gradually became bolder in their modifications of the traditional category-system. Pierre Grégoire's *Syntaxes* (1575–6), a bold attempt at an epitome of 'all the sciences and arts', devoted separate sections to mechanical arts, including a separate discussion of painting as well as of the traditional topics of cloth-making, war, navigation, medicine, agriculture, hunting and architecture. Bacon's classification seems to have been especially influential. Naudé's discussion of the formation of a library, for example, adopted a Baconian framework. The Italian bishop Antonio Zara

---

[64] Findlen (1994), 3, 50; cf. Lugli (1983); Impey and Macgregor (1985); Pomian (1987).

put into practice what Bacon was preaching with his system of thirty-six subjects arranged in the three master categories of memory, intellect and imagination. Ephraim Chambers divided knowledge into the products of the senses, reason and imagination.[65] D'Alembert discussed the ideas of Bacon in his prelimary discourse to the *Encyclopédie*.

However, a still more profound change in the organization of encyclopaedias began to be visible from the early seventeenth century onwards: alphabetical order. Alphabetical order had been known in the Middle Ages. What was new in the seventeenth century was that this method of ordering knowledge was becoming the primary rather than a subordinate system of classification. Today the system may seem obvious, even 'natural', but it appears to have been adopted, originally at least, out of a sense of defeat by the forces of intellectual entropy at a time when new knowledge was coming into the system too fast to be digested or methodized. Its gradual spread will be discussed in more detail in chapter 8 below.

THE ADVANCEMENT OF LEARNING

A number of changes in conceptions of knowledge have been noted in the course of this chapter, among them the increasing concern with figures. The use of figures or 'statistics' was associated with the new ideal of impersonal or impartial knowledge, of what would later be called 'objectivity' (above, 26). Two other changes in the course of the early modern period also deserve to be emphasized.

In the first place, a shift took place in the relative importance of liberal and useful knowledge, the latter being stressed by Descartes, Bacon and Leibniz as well as by Bacon's many followers such as John Durie, Samuel Hartlib, Robert Boyle, Joseph Glanvill and Hans Sloane. The *Essay toward Promoting All Necessary and Useful Knowledge*, published in 1697 by Thomas Bray, was typical of its time. Although the rhetorical claim to usefulness was traditional, the emphasis on the uses of practical knowledge was an innovation. Reversing the dictum of the French architect in Milan in 1400 (above, 83), the Baconians might well have said in 1700 that 'theory is worthless without practice', *scientia sine arte nihil est*.

By the eighteenth century, useful knowledge had become respectable. Under its new constitution of 1699, the French Academy of Sciences placed more emphasis on engineering and other forms of applied science, an emphasis which culminated in its multi-volume

---

[65] Yeo (1991).

Description of Crafts and Trades (1761–88).[66] A biographer of the alchemist-economist Johann Joachim Becher described him in its title as 'the model of a useful scholar' (*Das Muster eines Nützlich-Gelehrten*). The *Gentleman's Magazine* remarked in May 1731 that 'Our knowledge should be in the first place, that which is most useful, then that which is most fashionable and becoming a Gentleman.' In the same year, in Dublin, a society was founded 'for the Improvement of Husbandry', its purpose being 'to bring practical and useful knowledge out of libraries into the light of day'. Agricultural societies were founded all over Europe to spread knowledge which would be useful to farmers. The Erfurt Academy of Useful Sciences, founded in 1754, had similar aims, like societies founded in Philadelphia (1758), Virginia (1772) and New York (1784). Diderot and the French scholars associated with the *Encyclopédie* had similar views.

In Russia, the western knowledge which Tsar Peter the Great was so keen to introduce was exemplified by the schools which he founded to teach mathematics and navigation as well as by the fact that the first secular book to be printed in Russia was Leonty Magnitsky's *Arithmetic* (1703). For this kind of practical knowledge a new Russian word was coined, *nauka*. It is this word, usually translated into English as 'sciences', which was used to describe the new Academy of Sciences in St Petersburg. The original associations of the term *nauka* were not academic at all but military, naval, technological and economic.

Looking back, it is tempting to describe the first half of the seventeenth century as a brief 'age of curiosity'. It was the time that the words 'curious', *curiosus* or *curieux* came to be used much more frequently. The religious criticisms of 'curiosity' had at last been virtually banished from the secular sphere, while the secular criticisms of 'useless' knowledge were not yet vocal. In the second place, there was a shift in conceptions of knowledge, to borrow the famous phrase of Alexandre Koyré, 'from the closed world to the infinite universe', a new vision of knowledge as cumulative. Novelty lost its pejorative associations and became a recommendation, as in the titles of such books as Kepler's *New Astronomy* and Galileo's *Discourse Concerning Two New Sciences*.[67]

The best-known expression of this vision of progress is Francis Bacon's, in the book appropriately entitled *The Advancement of Learning* (1605). On the title-page and in the text of more than one of his books (figure 11), Bacon made use of a striking image which

[66] Briggs (1991), 40, 65.
[67] Thorndike (1951); Rossi (1962), 68–102.

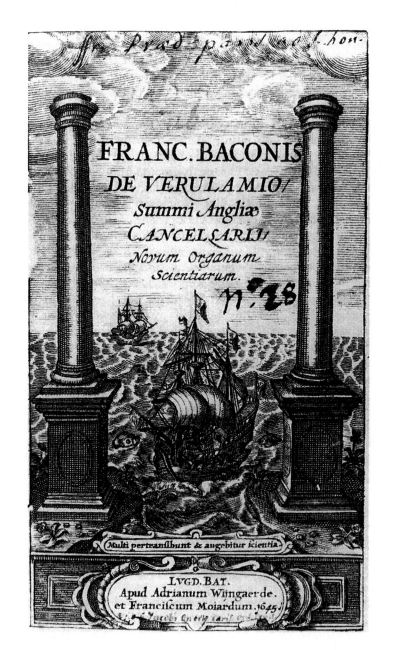

FRANC. BACONIS
DE VERULAMIO/
Summi Angliæ
CANCELLARII
Novum Organum
Scientiarum.

n.º 28

Multi pertransibunt & augebitur scientia.

LVGD. BAT.
Apud Adrianum Wijngaerde.
et Franciscum Moiardum. 1645.

11A, 11B   ENGRAVINGS, FRONTISPIECES, F. BACON, *INSTAURATIO MAGNA* (1620): PARIS, BIBLIOTHÈQUE DE LA SORBONNE PHOTO JEAN-LOUP CHARMET (FONDS V. COUSIN, 5525 RÉS.); AND *SYLVA SYLVARUM* (1627): CAMBRIDGE UNIVERSITY LIBRARY (LE 24.25)

symbolizes his desire to change the system. It is the image of the 'intellectual world' (*mundus intellectualis*) illustrated by an engraving of a globe or alternatively, a ship sailing beyond the Pillars of Hercules in search of new territories. 'It would disgrace us', he wrote in his *Refutation of Philosophies*, 'now that the wide spaces of the material globe, the lands and seas, have been broached and explored, if the limits of the intellectual globe should be set by the narrow discoveries of the ancients.' The English Baconian Joseph Glanvill adopted the motto of the emperor Charles V, PLUS ULTRA ('beyond', that is, beyond the Pillars of Hercules) as the title of one of his books, and Leibniz too wrote the phrase at the head of a manuscript on which he was working in the 1670s, concerned with the advancement of learning.

Bacon's ambition was clearly that of an intellectual Columbus who would 'redraw the map of learning'. For a concrete example of the advancement of knowledge, we may turn to maps themselves. Atlases, like encyclopaedias, tended to become larger and larger in successive editions. Ortelius asked his readers to send in information which might improve his atlas, and some readers responded.[68] The idea of the advancement or 'improvement' of knowledge recurs again and again in England, linking the millenarian enthusiasms of the 1650s to the more limited hopes of the 1660s and beyond, expressed in Joseph Glanvill's *Plus Ultra* (another allusion to the Pillars of Hercules) and in John Locke's *Essay Concerning Human Understanding* (1690). Another vivid example comes from a short treatise on the function of the 'library-keeper' published by John Durie in 1650, in which he argues that a university librarian ought to be bound to give an annual 'account' of 'his profit in his trade', in other words the increase in acquisitions, described as 'the stock of learning'.[69] In the eighteenth century, the ideal of intellectual exploration was sometimes summed up by a quotation from Horace, taken out of its original context and turned into the slogan 'Dare to know' (*sapere aude*).[70]

The modern academic ideal might be viewed as the routinization of these seventeenth- and eighteenth-century aspirations. Intellectual innovation, rather than the transmission of tradition, is considered one of the major functions of institutions of higher education, so that candidates for higher degrees are normally expected to have made a 'contribution to knowledge', and there is pressure on academics – despite the counter-pressures described in chapter 3 above – to colonize new intellectual territories rather than to continue to cultivate old ones.

---

[68] Jacob (1992), 88, 112.
[69] Webster (1975), 100–245.
[70] Venturi (1959).

CONCLUSION

The *Encyclopédie* offers an excellent view of what d'Alembert (following Bacon) called the 'map' of learning at the end of our period.[71] Successive editions of the book – and its rivals – reveal an increasingly acute awareness of the progress of knowledge. All the same, the classification of knowledge propounded by d'Alembert in his 'preliminary discourse' and presented in tabular form by Diderot is balanced between tradition and innovation. Looking back from our own time, this scheme looks traditional, especially the idea of the tree of knowledge and its branches, the distinction between the liberal and the mechanical arts and the discussion of the *trivium* of grammar, logic and rhetoric.

Viewed from 1500, on the other hand, a number of innovations would have stood out. The tree of knowledge had been trimmed.[72] Mathematics was promoted to the first place and discussed before the *trivium*. Theology was subordinated to philosophy, subverting the traditional hierarchy (and shocking the reviewer of the book in the *Journal des Savants*). As the engravings as well as the text reveal, the mechanical arts were taken even more seriously than in the encyclopaedias of Alsted and Zara, illustrating the increasing rapprochement between academic and non-academic knowledges.

Finally, the arrangement of the articles was alphabetical, although it was countered up to a point by the elaborate system of cross-references. Independently of the practical reasons for which it was adopted, the use of alphabetical order both reflected and encouraged a shift from a hierarchical and organic view of the world to one which was individualistic and egalitarian. In this respect we might speak of 'the content of the form', reinforcing the editors' ambition to subvert the social hierarchy in some respects at least. For the *Encyclopédie* was a political as well as an intellectual project. The politics of knowledge will be examined in more detail in the following chapter.

[71] Dieckmann (1961); Gandt (1994); Malherbe (1994), especially 29–31.
[72] Darnton (1984).

6

———— ∞∞∞ ————

CONTROLLING KNOWLEDGE:
CHURCHES AND STATES

The exercise of power perpetually creates knowledge and conversely,
knowledge constantly induces effects of power.

Foucault

Every accumulation of knowledge and especially such as is obtained by
social communication with people over whom we exercise dominion . . .
is useful to the state.

Warren Hastings

CHAPTERS 2–5 were mainly concerned with the academic world,
with its denizens, its institutions and its classifications. Politics is far from absent from this world, as earlier discussions
of the defence of intellectual territory and the resistance to innovation will have made abundantly clear. However, it is time to widen
the scope of this survey and turn to the politics of knowledge in the
sense of the collection, storage, retrieval and also the suppression of
information by the authorities, whether in the Church or in the state.
The increasing efforts made in this domain are perhaps the best evidence of the rise of the concern with useful knowledge discussed in the
previous chapter.

The dependence of all governments on information was analysed
nearly half a century ago in a classic study by the American political
scientist Karl Deutsch.[1] Some aspects of this theme have been studied
quite intensively of late. A number of monographs have been devoted
to the history of espionage and more generally to the information
on which governments based their foreign policies.[2] The history of
census-taking in a number of European countries has been investigated.[3] The 'information order' in empires, especially in Spanish
America and British India, has been studied in relative detail.[4] On the

---

[1] Deutsch (1953).
[2] Carter (1964); Agrell and Huldt (1983); Bély (1990); Marshall (1994); Preto (1994).
[3] Glass (1973); Herlihy and Klapisch (1978); Rassem and Stagl (1980); Buck (1977, 1982).
[4] Bayly (1996); Cohn (1996); Mundy (1996); Edney (1997); Drayton (1998).

negative side, the workings of religious and political censorship in different places have been the object of scores of monographs.[5]

Thanks to these studies, the general trend to the accumulation of more and more information in the early modern period seems fairly clear, as well as the tendency to arrange it in tabular or statistical form. One might even speak of the ideal, in some quarters, of the 'surveillance state', although it is as well to remember that early modern governments lacked the large numbers of officials which would have been required by any serious attempt to control the lives of all the people living within their frontiers. In practice, they collected information in order to respond to specific problems or crises such as sedition, plague and war, although a long-term trend towards the collection of information to help with routine practices of government is also visible, especially from 1650 onwards.

More obscure is the precise chronology, geography and sociology of this accumulation of information and the various reasons underlying it. In this chapter I shall approach these problems in a comparative manner, with special reference to empires, viewing the extension of knowledge as a precondition as well as a consequence of the expansion of empire – Portuguese, Spanish, British, French, Swedish or Russian (the Dutch Empire, which was more of an economic than a political enterprise, will be discussed in the following chapter). The rise of geography as an academic subject at this time (above, 100) was surely no accident.[6]

The problem is to specify the ways in which power and knowledge support each other, as two recent studies of imperial India show. In one of them, the conquest of India is presented as 'a conquest of knowledge', the invasion of 'an epistemological space', and the author's emphasis falls on the ways in which the British conquerors employed their knowledge of Indian languages or laws in order to impose their rule more effectively. In the other, the traditional 'information order' of Mughal times receives more attention. It is argued that the British began by relying on indigenous informants and Mughal techniques of information gathering. The replacement of these techniques by a more 'scientific' system relying on British observers insulated the new rulers of India from the knowledge of local attitudes and sentiments and so allowed the rebellion of 1857 to take them by surprise.[7]

---

[5] Siebert (1965); Santschi (1978); Duke and Tamse (1987); Roche (1989); Myers and Harris (1992).

[6] Cormack (1997).

[7] Cohn (1996), 16, 53; Bayly (1996), 56–96, 315–37; Pinch (1999), esp. 394–5.

Ideally, a comparative history of the kind undertaken here should reveal not only similarities and differences but also interactions – whether in the form of competition or in that of appropriation – between states, regions or domains of concern. Two examples of interaction stand out in this period, the exchange of techniques of information gathering between churches and states, and that between peripheries and centres. There is at least a *prima facie* case for arguing that in these respects it was often – though not always – the state which learned from the Church, while the centres of empire were surveyed using methods which had first been developed in order to govern far-flung provinces. To test these hypotheses, the following pages will examine the processes of collecting, storing, retrieving, using and suppressing different kinds of information.

THE RISE OF BUREAUCRACY

Governments have been interested in collecting and storing information about the people under their rule from the time of the ancient Assyrians, if not before. As a contemporary sociologist puts it, 'all states have been "information societies", since the generation of state power presumes reflexively monitored system reproduction, involving the regularized gathering, storage and control of information applied to administrative ends.'[8] The ancient Romans attempted to carry out complete censuses of the population. After the Norman Conquest of 1066, the new king of England ordered a survey of population, animal as well as human. However, 'Domesday Book', as this survey was called, was an extraordinary case, and the register was rarely consulted in the two centuries following its compilation.[9] It was only in the early modern period that the regular and systematic collection of information became part of the ordinary process of European government. The increasing centralization of administration both required and enabled early modern rulers to know much more about the lives of the governed than had been known in the Middle Ages.

With centralization came the rise of 'bureaucracy' in Max Weber's sense of the term. Unlike Mannheim (above, 8), Weber is not usually remembered as a sociologist of knowledge, but his famous theory of bureaucracy actually made a major contribution to the subject. After all, Weber defined bureaucracy as 'the exercise of control on the basis

---

[8] Giddens (1985), 178.
[9] Clanchy (1979), 19.

of knowledge'. He linked this 'rule of the office' to impersonal government on the basis of formal regulations and written communications submitted through the proper channels.[10]

In early modern Europe, one of the main developments in the history of the state was the trend towards bureaucracy in Weber's sense, together with a tendency to bureaucracy in the colloquial, pejorative sense of 'red tape' and to what was known in the sixteenth century as the 'rule of the secretaries' (above, 24).[11] One indicator of the rise of bureaucracy in both senses was the growth in the numbers of officials. Another, even more visible, was the rise of the purpose-built office, as in the case of the Uffizi in Florence (a complex of offices, as its name implies, before it became an art gallery), and in that of Versailles, where part of the new palace was constructed for the use of civil servants.

Rulers themselves were turning into bureaucrats as well as employing bureaucrats. The classic case is that of Philip II of Spain, who was nicknamed by his subjects 'the king of paper' (el rey papelero), because of the number of hours he spent at his desk and the number of documents generated by his attempts to learn about and control the lives of his subjects. Indeed, the king's almoner complained to his master about this escapism into a paper world.[12] The Escorial may well have become the centre of the greatest mass of official documents to have been collected since the later Roman Empire, another organization based on paper and paper-work.[13]

Philip II was not unique as royal bureaucrat. The rise of what we might call the 'paper state' in the early modern period was a general European phenomenon. Louis XIV boasted in his memoirs that he was 'informed about everything'. He too spent long hours at his desk or at meetings of councils and committees. So did the leading rulers of the Enlightenment, notably Frederick the Great of Prussia, Catherine the Great of Russia and Maria Theresa and Joseph II of Austria. The rise of committees and of boards (small groups acting by majority vote and known in Sweden and Russia as 'colleges'), is one of the main administrative innovations of the period. As Leibniz wrote to Peter the Great, 'There cannot be good administration except with colleges: their mechanism is like that of watches, whose wheels keep each other in movement.'

The main story to be told here is one of the accumulation of information, both responding and leading to the increasing desire of

---

[10] Weber (1920), vol. 1, 339.
[11] Nigro (1991).
[12] Parker (1998), 48.
[13] Kelly (1994).

rulers to control the lives of the general population, whether to tax them, conscript them into the army, or feed them in time of famine. However, the fact that knowledge was accumulating somewhere in the administration did not mean that it always reached the ruler or official who needed it. The larger the organization, the greater the danger that the information which enters it does not reach the top. In other words, historians like governments need to concern themselves with what might be called the 'mobilization' of information.[14]

The extent to which the practices and trends discussed in this chapter were confined to the western world is a question which, despite its importance, the secondary literature does not allow us to discuss in any detail. It is clear enough that the governments of some large Asian states, among them China, the Ottoman Empire and Mughal India, were very much concerned with the gathering of information. Censuses of the Chinese Empire were carried out in 1380, for example, and again in the 1390s. Numerous printed guidebooks and encyclopaedias were produced for the use of Chinese officials. In the Ottoman Empire, the records of the land surveys carried out at regular intervals for tax purposes, many of them still preserved in archives, are impressive. In Mughal India too there was an official interest in statistical data as well as an elaborate system of intelligence gathering for the purpose of surveillance.[15] Maps, plans and charts were no western monopoly. They were already a tool of government in this period in China, Japan and the Ottoman Empire, as the example of Piri Reis (above, 55) may remind us.[16]

Until more systematic comparisons have been carried out a firm conclusion would be premature. My impression is that around 1450 the major governments of Europe still lagged behind China and the Ottoman Empire in the extent of their information-gathering services. After 1600, on the other hand, the lead was taken by Europe, or more exactly by some European governments. In the account which follows the more bureaucratized states will be privileged, whether they were large states like France or small states like Sweden.

THE CHURCH AS MODEL

It is at least arguable that the first European bureaucracy was not secular but ecclesiastical. In the thirteenth century, Pope Innocent III

---

[14] Boulding (1966); Innes (1987).
[15] Barkan (1958); Hucker (1968); Metzger (1973); Thiel-Horstmann (1980); Bayly (1996), 10–55.
[16] Soucek (1992); Unno (1994); Yee (1994a).

was already concerned with the retrieval of information from official registers. In the Middle Ages, according to a recent historian of written records, 'Royal chanceries were slower than the papacy in developing scribal techniques for administration.'[17] This is scarcely surprising. After all, the Catholic Church was an institution built on a grander scale than any European monarchy, while the clergy once held a quasi-monopoly of literacy. The papal bureaucracy in particular built on a medieval tradition but it developed further in what might be called a Weberian direction in the sixteenth and seventeenth centuries. Pope Sixtus V, for example, established a number of specialized committees or 'congregations' in the course of his short but vigorous reign. In domains as diverse as archives (below, 138) and finance (notably the development of budgets, in other words regular financial forecasts), the Papacy was a pioneer.[18]

After the Council of Trent, which concluded its deliberations in 1563, the parish priests of the Catholic Church were required to keep registers of births, marriages and deaths. Bishops were expected to visit their dioceses regularly in order to assess their spiritual state. These episcopal visitations, which had been somewhat sporadic earlier, became regular events after Trent, generating a mass of records concerning the physical state of churches, the level of education of the parish priests, the number of confraternities and the morality of the laity.[19]

The Counter-Reformation Church also has its place in the history of statistics. Censuses of 'souls', as they were called, were regularly carried out as a way of verifying that parishioners were making the 'Easter duties' of annual confession and communion required of them by the Council of Trent. As a further check, parish priests were ordered to issue tickets or *schedae* to their parishioners, tickets which had to be returned to the priest at confession or communion. The increasing fear of heresy as well as the development of numeracy contributed to the rise of statistics.

Visitations of this kind took place in Protestant as well as Catholic Europe. In Lutheran Germany, for instance, there were regular inspections of parishes in the sixteenth century. In England after the Reformation, new bishops produced 'interrogatories' in order to investigate the dioceses of Gloucester and Worcester (eighty-nine questions, 1551–2) and Norwich (sixty-nine questions, 1561). In Lutheran Sweden and Finland, the church examination registers of the

---

[17] Clanchy (1979), 215; Stock (1983), 37.
[18] Partner (1980, 1990); Prodi (1982).
[19] Burke (1979); Mazzone and Turchini (1985).

seventeenth and eighteenth centuries have been intensively studied by historians concerned with the rise of literacy. The detailed records of the interrogation of householders by the clergy and their classification according to competence ('reads well', 'reads a little' and so on), are – like the records of the Inquisition – a remarkable illustration of the official passion for precise information.[20]

As the Catholic surveys after the Council of Trent were stimulated by the fear of heresy, which the Council had been summoned to suppress, so the English surveys were stimulated by the fear of dissent from the Church of England. In 1676, for instance, the bishop of London carried out a survey of Dissenters, known after him as the 'Compton Census'. The elaborate questionnaire issued by the archbishop of York to his parish clergy in 1743 also betrays these preoccupations. 'What number of families have you in your parish? Of these, how many are Dissenters? . . . Is there any public or charity school? Is there in your parish any Almshouse, Hospital, or other charitable endowment? How often is the public service read in your church? . . . How often, and at what times do you catechize in your church?'[21] The link between the collection of information and the desire of the religious authorities to control their flocks will be clear enough.

The ecclesiastical institution most concerned with knowledge gathering was the Inquisition, in Spain, Italy and elsewhere. People suspected of heresy were interrogated in an extremely systematic manner about their age, place of birth and occupation as well as about their beliefs, and whatever they said was recorded with great care. The archives of the various Inquisitions therefore constitute a 'data bank' from which social historians have learned much, especially in the last generation. However, the collecting of information by inquisitors deserves the attention of historians not only as a source but also as a phenomenon in its own right, as a leading early modern example of the pursuit of knowledge for the sake of control.[22]

It is tempting to speculate whether the the methods of the Church were adapted to the needs of the state by the three cardinals who were so prominent in secular government in the middle of the seventeenth century, Richelieu and Mazarin in France and their contemporary Melchior Khlesl in the Habsburg Empire. In any case, interaction between the temporal and spiritual powers in the domain of knowledge is a theme which will recur in these pages.

---

[20] Strauss (1975); Johansson (1977).
[21] Ollard and Walker (1929–31); Jukes (1957).
[22] Henningsen and Tedeschi (1986).

So far as the gathering of information is concerned, it may be useful to distinguish the knowledge acquired by rulers about their neighbours, rivals or enemies, from the knowledge they possessed about their own domains, whether empires or 'mother countries'.

FOREIGN AFFAIRS

In the field of foreign affairs, it is appropriate to begin with the Republic of Venice, since the Venetians were among the first European powers to adopt the system of resident ambassadors, as much to gather information about other countries as to negotiate with them. The Venetian government expected to receive from its representatives abroad not only regular dispatches but also formal reports at the end of the mission (three years or so), the famous *relazioni*, which described the political, military and economic strengths and weaknesses of the state to which the ambassador had been accredited.[23] Venetian ambassadors were also asked to circulate information abroad. For example, when the pope laid Venice under interdict in 1606, the Venetian ambassador to Paris was instructed to ensure that the French were informed about the Venetian side of the question.

Other governments imitated Venice, but rather less systematically. The new but proliferating genre of treatises on the duties of ambassadors generally stressed the importance of sending information home, as Frederick Marselaer did in his *Legatus* (1626). Reports in the style of *relazioni* exist in other countries, like Sir George Carew's penetrating account of the French court in the age of King Henri IV, but the practice was less regular in other states than was the case for Venice.

Ambassadors collected information not only by keeping their eyes and ears open, but also via a network of assistants, agents or 'informers', not to say spies, whether they were employed full-time or part-time, like the Venetian merchants in Istanbul who regularly sent political information home. The 'secret service' (as it was already known by 1583, at least in Naples), was an elaborately organized enterprise in the early modern period, complete with codes, false addresses, safe houses and double agents. The Venetians were particularly skilled practitioners of both espionage and counter-espionage and frequently infiltrated foreign embassies for these purposes.[24]

By the seventeenth century, other states were catching up with Venice in these respects. Sir Henry Wotton, British ambassador in

---

[23] Mattingly (1955), 109–14; Queller (1973); Toscani (1980).
[24] Mattingly (1955), 244–6, 259–61; Preto (1994), 90, 133–4.

12   WOOD-CARVING, *THE SPY* (SEVENTEENTH CENTURY):
COURTESY OF SCUOLA GRANDE DI SAN ROCCO, VENICE

Venice, employed spies in Milan (which then formed part of the
Spanish Empire), to send him information about the movements of
Spanish troops (figure 12). He also employed agents in Rome and
Turin, and intercepted the letters of Jesuits in particular (the art of
opening letters unobtrusively was already quite well known). The
value of the information which Wotton acquired by this means may
be gauged from the fact that the Doge sometimes gained his knowledge
of the plans of the governor of Milan from the British embassy.[25]

For their part, the Spanish government have been described by a historian of diplomacy as having 'a far-flung, well-organized, extremely
effective network for gathering information'. Don Diego Hurtado de

---

[25] Burke (1998a), 103.

Mendoza, the Spanish ambassador in Venice between 1539 and 1547, organized a network of spies in the Ottoman Empire, while the Count of Gondomar, Spanish ambassador to London in the early seventeenth century, paid large salaries to leading members of the government (£1,000 each to the Lord High Treasurer and the Lord High Admiral), for informational services rendered. Conversely, later in the century, the clerk to the Spanish ambassador received £100 a year for passing information to the British.[26] In France, too, numerous spies were employed by the government and its ambassadors.[27] Groups of Protestant exiles in England and elsewhere were infiltrated, and art collecting was sometimes used as a cover for espionage. The connoisseur Roger de Piles, for example, was sent to the Dutch Republic, officially to buy paintings for King Louis XIV and in fact to gather political information. The Dutch penetrated his cover and Piles spent some time in prison, using his enforced leisure to write a book about art criticism which became a classic in its field.[28]

INFORMATION AND EMPIRE

In his celebrated and controversial study, which extended the ideas of Foucault about power and knowledge into new regions, the critic Edward Said discussed what he called 'orientalism' as a western system of both representation and domination.[29] He began his story in the years around 1800, with the role of scholars in Napoleon's Egyptian campaign. The systematic gathering of knowledge by European powers in order to dominate other parts of the world can be found much earlier.

For example, the early modern seaborne empires – Portuguese, Spanish, Dutch, French and British – all depended on the collection of information. In the first instance they needed information about routes to the Indies or to Africa. Hence the appointment of royal cosmographers in Portugal and Spain, specialists who were expected to supply information on astronomy, geography and navigation. Records of what was known, often in the form of charts, were stored, as we have seen (above, 61) in the Armazém de Guiné and the Casa da India in Lisbon and in the Casa de Contratación in Seville. Jorge

---

[26] Carter (1964), esp. 6, 123; Echevarria Bacigalupe (1984); Marshall (1994), 134–5, 247.
[27] Bély (1990).
[28] Mirot (1924).
[29] Said (1978).

de Vasconcelos, for example, the head (*provedor*) of the 'warehouses' of Africa and India at the beginning of the sixteenth century, was in charge of charts, which were issued to pilots and captains when they left Portugal and given back on their return.[30]

In the age of Louis XIV, the powerful minister Jean-Baptiste Colbert has been described as 'the information man' because he was so much more systematic than his predecessors in this respect.[31] Colbert collected information about the Middle East and Far East for a mixture of economic and political reasons. It was on his initiative that an East India Company (the *Compagnie des Indes Orientales*), was founded in 1664 in order to compete with the English and Dutch. The minister sent the abbé Carré to India in 1666 with the director of the company, apparently to act as an informer, and Carré reported back to Colbert in 1671.[32] Similar interests were shown by three successive secretaries of state for the navy: Louis de Pontchartrain; his son Jérôme, comte de Maurepas (who succeeded him in 1699); and Jérôme's son, also comte de Maurepas, who replaced his father in the post in 1723. Official expeditions were sent to South America, for example, and observations were made by engineers, astronomers and botanists 'by order of the king', a phrase they were proud to use on the title-pages of their publications.[33]

When parts of other continents were incorporated into European empires, it became necessary to acquire systematic knowledge of the land, its resources and its inhabitants. The example of the Spanish government is particularly revealing in this respect. Charles V was already making enquiries of the archbishop of Mexico in 1548, but the systematic collection of information about the New World began in the 1570s. An important role in the knowledge-gathering process was played by Juan de Ovando, who was appointed visitor to the Council of the Indies in 1569, and was shocked to discover how poorly informed the councillors were about the New World. In the same year he sent out thirty-seven-point questionnaires to local officials in Mexico and Peru, followed by more elaborate ones. By this time the questionnaire was a familiar tool of government in the Church, regularly employed in episcopal visitations as well as by the Inquisition. Ovando, himself a churchman, seems to have adapted ecclesiastical methods to the service of the state.[34]

[30] Goodman (1988), 50–87.
[31] Hoock (1980); Meyer (1981), 222.
[32] Burke (1999b).
[33] Burke (2000b).
[34] Burke (1979).

It was Ovando who sent the physician Francisco Hernández to New Spain to study its natural history (above, 60).[35] He was also responsible for the creation of the new official post of 'geographer-historian' (cosmógrafo-cronista). Its first holder, Juan López de Velasco, was Ovando's former secretary. In his turn, in 1577, Velasco sent out a printed questionnaire to the municipal authorities of New Spain, concerning the natural history of each region, its mines, local history and so on. Among the questions, or more exactly orders, were the following:

> State who was the discoverer and conqueror of said province . . . state to whom the Indians belonged in heathen times . . . and the form of worship, rites and customs they had, good or bad. State how they were governed; against whom they carried on warfare; the clothes and costumes they wore and now wear and whether they used to be more or less healthy anciently than they are now, and what reasons may be learned for this.[36]

In the context of the history of knowledge, this document is of interest for a number of reasons. It reminds us that the questionnaire was not the invention of nineteenth-century sociologists, but the adaptation to academic purposes of a traditional administrative procedure used by episcopal and secular officials. It also reveals that the government was already aware of, and concerned about, the terrible decline in the population (due in the main to the import of European diseases to which the Indians had built up no resistance), a decline which historians of Spanish America rediscovered in the 1950s. It is also significant that the questions were not narrowly utilitarian. They reveal the interests of a humanist in government service.

Russia in the eighteenth century offers another striking example of an imperial government concerned with gathering information. Peter the Great sent his German librarian, J. D. Schumacher, to the Dutch Republic in 1721 to acquire information about Dutch technology, in other words to engage in what is now called 'industrial espionage' (below, 154).[37] The tsar's interests extended to the eastern limits of his empire. Another German, Daniel Messerschmidt, was ordered to spend seven years in Siberia (1720–7) in order to collect information about the region, while the Russians Fedor Luzhin and Ivan Evreinov and the Dane Vitus Bering were sent to Kamchatka to discover

---

[35] Bustamante García (1997).
[36] Cline (1964); Goodman (1988), 65–72; Mundy (1996).
[37] Davids (1995), 338.

whether or not there was a land link between Asia and America.[38] In similar fashion, the expedition to Lapland in the 1730s by the famous botanist Carl Linnaeus was made not only for the advancement of science but to provide the Swedish government with information about the mineral and other resources of that part of the empire.[39]

Catherine the Great showed similar interests to Peter's. Sir Samuel Bentham (the brother of the more famous Jeremy) was employed in her service from 1780 to 1795, mapping Siberia and studying its mineral and human resources. The official instructions to the members of the expedition to Siberia during Catherine's reign (printed in the appendix to Martin Sauer's contemporary *Account of a Geographical Expedition to the Northern Parts of Russia*), included the following points, expressed (as in the case of Ovando) in the imperative mode: 'Observe their dispositions and different corporeal qualifications; their government, manners, industry, ceremonies and superstitions, religious or profane; their traditions, education and manner of treating their women; useful plants, medicines and dyes; food, and manner of preparing it; habitations, utensils, carriages and vessels; manner of life and economy.'[40] Although the manner of treating women was not infrequently used as an indicator of civilization, its emphasis also suggests the personal involvement of the empress in this knowledge-gathering expedition.

The influence of the expedition of Captain Cook on the Russians is also worth noting. Joseph Billings, who had served with Cook before joining the Russian navy, was put in command of this expedition precisely because of his experience of exotic places. The mixture of useful information with knowledge which had no obvious practical value for the rulers of an empire is reminiscent of Velasco's sixteenth-century questionnaire. The desire for control was obviously a major stimulus to the collecting of information by early modern states and especially empires, but curiosity also played its part, and information was collected not only because it was immediately useful but in the hope that one day it might be.

Government patronage of research, already discussed in the case of scientific academies (above, 45), extended to the most distant parts of empire and even beyond. An early example is the expedition to Brazil mounted by Johan Maurits of Nassau (1637–44), complete with artists such as Frans Post and men of learning such as the physician Willem Piso to study and record the local fauna and flora. The famous

---

[38] Golder (1922), 6–8; Anderson (1978), 128–36; Shaw (1996).
[39] Koerner (1996).
[40] Reinhartz (1994).

scientific expedition to Peru in 1736 by a group of French savants was supported by the minister Maurepas, and described in the printed account as 'a voyage made at the order of the king'.[41] Again, the Danes mounted an official expedition to Arabia in 1761. The German theologian Johann David Michaelis was interested in the region for the light it threw on the interpretation of Scripture, and found a patron in Count Bernstorff, minister to the king of Denmark. Hence the appointment of the scholar Carsten Niebuhr as a Danish lieutenant of engineers, in charge of a team which included a philologist, two naturalists and an artist.

The knowledge gathered in expeditions such as these may not have been immediately useful, but it was not politically neutral either. Like the government-funded academies of Paris, Berlin, St Petersburg and Stockholm, these expeditions were a good investment. As we say today, it gave the sponsoring governments a good image. Contemporaries too were well aware of this point, witness the remark of Fontenelle, secretary to the French Académie des Sciences, in his obituaries of the academicians, about the 'wise policy' of Colbert in supporting learning, thus glorifying Louis XIV and giving the French an intellectual empire (*l'empire de l'esprit*). By the later eighteenth century, the growing number of these expeditions was already causing alarm in some quarters. The Dutch writer Cornelis de Pauw, for instance, in his 'Philosophical Researches' on the Americans (1770), complained in his preface that the price of the clarification of some points of geography was the destruction of part of the globe. 'Let us place limits on this passion to invade everything in order to know everything' (*Mettons des bornes à la fureur de tout envahir pour tout connaître*).

INTERNAL AFFAIRS

As the example of Domesday Book reminds us, rulers have long been concerned to know their people and their territories. One manner of acquiring this knowledge was to make a tour of the region. A famous example from the sixteenth century was the 'tour de France' made in 1564–6, soon after his accession, by the child-king Charles IX. This direct method continued throughout the period. Frederick the Great, at least early in his reign, travelled his kingdom so as to be well-informed about it. Catherine the Great's visit to New Russia in 1787 is well known, thanks to the story of the way in which she was

---

[41] Boxer (1957); Burke (2000b).

supposed to have been deceived by her favourite, Gregory Potemkin, who ordered the construction of a model village which was re-erected in several places for the empress to inspect again and again.[42]

Increasingly, however, ruler-bureaucrats lacked the time to travel extensively in their kingdoms. They had access to far more information than their predecessors, but it came to them at second hand, in the form of reports. Frederick the Great, for instance, instructed his officials to travel in order to get to know their regions and to send him news about what they had found. One of the pieces of advice which Leibniz gave to Tsar Peter the Great was to 'have an exact description of the country made'.

For an example of the new system at work we may return to the desk-monarch *par excellence*, Philip II. It was in Philip's time that detailed reports, now known as the *Relaciones topográficas*, were made of some 600 villages in one region of Spain, New Castile. These reports are derived from the responses to questionnaires (*interrogatorios*) sent out 1575 and 1578 (fifty-seven questions or *capítulos* in the first case, forty-five in the second). Some of the questions deal with practical questions of administration, privileges, the quality of the land and the number of hospitals. Others, however, concern the religious life of the inhabitants, their favourite saints and festivals, supporting the theory that episcopal visitations were taken as a model. Another possible model was the humanist 'chorography', a historico-geographical description of a particular region. The parallel with the survey of New Spain in 1569 discussed above (127) will be obvious enough. The *Relaciones topográficas* offer one example of a survey of the centre following the model of a survey of the periphery.[43]

Colbert was another lover of questionnaires. In 1663 he instructed his representatives in the provinces, the *intendants*, to send him information about their areas of responsibility. Shortly afterwards he gave instructions for a series of surveys (*enquêtes*).[44] He may have borrowed the idea of the questionnaire from the Church, but his sophisticated methods in turn influenced the Church. It does not look like coincidence that particularly elaborate ecclesiastical questionnaires were issued by the archbishop of Rouen (Colbert's son) and the archbishop of Reims (the brother of Colbert's rival Louvois).[45]

Visits and questionnaires do not exhaust the means at the disposal of early modern governments for acquiring information for the

---

[42] Boutier, Dewerpe and Nordman (1984); Wolff (1994), 130–4.
[43] Cline (1964), 344; Bouza (1992), 90–100; Parker (1998), 59–65.
[44] Meyer (1981), 105.
[45] Venard (1985), 37.

purpose of control. The period was marked by the rise of various equivalents of the modern 'identity card'. In times of plague, Italian Health Boards required travellers to carry passes (known as *bollette*, or *bollettini*) to limit the spread of infection. The traveller Philip Skippon, who received such a *bollettino* in Mantua in 1664, noted that he was described in it as an Englishman coming from Verona, twenty years old, with a beard, brown hair, dark eyes, and a normal complexion. Passports, originally safe-conducts in wartime, were extended to peacetime in eighteenth-century France. After 1777, people of African origin were required to carry special passbooks or *cartouches*.[46] Again, the Russian government began to require travellers to carry internal passports in the early eighteenth century. These passports began to be printed in 1743, and like the Italian *bollettini* they included a physical description of the traveller. Originally fiscal in purpose (to prevent the evasion of the poll tax), these passports became a means for the government to control the movements of the population.

To call the Russian system a 'police state', as some historians have done, may be something of an exaggeration, given the relatively small numbers of officials active in that vast country, but the will to gather information for the purposes of control was certainly present in late eighteenth-century Russia. A. A. Viazemskii, procurator-general of the Senate, built up a network of informers in the provinces. The Great Commission of 1767 and the requirement, in 1775, that governors produce regular reports on their provinces, also boosted the amount of information available to officials in St Petersburg.[47]

Paid domestic spies or 'informers' were another tool of government which goes back at least as far as the secret agents of Roman emperors, the *schola agentium in rebus* or more colloquially the *curiosi* ('snoopers'). In Spain in the early seventeenth century, informers were stationed even in the royal palace, and the post of 'principal spy' (*espía mayor*) had been created.[48]

The encouragement of denunciations of rule-breakers by their neighbours was another common technique, apparently learned by the state from the Church, which had long been concerned with the detection of heresy, blasphemy and immorality. The appointment in sixteenth-century Venice of a group of officials known as 'Inquisitors of State' paid homage to the ecclesiastical origins of this institution. Of the government of Henry VIII of England it has been remarked that paid informers were not employed because they were unnecessary.

---

[46] Cipolla (1976), 25; Burke (1987), 126; Bély (1990), 610ff, 621, 624, 652.
[47] Raeff (1983), 225–8; Le Donne (1984), 125–8.
[48] Blum (1969); Elliott (1986), 316.

'Information came and did not have to be sought.' The same point might be made about Venice, where the government made use of the so-called *bocchi di leone*, letter-boxes in the shape of lions' mouths in which the public could place their denunciations, signed or unsigned. By the mid-seventeenth century, specialization had taken place and different kinds of denunciation (of bandits, extortion, gambling, political corruption or irreverence in church) were supposed to be placed in different boxes.[49]

Thanks to these methods, governments were becoming increasingly well-informed. A seventeenth-century Scottish traveller to France, Sir John Lauder, recorded in his memoirs the story that Cardinal Richelieu 'knew all things that passed through France as if he had been present, and two of the most intimate should not have spoken ill of him at Poitiers but he should have known it ere four days at Paris. Some imputed it to a familiar spirit he had, others to his spies he had everywhere.' In both cases, the cardinal's methods were viewed as diabolical. The process did not end with Richelieu. The Paris of Louis XIV and Louis XV was closely observed by paid informers, better known as *mouches*, so many flies on the walls of cafés and other places where sedition might be heard. By 1720 they were at their posts in some forty cafés in the capital. By the end of the eighteenth century, French police records or *dossiers* already included personal files on major suspects complete with portraits.[50]

MAPPING THE STATE

A good deal of the information which interested government officials was recorded in the form of maps (figure 13). The 'emergence of cartography as a tool of government' was a major trend in this period, whether the purpose of the map was to establish boundaries, to defend the state against its enemies or to facilitate planning and thus to rationalize administration.[51] For example, Philip II encouraged the mapping of the Iberian peninsula in the 1560s. Pedro de Esquivel, professor of mathematics at the university of Alcalá, was asked to carry out a survey of Spain, although he died soon after his appointment and the project lapsed.[52] The Portuguese cosmographer Francisco Domínguez spent five years in New Spain from

---

[49]   Preto (1994), 168ff; Elton (1972), 331.
[50]   Cobb (1970); Williams (1979), 104–11.
[51]   Buisseret (1992); Biggs (1999).
[52]   Goodman (1988), 65–6; Parker (1992).

13 DETAIL FROM J. CASTALDUS, *Romania*, IN ORTELIUS, *THEATRUM ORBIS TERRARUM* (ANTWERP, 1570)

1571 onwards, carrying out a survey of the territory. The 1577 questionnaire sent to Philip's dominions in the New World included a demand for maps, some of which still survive.[53]

In France, Cardinal Richelieu, the virtual ruler of the state, commissioned a map of France in thirty sheets which was completed in 1643. Colbert was another enthusiast for cartography, who demanded maps of each province. In 1668, he asked the Academy of Sciences to recommend ways of increasing the reliability of maps. In 1679, Louis XIV approved a proposal from Colbert to undertake a more accurate map of France (so much work was required that the map itself was not ready until 1744, a generation after the king's death).[54] French cartography of this period vividly illustrates the process of what some sociologists call the 'scientification' of knowledge. The Royal Observatory was used for cartographic purposes, the astronomer Gian-Domenico Cassini worked with the military engineer Sébastien de Vauban to improve military surveys, while his former pupil Guillaume Delisle, chief geographer to the king, and his grandson César-François Cassini both contributed to the map of France mentioned above.[55] There were good political as well as military reasons for this concern with accuracy. At the congress of Utrecht which ended the War of the Spanish Succession at the end of the reign of Louis XIV, maps were used to ensure that no dispute would arise later over what had been agreed.[56]

It was only to be expected that Tsar Peter the Great would be interested in mapping and surveying. The German geographer Johan Baptist Homann was commissioned by the tsar to map Russia, and students at the naval academy were used to collect information for him. Peter himself met the geographer Delisle in Paris in 1717, and suggested corrections to his map of Russia, while in 1721 the tsar himself gave detailed instructions to geodesists.[57]

The case of Britain illustrates once again the general point that in many of the domains discussed in this chapter, the periphery was surveyed before the centre. The Board of Trade proposed the mapping of the colonies in 1720. Military surveyors mapped Scotland (1747–55), a project linked to road building and the 'pacification' of the Highlands after the great rebellion of 1745. There followed the mapping of Quebec (1760–1), Bengal (1765–77) and Ireland (1778–90). England itself, on the other hand, began to be surveyed only at

---

[53] Alvar Ezquerra (1993).
[54] Hahn (1971), 2; Konvitz (1987); Buisseret (1992).
[55] Pelletier (1990).
[56] Bély (1990), 461.
[57] Anderson (1978), 131–6.

the end of the century, partly in response to the threat of invasion at the time of the French Revolution. The 'Ordnance Survey' betrays its military origins by its very name, since it was organized by the Master-General of the Ordnance, presumably because the transport of artillery requires accurate knowledge of the terrain.[58]

THE RISE OF STATISTICS

One of the reasons for the rise of official interest in maps was their presentation of quantitative information, shown to scale. Early modern rulers and their ministers were increasingly concerned with figures as well as facts. They were especially concerned to know how many people lived in their dominions. Earlier governments had only been able to make 'the wildest of wild guesses'. The English government, for instance, believed that the country had 40,000 parishes in 1371 when the true figure was around 8,600.[59] In an age when the size of armies was increasing as rapidly as in the seventeenth century, governments could no longer afford this kind of ignorance.

Information about births, marriages and deaths also began to be collected. One stimulus to such collecting was the plague, which struck Italy, for example, with particular force in 1575 and 1630, and London in 1665. There were other reasons for a growing interest in demography. In the middle of the seventeenth century, in the Dutch Republic, the lawyer-statesman Jan de Witt was already using mortality figures in order to set up an annuity system administered by the government. In Sweden, where the government was concerned to stimulate population growth on the principle that 'a plenitude of poor people is a country's greatest wealth', the clergy were ordered in 1736 to provide annual figures of births and deaths in their parishes, and a national census was ordered in 1748. A census bill was put before the British Parliament in 1753; it is equally revealing of the climate of opinion at this time that the bill was proposed and that it was defeated, like the proposal of 1758 for compulsory registration of births, marriages and deaths.[60] From the later eighteenth century onwards, the national census became a regular event in one western country after another. A census of Denmark and Norway was carried out in 1769. A census of Spain was also made in 1769, followed

---

[58] Seymour (1980), 4, 15, 45; Edney (1997).
[59] Lander (1969), 166.
[60] Buck (1982); Johannisson (1990), 351.

by the newly independent USA (1790), the UK (1801) and France (1806).[61]

On a smaller scale, there were many precedents for the national census, whether at the level of the city or that of the diocese. Early examples of the awareness of the uses of information presented in figures come from the city-states of Florence and Venice as early as the fifteenth century. Florence and Venice may have been pioneers because they were small – small is efficient as well as beautiful. Florence and Venice were also republics dominated by merchants with an 'arithmetical mentality' encouraged by the educational system, notably the abacus-schools which ensured unusually widespread numeracy. It is obviously easier for governments to collect this kind of information when private individuals are already aware of its value.[62]

For whatever reason, a census of the city and its territories took place in Florence in 1427, essentially for tax purposes.[63] The survey turned out to be so expensive to carry out that it was rarely repeated, but the example of Florence was followed elsewhere. In the province of Holland, for instance, the *Enquiry* of 1494 and the *Information* of 1514 were village-by-village surveys, responses to a questionnaire about the numbers of hearths and the taxes. The government of Henry VIII ordered the parish clergy to keep registers of births, marriages and deaths. By the sixteenth century, the Venetian government, which also used the parish clergy as information-collectors, was using printed forms in order to ensure that that information was presented in a more or less standardized manner, in tables with headings which included men, women, boys, girls, servants and gondolas. The British government also used the clergy in the 1690s to collect information about the poor.

The officials of territorial states not only employed the clergy but also learned from the ecclesiastical precedents mentioned earlier, and ordered more (and more detailed) social surveys from the late sixteenth century onwards than before. It is no surprise to discover that a Spanish census was carried out in 1590–1, soon after the non-statistical survey of New Castile described earlier. In the seventeenth century, among certain European governments at least, there developed an increasing interest in quantitative data, known in England as 'political arithmetic' and in France as *calcules politiques*.[64] From 1635 onwards, for example, the British Board of Trade

---

[61] Glass (1973); Pearson (1978).
[62] Burckhardt (1860); Goldthwaite (1972).
[63] Herlihy and Klapisch (1978).
[64] Letwin (1963); Glass (1973); Holmes (1977).

concerned itself with the population of the American colonies. Late seventeenth-century England was the age of William Petty (who advocated the foundation of a central office for statistics), John Graunt, Gregory King, and King's friend Charles Davenant (Inspector of Imports and Exports) and their attempts to calculate the wealth and population of Britain and Ireland.[65]

Petty, who moved in the circles of Marin Mersenne in Paris and Samuel Hartlib in London (above, 66, 67), was a believer in what he called 'political arithmetic', defined as 'the art of reasoning by figures upon things relating to government'. He was interested in questionnaires, and his manuscript 'method of enquiring into the state of any country' listed fifty-three questions, on wages, prices, population, diseases, public revenue, officeholders and so on, not forgetting games, 'court beauties' and 'What are the books that do sell most', another example of the mixture of utility with wider forms of curiosity.[66]

In France, Richelieu and Colbert were thinking along similar lines. Richelieu ordered a number of 'inquiries' (enquêtes), including demands for precise figures. Almost immediately after coming to power in 1661, Colbert ordered a census of trees in royal forests, thinking of the needs of the navy. In 1667, he ordered parish registers to be kept. In 1669, his forest ordinance gave instructions for the management of these resources on what have been called 'Baconian lines'.[67] In 1670, he ordered the monthly publication of baptisms, marriages and burials in Paris. Colbert was also extremely interested in trade figures. He expected to receive regular news about prices in different regions of France, while the French ambassador to the Dutch Republic was instructed to provide details about the number of Dutch ships and the amount of French wine they imported.[68]

Colbert was not alone in his concern for figures. It was shared by the reforming circle around the heir to the French throne, the duc de Bourgogne, at the end of the century. In 1697, a nineteen-point questionnaire was sent to the intendants to provide information for the duke's political education. As one member of the circle, Archbishop Fénelon, put it, playing on the ecclesiastical resonances of this pastoral image, 'What would one say of a shepherd who did not know the number of his flock?' Another member of the circle, Marshal Vauban, much interested in what he called les statistiques – in other words, information useful to statesmen – developed a method for

---

[65] Innes (1987); Brewer (1989).
[66] Buck (1977, 1982); Rassem and Stagl (1994), 289–91.
[67] Grove (1996), 155.
[68] King (1949), 185–7; Meyer (1981).

calculating populations and attempted in a treatise published in 1707 to measure the French standard of living.[69]

By the eighteenth century, when Sir Robert Walpole noted that the House of Commons preferred 'figures of arithmetic' to 'figures of rhetoric', survevs of this kind were becoming increasingly elaborate as well as spreading to other parts of Europe. The statistical tables (*Staatstafeln*) which Leibniz had recommended in the 1680s became a part of everyday government in Prussia in the time of Frederick the Great. In Russia, a census was begun in connection with the new poll tax (1718). In Sweden, the astronomer Wargentin was given the task of analysing the statistics of births and deaths (which the clergy had been ordered to furnish), in some articles published in the journal of the Academy of Sciences in 1754–5. In 1756 the Swedish government appointed a permanent body concerned with statistics, the Tabellkommission, with Wargentin as one of its members.[70]

The concern of rulers with numbering the people, and sometimes the animal population as well, was not always taken well by their subjects, who suspected, often with reason, that such investigations would be followed by an increase in demands for higher taxes or military service. The term 'Domesday Book' was not intended as a compliment. There was vocal opposition to the census in Parma in 1550, in Naples in the 1590s and in France in 1663, when it was claimed that 'to count families and animals is to enslave the people' (*faire le dénombrement de familles et du bétail, c'est mettre le peuple dans une grande servitude*). Such objections could still be heard in England in the eighteenth century.[71] No wonder that one of the first actions of many early modern rebels was to burn official records.

INFORMATION STORAGE AND RETRIEVAL

As they increased in volume, the records needed to be housed in special repositories, the archives, with special keepers, professional archivists, with catalogues, indexes and so on.[72] Medieval governments already produced and preserved a mass of documents. King Philippe Auguste of France set up the 'treasury of charters' (*Trésor des Chartes*) later kept in the Sainte Chapelle in Paris, while the rolls

---

[69] Esmonin (1964), 113–30; Rothkrug (1965), 107n, 284–6; Rassem and Stagl (1994), 342–5.

[70] Nordenmark (1939), 232–69; Confino (1962), 160–4; Reichmann (1968); Glass (1973); Rassem and Stagl (1980), 18; Klueting (1986).

[71] Burke (1987); Glass (1973), 19.

[72] Bautier (1968).

of parchment generated by a relatively small medieval kingdom, England, continue to fill an impressive number of shelves in the Public Record Office. However, during the Middle Ages, documents were often kept with other precious objects in treasuries, and they were constantly moved from place to place following their owners. The main obstacle to the development of a state archive in the Middle Ages was the mobility of the monarchs. Such collections of official documents as existed were decentralized.[73]

The early modern period was a turning-point for several reasons. In the first place, the invention of printing turned manuscripts into a particular kind of document and encouraged them to be stored separately, in a particular part of a library or in a building of their own. In the second place, the growing centralization of government resulted in an unparalleled increase in what Philip II once called 'those devils, my papers' (he sometimes signed 400 documents in a single day). In the case of rulers such as Louis XIII of France, who were not prepared to spend as many hours at their desks as Philip II, secretaries were authorized to forge the royal signature. In the third place, there was the settling down of governments in the Uffizi, the Escorial, Versailles, Whitehall and so on. The second trend made archives necessary while the third made archives possible. The centralization of government was followed by the centralization of documents.[74] In the course of the sixteenth and seventeenth centuries, a number of depositories were set up or at least reorganized, mainly in order to allow officials to retrieve information without too great a delay. Documents which had previously been treated as the private property of officials – even Richelieu left his papers to his niece – were now deemed to belong to the state.

As in other domains discussed in this chapter, the Counter-Reformation Church seems to have been a pioneer. Among the popes of the period, three took a particular interest in the archives of the Vatican. In 1565, Pius IV asked the cardinal-librarian to create an archive, and in the following year, a papal bull ordered the organization of stores for documents in each diocese. In 1591, Gregory XIII forbade the consultation of documents in the archive without his permission. In 1612, Paul V founded a special secret archive. Part-time and later full-time archivists were appointed to look after and to index the documents.[75] The papal model was gradually followed elsewhere in the Church. In Toledo, for instance, the provincial council

---

[73] Clanchy (1979), 138ff; Guénée (1980), 91–100; Wernham (1956), 13.
[74] Ranum (1963); Bautier (1968); D'Addario (1990); Parker (1997), 28–9.
[75] Marini (1825); Gasparolo (1887).

ordered the foundation of an episcopal archive in 1582. In Milan, a mid-seventeenth-century archivist to the archbishop had the volumes of visitations bound, presumably to facilitate rapid consultation.

In the case of the state, the maxim that small is efficient may be illustrated by the case of Sweden, the government's concern for archives being shown by the appointment of official archivists from the beginning of the seventeenth century, beginning with Johan Bure, appointed state archivist (*riksarchivar*) in 1609. In England, a new State Paper Office was founded by Queen Elizabeth, and the post of Keeper of the State Papers by her successor James I. The governments of Spain and France were becoming particularly archive-conscious at this time. In the history of the Spanish archives, Philip II played a characteristic personal role. As regent in 1545, Prince Philip had already ordered the storage of state papers in the castle of Simancas. After he came to the throne, Philip II put the historian Jerónimo Zurita in charge of collecting official papers, while the king himself cut up documents to classify and store. In the seventeenth century, the energetic Count-Duke of Olivares, Philip IV's first minister, concerned himself with the discovery, classification and relocation of scattered documents. In the eighteenth century, a special archive for American documents, the Archivo de Indias, was created in Seville.[76]

In France, the seventeenth century was the age of the ordering of the archives, first by the scholar Théodore Godefroy (1615), then by Richelieu and later by Colbert. Richelieu, for example, was concerned with the details of the location and classification of particular kinds of document. Colbert's correspondence includes frequent orders to subordinates to search archives, and the minister insisted on the making of inventories of older archives and copying the documents found there (258 volumes of copies of documents found in the south of France were compiled between 1665 and 1670). Louis XIV's foreign minister Torcy was especially interested in the archives concerning foreign affairs and created a special depot for them in 1710. When Louis XIV came to power, no department of state had an archive, but at his death they were all depositing their records in fixed places.[77]

These archives were not created for the convenience of historians, but existed for the sake of administrators. They were part of the *arcana imperii*, 'secrets of state', a phrase used with increasing frequency in the seventeenth century expressing the concern of officials with infringements of their monopoly of certain kinds of political

[76] Ballesteros Beretta (1941); Cline (1964); Parker (1998), 66.
[77] Boislisle (1874), iii; Baschet (1875), 26–9, 37, 93–103; Church (1972); Pomian (1972); Kolmar (1979); Saunders (1991).

information. It was an important moment in the history of the state when the officials gradually shifted from working at home, and so treating state papers as their private property, to working in offices and keeping the papers in archives. A monopoly of information (certain kinds of information, at any rate) was a means to achieve a monopoly of power.[78] Only with the French Revolution was the principle of public access to archives proclaimed, and practice lagged behind theory.

CENSORSHIP

Much of the information discussed so far was 'TOP SECRET', as the British army used to describe it. For this reason and others a system of control or censorship was in operation. In Venice, for example, access to archives was strictly controlled. Even the doge was not allowed to enter the archive alone. Only members of the Senate could enter the archive, and only members of the Collegio could remove documents. To avoid the temptation to read the papers in his care, the keeper of the archive was supposed to be illiterate.[79]

The most famous and widespread censorship system of the period was that of the Catholic Church, associated with the 'Index of Prohibited Books'. The Index was a printed catalogue – perhaps better described as an 'anti-catalogue' – of the books which the faithful were forbidden to read. Actually there were many local indexes but the important ones were those issued by papal authority and binding on the whole Church.

The Index appears to have been invented as an antidote to Protestantism and printing. At the Reformation, the Protestants claimed that knowledge was on their side. The Englishman John Foxe, for example, author of a famous 'book of martyrs', claimed that 'either the pope must abolish knowledge and printing, or printing must at length root him out.' To this claim the Index offered a response. It was an attempt to fight print with print, to control the book population. The model index, issued in 1564, began with a set of general rules forbidding three main types of book: the heretical, the immoral and the magical. Then came an alphabetical list of authors and titles, the authors divided into 'first class' (all their writings being prohibited) and second class (in which case the ban extended only to specific works). The censorship system was complex, with three rival

---

[78] King (1949), 147–53.
[79] Baschet (1875), 175–6.

institutions competing to control it in Rome itself. It was resisted by printers, booksellers and readers, often with success. It may have been counter-productive, encouraging the curiosity of the faithful.[80] All the same, it did obstruct the circulation of knowledge in the Catholic world.

Most of the books on the Church's list were works of Protestant theology, but the list also included some books on other topics which happened to have been written by heretics. For example, in 1572, a professor of medicine at the university of Padua found it difficult to acquire a copy of Zwinger's famous encyclopaedia (above, 95) because it was the work of a Protestant, while a Madrid bookseller found himself in trouble in 1618 for similar reasons, when Conrad Gesner's treatise on fish was found in his shop.[81] In similar fashion the *Acta Eruditorum* of Leipzig, one of the most famous learned journals of the seventeenth century, was suspect because of its Protestant editors.

The Catholic Church was not alone in its concern with controlling the book population. Protestant censorship began as early as the 1520s in Strasbourg, Zurich and Saxony, the works prohibited including not only Catholic polemic but also the works of radical reformers such as the Anabaptists. In Geneva too there was a censorship system, and the authors of books had to obtain permission to print from the town council or later from the committee which oversaw education, the 'Scholarchs'.[82] If Protestant censorship is virtually forgotten while Catholic censorship is still remembered, this is probably a result of the fact that the Protestants were decentralized, not to say divided, so that their attempts to suppress certain kinds of book were necessarily less effective.

Like the churches, and following the model of the churches, the states of early modern Europe organized a system of censorship of the printed word, fearing 'sedition' as much as the churches feared heresy. Even the more tolerant parts of Europe, such as Venice, the Dutch Republic and England, placed some restraints on freedom of communication. Spinoza's *Theologico-Political Treatise*, for example, was banned by the Dutch States-General in 1674. In England, in the reign of Queen Mary I, the English government regulated the English book trade by establishing the Company of Stationers, to which all printers had to belong. In the reign of her successor Queen Elizabeth, printing was confined to London, Oxford and Cambridge in order to bring it under more effective supervision.

---

[80] Prosperi (1997).
[81] Pardo Tomás (1991), 298; Infelise (1999b), 55.
[82] Santschi (1978).

All the same, relatively open information systems such as those obtaining in the Dutch Republic and Britain may be contrasted with relatively closed ones in Spain, Austria and Russia, with France somewhere in between. In the case of the Dutch Republic, a decentralized political structure in an urbanized region dominated by merchants provided the conditions for information to circulate with unusual freedom via speech and writing as well as print. Dutch diplomacy has been described as 'notoriously public', while confidential documents were not infrequently sold to outsiders (below, 147). Foreign visitors to the Republic remarked on the ease with which they could obtain information about Dutch technology (below, 154).[83]

In England, control of the press collapsed in the middle of the seventeenth century under the Commonwealth, but it was reimposed by the Licensing Acts. According to the Licensing Act of 1662, law books had to be inspected by the Lord Chancellor, history books by a secretary of state, and most other kinds of book by the archbishop of Canterbury and the bishop of London. The lapse of the Licensing Act in 1695 ended not only censorship but also the control of printing through the Stationers' Company, a control which had lasted some 140 years. The press was now free from pre-publication control. In other words, 'Everyone was free to publish what he pleased, and to take the consequences.'[84]

In Louis XIV's France, the lieutenant-general of police, La Reynie, exercised a strict control of the press from 1667 to 1697. In similar fashion to the English under Elizabeth, Colbert tried to concentrate Paris printing in a few hands so that it would be easier to control. In 1701 there were only fifty-one printing shops in Paris compared with seventy-five in 1644 and 181 in 1500. Books were still being burned in public in the eighteenth century, among them Voltaire's *Philosophical Letters* (1733) and Rousseau's *Emile* (1762), but some censors, notably Malesherbes, who held the office of *directeur de la librairie* from 1750 to 1763, believed in the freedom of the press. On one occasion Malesherbes warned Diderot in advance that the police were coming to search his house and confiscate copies of the *Encyclopédie*, and even offered to hide this compromising material in his own home.[85]

Fear of sedition was not the only reason for government censorship. The publication of secrets was another concern. For example, knowledge of the Indies and Africa was treated as a state secret by the Portuguese. In 1504, King Manuel forbade chart-makers to

---

[83] Davids (1995).
[84] Siebert (1965); Sutherland (1986), 25.
[85] Martin (1969); Phillips (1997); Birn (1983, 1989).

represent the West African coast beyond the Congo, and required existing charts to be submitted for censorship.[86] The now famous account by the Portuguese apothecary Tomé Pires of his travels in the East, the *Summary of the Orient*, addressed to King Manuel, was originally kept secret because of the information about spices which it contained. The Italian translation of Pires which appeared in 1550 in Ramusio's famous collection of voyages lacked the section on spices, as if the manuscript had been censored. The government's anxiety on this score may have been justified, since in 1561 the French ambassador to Lisbon was instructed to bribe a Portuguese cartographer to provide a map of southern Africa.[87] This Portuguese preoccupation with the secrecy of information lasted a long time. In 1711, *Culture and Opulence of Brazil*, a treatise on the Brazilian economy published under the pseudonym of Antonil by an Italian Jesuit who lived there, was immediately suppressed, apparently out of fear that foreigners would learn the routes to the Brazilian gold mines.[88]

The Portuguese anxiety over the publication of confidential information was an extreme case of a general tendency. For example, a certain Lazzaro Soranzo was arrested by the Council of Ten in 1598, following his publication (in Ferrara) of an anti-Turkish treatise which the Venetian government considered to have divulged confidential information about the Ottoman regime.[89] Maps and plans in particular were politically sensitive. One might not have thought that the Venetian patrician Daniele Barbaro's commentary on the treatise by the Roman architect Vitruvius (1556) was a politically dangerous work, but objections were made to its publication on the grounds that the illustrations of fortifications might help the enemies of Venice. The French geographer André Thevet, in a letter to the king prefixed to his *Cosmography* (1575), explained his refusal to include plans of French cities and fortresses in political terms, 'not considering it a good idea to reveal French secrets to foreigners' (*ne trouvant bon de découvrir aux étrangers les secrets d'icelle*).[90]

In order to keep information secret it was normal for governments to use codes, which developed in this period in parallel with the rise of diplomacy. The Italians were pioneers in both areas. The cipher secretaries of Venice and Rome were celebrated for their skills, while

---

[86] Lach (1965), 151–3; Teixeira de Mota (1976).
[87] Buisseret (1992), 106.
[88] Cortesão (1944), lxv–lxviii; Lach (1965), 151–4.
[89] Preto (1994), 433.
[90] Buisseret (1992), 111.

another Italian was responsible for coding the letters of Philip II.[91] If the Italians were not also pioneers in the art of misinformation, in other words of spreading false rumours, they were among the first to discuss the subject openly in books such as Giovanni Botero's *Reason of State* (1589).[92]

THE DIFFUSION OF INFORMATION

Controlling information was not easy. The frontier between the public domain and the *arcana imperii* was frequently transgressed, and a good deal of political information was diffused, whether officially or unofficially. It was sometimes argued, notably by the friar Paolo Sarpi, adviser to the Venetian government in the early seventeenth century, that spreading information was a more effective political weapon than suppressing information.[93] Some regimes were particularly open in this respect, among them the Dutch Republic; England during the Civil War and again after 1688; and Sweden during the so-called 'age of liberty', especially the six years from 1766 to 1772.

Although the archives were not open to everyone, it was possible to gain access to them for particular purposes. Despite his image as the founding father of modern historical writing, Leopold von Ranke was not the first archive-based historian. In early modern times, official historians such as Gianbattista Adriani in Florence, William Camden in England and Samuel Pufendorf in Prussia and Sweden were granted access to official documents in order to explain and justify the policies of the governments which employed them. The students of Torcy's political academy (above, 47) used his new *Dépot* as part of their political education. In 1714, a French scholar, Hyacinthe d'Arche, was authorized to consult the archive in the Tower of London which English scholars such as John Selden had long been using.[94]

There was a long tradition of the use of local records for local reasons such as deciding disputes over inheritance. Parish registers were consulted for a variety of purposes. For example, in his treatise on the decline of Spain and the ways to remedy the situation, a canon of Toledo, Sancho de Moncada, used parish registers to show that marriage rates had declined. The English parish registers were laid

---

[91] Kahn (1967), 106–81.
[92] Dooley (1999), 82–6, 117, 127.
[93] Dooley (1999), 32.
[94] Bély (1990), 328–9, 460.

under contribution by the scholar George Hickes in an attack on the Scottish Presbyterians in 1677 in which he observed that the illegitimate birth-rate was higher in the country of 'these Pharisees' than it was elsewhere.[95]

Governments sometimes needed to make information public for their own purposes. It was obviously to their advantage to spread the knowledge of laws and other regulations, which were regularly proclaimed aloud as well as printed and posted in public places.[96] The problem, from their point of view, was to keep a balance between giving the public too little information, a situation which encouraged the spread of wild rumours, and giving them too much, which encouraged ordinary people to comment on affairs of state.

Official newspapers such as the Paris *Gazette* presented selected news items from the government's point of view. A foreign observer commented in 1639 that 'the French make a wondrous good use of it in giving what impressions they think good to their subjects.' In 1658, for example, the government discussed the need to ensure that the editor of the *Gazette* made favourable remarks about the king of Sweden, a French ally at this time.[97] The French model was soon followed in London and elsewhere. Two editors of the London *Gazette*, Lord Arlington and Sir Joseph Williamson, were also spymasters, so access to confidential information presented no problem for them.[98] Since the news in official newspapers was not always trusted by the readers, governments sometimes found it in their interest to leak information to unofficial sources, such as the manuscript newsletters which circulated in eighteenth-century France.[99]

Confidential information about foreign affairs was particularly likely to come to light, since it was in the interest of each country to discover, and sometimes to reveal, the secrets of their rivals and enemies. In London, Paris, Vienna and elsewhere it was common practice to open the letters sent to and from ambassadors, resealing them with care to prevent discovery. In Celle, for example, in the domains of the Duke of Brunswick, the local officials passed information to William III of England which they had gleaned from French, Danish and Swedish dispatches. In wartime, couriers might be ambushed and their letters seized. In Richelieu's time, for example, the French waylaid a Spanish courier in a forest near Loches. Important letters

---

[95] Thomas (1971), 156.
[96] Fogel (1989).
[97] Dahl (1951), 36.
[98] Marshall (1994), 28–30.
[99] Moureau (1995).

were usually written in code, but governments employed skilled code-breakers, not infrequently mathematicians, such as François Viète, who served Henri IV of France, and John Wallis, who served both Cromwell and William III. On occasion captured dispatches would be printed in order to reveal the enemy's duplicity. Both Catholics and Protestants had recourse to this technique during the Thirty Years War, in order to pin the 'war-guilt' on the other side, the rival collections of documents being entitled the *Anhalt Chancery* and the *Spanish Chancery*.[100]

The unofficial publication of confidential information was also a frequent occurrence. Machiavelli's notorious *Prince* should perhaps be regarded in this light, since it was a manuscript treatise offering advice to a particular ruler, a long memorandum as it were, which was only published after the author's death. Treatises on diplomacy made the practices of ambassadors and their secretaries part of general knowledge. One of the best-known of these revelations of 'trade secrets' in print was the work of a Dutch diplomat who was also active both as a writer of newsletters and as a spy (for the English), Abraham Wicquefort, author of *The Ambassador*, published in French in 1680.

The Republic of Venice was particularly concerned to keep its political secrets, but a government which consisted of 2,500 patricians alternating in office was bound to include some moles. The famous *relazioni* (above, 123) were read by a considerably wider group than those for whom the reports were intended. Some of these documents were copied and even found their way into print. A biography of Charles V, for example, published in 1567 by the professional writer Francesco Sansovino, made use of *relazioni* by two Venetian ambassadors to the imperial court.[101] By the seventeenth century at the latest, *relazioni* were on sale in certain European cities, notably Rome (to the shock of some Venetian ambassadors). For example, ambassador Renier Zen's description of Rome, written in 1623, was available for borrowing from the library of a Roman monastery later in the decade.[102] The ex-secretary to the French ambassador to Venice, Amelot de la Houssaie, was able to use letters, memoirs and *relazioni* for a history of Venice (1685) which made public what the author described in his preface as 'the mysteries of power' (*les mystères de la domination*). Copies of *relazioni* were and still are be found in a number of the major public and private libraries of Europe. Ranke

---

[100] Koran (1874); Kahn (1967), 106–81; Oakley (1968); Marshall (1994), 85–95.
[101] Morel-Fatio (1913), 152.
[102] Dooley (1999), 32.

discovered some in Berlin and Vienna before he carried out research in Venice itself.[103]

It was only to be expected that sooner or later someone would be enterprising and bold enough to print some *relazioni*. This step was taken by the printer who edited an anthology of texts under the name of *Political Treasury*, published in Paris (with 'Cologne' on the title-page) in 1589.[104] Later editions appeared in Milan and Vicenza. Three more *relazioni* by Venetian ambassadors to Rome were published in 1672 under the title *The Treasures of the Court of Rome*. The place of publication was given as 'Brussels' and there was no printer's name on the title-page. Even more remarkable was the publication in 1547 of an interrogation of a suspect heretic by the Inquisition, under the title of *Articles Proposed to Fra Baldo*.[105] The history of moles is a long one. Secrets are of course divulged for various reasons, political or idealistic as well as economic. However, the invention of printing reinforced the profit motive by enlarging the potential market. The market for knowledge in early modern Europe is the subject of the following chapter.

---

[103] Baschet (1870), 348–52; Tucci (1990), 99–107, at 100; Preto (1994), 66.
[104] Heath (1983); Balsamo (1995).
[105] Prosperi (1996), 162.

7

⁓

SELLING KNOWLEDGE:
THE MARKET AND THE PRESS

Scientia donum dei est, unde vendi non potest.
(Knowledge is a gift of God, so that it cannot be sold.)
Medieval aphorism

Learning is itself a trade.

Johnson

The ideas of religious liberty and freedom of conscience
merely gave expression to the sway of free competition within
the domain of knowledge.

Marx

ONE reason for saying that we live in an information society is that the production and sale of information makes a considerable contribution to the more developed economies. Some North American economists had already noticed this point a generation ago. In the 1960s, one of them was arguing that his colleagues had neglected 'the commodity aspects of knowledge', describing machines as 'frozen knowledge' and suggesting that economic development was 'essentially a knowledge process'. At much the same time, another economist published a book-length study of knowledge as a product, considering its stocks, costs and prices.[1] More recently, there has been a flood of books and articles on the information industry, information marketing, information services and information management.[2]

Once again it is worth posing a question which has recurred in this essay: What exactly is new in all this? I have no intention of denying the importance of the recent trends towards the commodification of knowledge.[3] All the same, it is worth trying to place these trends in the perspective of more gradual changes over the longer term. In this

---

[1] Stigler (1961); Machlup (1962); Arrow (1965); Boulding (1966).
[2] Bell (1976); Machlup (1980–4); Rubin and Huber (1986); Fuller (1992), etc.
[3] Schiller (1996).

context it is important but not sufficient to invoke the British Copyright Act of 1709, passed, according to its preamble, 'for the encouragement of learned men to compose and write useful books', in other words with knowledge rather than fiction in mind. It is necessary to range more widely and to go back much further. The idea of selling knowledge, for instance, is at least as old as Plato's critique of the sophists for this practice. The idea of knowledge as property (*possessio*) was formulated by Cicero. In ancient Rome, the term *plagiarius*, which originally referred to someone who stole a slave, was applied by the poet Martial to literary theft; the term *compilatio* also referred to plagiarism, viewed as a plundering of the original author.[4] In the Middle Ages, 'compiling' became respectable, suggesting that the sense of intellectual property was becoming less acute, but in the thirteenth century the traditional legal argument that knowledge was 'God's gift which cannot be sold' was challenged by the new principle that teachers should be paid for their labour.[5] In the fourteenth century, the poet Petrarch, in his book *On the Remedies of Fortune*, denounced people who viewed books as if they were a commodity (*quasi mercium*).

At the Renaissance, disputes over plagiarism became increasingly common despite (or because of) the difficulty of defining intellectual ownership. Renaissance humanists regularly accused one another of 'theft', while themselves claiming to practise no more than creative 'imitation'. By the seventeenth century, general discussions of the topic were appearing in print. Writers and printers disputed with one another over the property rights to a text. These disputes should be linked to the 'individualism', the emulation and the self-consciousness discussed by Jacob Burckhardt in his famous book on the Italian Renaissance. They are connected with the rise of the idea of 'genius', with the origins of 'originality', the decline of the notion of 'authority' and the 'birth of the author'. They also reveal changes in the balance between monopoly and competition in the field of knowledge, themes discussed in the mid-twentieth century by Karl Mannheim and Harold Innis.[6]

Two examples from Germany in the early sixteenth century illustrate the increasing preoccupation with property in texts and ideas. The first case, in 1533, was a dispute between two printers, from Frankfurt and Strasbourg respectively, over the use of plagiarized woodcuts to illustrate a treatise on herbs. The printer accused of plagiarism defended himself on the grounds that the spread of know-

---

[4] Lindey (1952); Hathaway (1989).
[5] Post (1932); Post, Giocarini and Kay (1955).
[6] Burckhardt (1860); Nisard (1860), esp. vol. 2, 12ff; Zilsel (1926); Mannheim (1929): Innis (1950); Viala (1985), 94–103; Chartier (1992).

ledge was a 'benefit to mankind'. The second case was a dispute between writers, in which a popularizer of natural philosophy was accused of plagiarism by a number of scholars including Conrad Gesner (the bibliographer discussed above, 92).[7]

So far as intellectual property is concerned, the movement known today as the 'scientific revolution' reveals not only ambiguity but also ambivalence. On the one hand, the ideal of making knowledge public for the good of humanity at large was taken very seriously. On the other, it is impossible to ignore the reality of bitter disputes between individuals over priorities in discovery, extending from the telescope to the calculus.

In the case of the telescope, a Dutch lens-grinder applied for a patent in 1608 for an instrument which made distant objects appear close. Galileo heard of this device through his friend Paolo Sarpi, a Venetian friar whose international network of correspondents made him something of an intellectual broker in the style of Mersenne (above, 25). Stimulated by the news, Galileo made a telescope of his own which was three times more powerful than the Dutch prototype. However, the Neapolitan natural philosopher Giambattista Della Porta wrote to an acquaintance that 'The invention of the eyepiece in that tube was mine, and Galileo, lecturer in Padua, has adapted it.'

In the case of the calculus, the protagonists in the dispute were Newton and Leibniz. Both scholars were working independently on the mathematics of the infinitesimal. Leibniz learned of Newton's work from the intellectual broker Oldenburg (above, 24) and wrote back hinting at his own discoveries. He wrote directly to Newton about the subject in 1676. These precautions did not prevent Leibniz being accused of plagiarism in a book published by a disciple of Newton in 1699.[8]

Ironically enough, co-operation is more visible in the field of agriculture, where new techniques were obviously profitable, than in pure mathematics. In the eighteenth century, many agricultural societies were founded in Britain, Italy, France, Russia and elsewhere in order to spread the knowledge of new techniques. Improvements in agriculture illustrate a major theme of this book, the interaction of knowledges, since information about these improvements travelled both upwards and downwards. Diderot, as always interested in things technical, wrote the article on agriculture in the *Encyclopédie*, discussing for example the innovations of the English farmer Jethro Tull and so bringing them to the notice of a wider public.[9]

---

[7] Eamon (1994), 110, 384. Cf. Tennant (1996).
[8] Merton (1957); Iliffe (1992); Findlen (1994), 324–5.
[9] Confino (1962), 158–9.

Even academic knowledge could become a commodity. Teaching for money was a traditional activity in schools and universities alike. Public lectures for fee-paying audiences became increasingly common in the seventeenth and eighteenth centuries. Théophraste Renaudot organized lectures of this kind in Paris, as we have seen (above, 66). The 'retailing of knowledge' in this way became part of the culture of London from the late seventeenth century onwards and of English provincial towns a generation later. In London in the eighteenth century, lectures on anatomy and surgery were advertised in the newspapers and the lecturers have been described as 'market-oriented'. The commercialization of medical knowledge may be illustrated by the increasing prominence in the newspapers of advertisements by 'quacks', in other words unofficial medical practitioners who promised marvels.[10]

Awareness of the links between knowledge and the market-place appears to have been growing in the seventeenth and eighteenth centuries. The Baconian John Durie described a good librarian as 'a factor or trader for helps to learning'. Thomas Sprat's history of the Royal Society is full of economic metaphors (the Society as a 'bank' or 'port' of knowledge, for example). The German scholar Johann Burchard Mencke published in 1715 a vivid denunciation of what he called the 'charlatanry' of the learned, in other words the art of self-advertisement by means of unusual clothes, pompous titles for themselves and their books, attacks on other scholars and the dedication of their own works to important people, dedications which Mencke described as sales masquerading as gifts.

The relation between the two spheres was two-way. As the epigraph to this chapter reminds us, Marx viewed new attitudes to knowledge as so many effects of the rise of capitalism on the cultural superstructure. However, as many scholars have argued and this chapter will attempt to illustrate, the effects of new knowledge on the economy were also substantial.[11]

THE RISE OF INTELLECTUAL PROPERTY

From the late Middle Ages onwards, we see increasing emphasis on the exploitation of knowledge for gain and the need to protect trade secrets as 'valuable intellectual property'.[12] The Renaissance architect

[10] Walker (1973); Porter (1989); Money (1993); Lawrence (1996), 163, 167–9.
[11] Landes (1998), 276–91.
[12] Eamon (1994), 75, 81.

Filippo Brunelleschi warned a colleague against people who claim credit for the inventions of others, and the first known patent was granted to Brunelleschi himself in 1421 for the design of a ship. The first patent law was passed in Venice in 1474.[13] The first recorded copyright for a book was given to the humanist Marcantonio Sabellico in 1486 for his history of Venice, and the first for an artist was given to Titian by the Venetian Senate in 1567 to protect prints of his work from unauthorized imitation.[14] Regulation began in a piecemeal way. Popes, emperors and kings gave privileges, in other words temporary or permanent monopolies, to protect particular texts, printers, genres or even new founts of type. The Emperor Charles V, for instance, issued forty-one 'letters of protection' (*Schutzbriefe*) of this kind in the course of his long reign. The copyright acts of the eighteenth century were a development from this earlier system of privileges.[15]

When analysing these examples, it is important not to impose modern categories on contemporary ones. It may be useful at this point to distinguish two conceptions of a text (or an image for that matter), the 'individualist' and the 'collectivist'. In the first case, the text is viewed as the property of an individual because it was the work of an individual brain. We live in a culture which is strongly individualist in this sense. In the second case, the text is viewed as common property because every new product draws on a common tradition. This view was dominant in the Middle Ages, as the tradition of copying shows. Scribes who copied manuscripts apparently felt free to make additions and changes. Conversely, scholars writing 'new' works felt free to incorporate passages from their predecessors. The trend to more individualist attitudes was assisted by the rise of print, which helped to fix as well as to diffuse texts. All the same, the process of change was not sudden or smooth, and examples of the survival of collectivist attitudes into the sixteenth and seventeenth centuries are not difficult to find, coexisting with the rise of privileges and patents.

Of course the idea of 'common property' is an ambiguous one. The question, Common to whom? needs to be asked, and the answer is often, 'Common to a social group', whether a guild or a government, rather than 'Common to everyone'. To spread information more widely might well be regarded as a kind of treachery. In the early modern period, the complementary if opposite concerns with keeping and with divulging trade secrets can be observed in a number of fields.

---

[13] Eamon (1994), 88–9.

[14] Gerulaitis (1976), 35–6; Landau and Parshall (1994), 362.

[15] Schottenloher (1933); Armstrong (1990); Feather (1994); Tennant (1996); Johns (1998), 326–79.

Spying, already discussed (above, 131) as part of the knowledge-gathering activities of governments, may also be viewed as an instance of the sale of information. The Dutch government regularly rewarded foreign ambassadors, Venetians for example, for passing on confidential information.[16] As we have seen (above, 147), official documents might be copied and sold. The French writer Amelot de la Houssaye was accused of selling documents stolen while he was secretary to the French embassy. The rise of newsletters in the seventeenth century turned political information into a commodity which was 'bought and sold in appreciable quantities for the first time'.[17] Rivalry in the pursuit of new technologies led to industrial espionage.

INDUSTRIAL ESPIONAGE

The advancement of learning was supported not only for its own sake but also for its economic effects. Bacon and his followers were interested in improvements in industrial processes such as dyeing and glass-making.[18] These improvements were diffused over Europe thanks to industrial espionage. In the analysis of such espionage, as in many other examples discussed in this book, it is important to avoid the projection of our concepts onto the past. Industrial espionage cannot be defined precisely in a period when entrepreneurs might be proud to show their technology off to foreign visitors. In the Dutch Republic, it was particularly easy for foreigners to discover how new machines worked. Hence it is only prudent to follow a leading scholar in the field and to speak of 'the espionage end of the information spectrum', linking it with attempts by governments or individual entrepreneurs to entice skilled workers from abroad to join them. The reason for the link is that craft knowledge was and is difficult to put in writing, so that the migration of techniques was linked to the migration of workers.[19]

A famous example of such enticement from the later seventeenth century, when governments were coming to take an increasing interest in trade and industry, was Colbert's attempt to attract Venetian craftsmen to France in order to discover from them the secret techniques of the glass-making industry. It is said that the Venetian ambassador to France liquidated some of these craftsmen before the secrets could be divulged. Foreigners went to Venice to discover the

---

[16] Rowen (1987); Bély (1990), 230ff.
[17] Cobb (1970); Tucci (1990); Infelise (1997, 1999a); Dooley (1999), 9.
[18] Webster (1975), 388–96.
[19] Harris (1985); cf. Cipolla (1972).

techniques. The Scottish mathematician James Stirling, nicknamed 'the Venetian', lived in Venice for about ten years in the early eighteenth century. He is supposed to have discovered the secret of Venetian glassmaking and then to have left Venice for fear of assassination.

The Venetians were not the only object of this kind of attention. In the eighteenth century, the Roman government invited a craftsman from Lyons to introduce the French method of dyeing silk and sent six weavers to Turin to learn Dutch methods. By this time the French, the Swedes, the Russians and the Austrians were all interested in acquiring English technology and workers. In England in 1719, there were protests against the emigration of skilled workers to France and Russia. The Austrian Joseph Emmanuel Fischer von Erlach (son of the famous architect), whose travels in England in the early 1720s were financed by his government, is said to have spied on English steam power. Swedish visitors to England reported back to the Board of Mines or the Iron Office in their own country about the machinery they had observed and sketched. In the 1780s, a French engineer travelled in England collecting information about Wedgwood pottery, stocking looms and other machines and took home with him three workers 'without whom the machines themselves would be quite useless'.[20]

COMMERCE AND INFORMATION

Commerce like industry depended on what has been called 'the search for information one lacks and the protection of information one has'.[21] International fairs at Besançon, Piacenza, Frankfurt and elsewhere were centres of exchange of information as well as commodities. Merchant culture was written culture and was already so in the Middle Ages. The fifteenth-century Florentine Giovanni Rucellai's claim that a good merchant always had inky fingers was in no way exceptional.[22] Trade routes were paper routes and trade flows depended on information flows.

In the sixteenth century, the letters home written from leading commercial cities in Europe and Asia by members of the merchant families of Genoa, Venice, Florence and elsewhere amounted to virtual 'data banks'. The Genoese merchant diaspora, for example, could be found in Antwerp, Seville, Lisbon, London, Cologne, Chios, Oran,

[20] Zacharias (1960); Robinson (1975); Lindqvist (1984), 95–178; Harris (1985, 1992, 1996a, 1996b); Davids (1995).
[21] Geertz (1979).
[22] Bec (1967); Heers (1976).

Aleppo and so on. The Fugger newsletters sent from different parts of the world to the family headquarters in Augsburg between 1568 and 1605 are further testimony to the importance and also the perceived importance of information in international trade.[23] One reason for the notorious commercial success of ethnic and religious minorities – Jews, Parsis, Quakers, Old Believers and so on – may have been their creation of information networks which were relatively inaccessible to outsiders.

Political and industrial spying was accompanied by commercial espionage. For example, Venetians and Spaniards both attempted to discover the secrets of Portuguese commerce with the East. When rumours about spices from India arriving in Lisbon reached Venice in 1501, the reaction of the government was to send an agent to Portugal to discover what was happening and report back to them. His report still survives. The Spanish pilot Juan de la Cosa was sent to Lisbon in 1503 for similar reasons. In situations of intense competition, marginal advantages in market information might be extremely profitable. No wonder that in 1478, some Venetians made a hole in the roof of the Doge's palace in order to discover the latest news from Istanbul. The great fifteenth-century merchant Jacques Coeur made use of carrier pigeons, while in Japan the brokers of seventeenth-century Osaka used fires, flags and carrier pigeons to relay information on market prices.[24] Information about commodities is itself a commodity, and there was a ready market for information about markets.

No wonder then that in 1661 the deputy governor of the English East India Company, Sir Thomas Chambrelan, asked an agent at Bantam to send him a report on the trade of Cambodia, Siam, China and Japan.[25] Information about past transactions was a guide to future strategies, so commercial companies and private firms came to keep registers and even archives. In 1609, for example, the court of the East India Company of London ordered the keeping of a register of letters to and from the company. Knowledge of the best trade routes was of great commercial value, so commercial companies, as we have seen (66), had an interest in knowledge of geography and navigation. In London, for example, the Russia Company paid for a translation into English in 1561 of the treatise on the art of navigation by Martín Cortés. The East India Company appointed Thomas Hood and Edward Wright to lecture to their members on mathematics and

[23] Doria (1986).
[24] Yazaki (1968), 235.
[25] Bassett (1960), 225.

navigation, and Richard Hakluyt to write their history. In France, it was the Compagnie des Indes which commissioned d'Anville's famous map of India (1752). Without exaggerating the similarities between the early modern period and the twenty-first century, we may say that companies were already acting as patrons of research.

INFORMATION AND THE VOC

A striking example of the awareness of the commercial value of information in this period comes from the history of the Dutch East India Company, known as the VOC (Vereenigte Ost-Indische Compagnie). The VOC has been described as a 'multinational', with information requirements not unlike those of an empire.[26] The success of the company has been attributed (among other things), to the 'efficient communications network' of the company, without equal among its rivals in this respect.[27] The VOC was interested in mapping its territories, and its maps and charts were constantly updated. Members of the famous Blaeu family of printers were employed as mapmakers to the VOC from 1633 to 1705, in other words as producers of manuscript maps containing secret information which did not appear in their famous atlases. The chartmakers had to swear an oath before the burgomaster of Amsterdam not to print the information in these charts and not to disclose it to anyone who was not a member of the company. The charts were loaned to pilots for use on voyages but were supposed to be returned. All the same, they were sometimes made available to foreigners at a price. A Dutch chart now in a French archive carries the inscription 'bought from a Dutch pilot'. In similar fashion, what the Company euphemistically called 'gratuities' gave the VOC access to information from both Dutch and foreign diplomats.[28] Political information was obviously important for the company. When the Italian Jesuit Martini was captured by the Dutch on his way home from China (above, 54), he was interrogated in Batavia and the VOC was extremely interested in his news of the fall of the Ming dynasty.

What was most remarkable in the information system of the VOC was the importance to the company of regular written reports. The stress on regular reports had analogues elsewhere in early modern Europe but in very different fields, notably the state of Venice, with

---

[26] Goody (1996), 116
[27] Steensgaard (1982), 238.
[28] Koeman (1970); Schilder (1976), 62–3; Smith (1984), 994.

its diplomatic *relazioni*, and the Society of Jesus, with its system of 'annual letters'. The VOC of course emphasized commercial information, especially in statistical form. From Batavia (now Jakarta in Indonesia), for instance, the governor-general and the council sent an annual report, known as a 'general letter' to the directors (the Heeren XVIII). More specific letters, still to be found in the archives in The Hague, included reports from regions and factories (Surat, for example), complete with statistical data.

These reports were summarized by Pieter van Dam, an advocate who worked for the VOC for more than fifty years and was asked by the directors to write a confidential account of company affairs for their own use. The VOC appears to have been relatively quick to develop an awareness of the importance for marketing strategies of the systematic collection of information, especially statistical information. A key figure in this respect was Johannes Hudde, a leading mathematician and a burgomaster of Amsterdam as well as a company director. Thanks to Hudde, sales figures were already being analysed in 1692 in order to determine the future policy of the company on pricing and the ordering of pepper and other commodities from Asia.[29] As in the case of reports, the closest parallels to the VOC's interest in statistics come not from rival companies but from the Catholic Church and the centralizing state (above, chapter 6).

Like these institutions, the VOC was unable to keep all its secrets. The English East India Company, for example, regularly acquired confidential information about the time of arrival and the contents of the cargo of VOC ships returning from Asia. The Dutch historian – and former newswriter – Lieuwe van Aitzema was able to include the transcript of a confidential report to the company on the situation in Asia in the fifth volume of his history of the Netherlands (first published 1657–68).[30]

THE RISE OF STOCK EXCHANGES

Bourses, which were among other things institutions for the exchange of information, were founded in Bruges (1409), Antwerp (1460), Lyons (1462), Amsterdam (1530), London (1554), Hamburg (1558), and Copenhagen (1624). Originally commodity markets, the bourses turned into markets in stocks and shares. A vivid description of the Amsterdam bourse was given by the Sephardic Jewish merchant Joseph

---

[29] Smith (1984), 1001–3.
[30] Poelhekke (1960); Smith (1984), 996; Rowen (1987).

Penso de la Vega in a dialogue in Spanish with the pleasing title *The Confusion of Confusions* (1688). This dialogue shows that the practice of speculation in company shares and even the division into 'bulls' and 'bears' had already become standard practice at this time (in England, the phrase 'buyer of bearskins' was in use by 1719 to refer to someone who buys the skin before the bear is killed).[31] In London, 'stockjobbers' (to use a term coined in the seventeenth century) frequented Jonathan's coffee-house in Exchange Alley to trade in news, notably news of the 'Great South Sea' (the Pacific Ocean, hence South America), in the years before the 'South Sea Bubble' burst in 1720.

Bourses were especially sensitive to any news which affected supply and demand. Vega, for example, discussed the effect on the market of news from the Indies and news of peace and war in Europe. No wonder that there was deliberate spreading of rumour in order to force prices up and down. A notorious instance from a somewhat later period was the rumour of Napoleon's death which reached London in 1814.[32]

Like speculating on the stock market, maritime insurance makes a good example of a business which is particularly sensitive to information. The insurance business developed in a number of centres, notably Genoa, Venice and Amsterdam, but from the end of the seventeenth century onwards, London took the lead. Like stockbrokers, insurers met in particular coffee-houses to exchange their news. At the end of the seventeenth century, Edward Lloyd was the proprietor of a coffee-house in Lombard Street, the old business district of the City, and his establishment was naturally frequented by merchants, many of them interested in information about the arrival or departure of ships. From this beginning it was a natural development for Lloyd to found a journal specializing in shipping news, and also to develop maritime insurance in London. It is for this reason that the Lloyd's of today still bears his name.[33]

PRINT AND THE SALE OF KNOWLEDGE

Acquiring knowledge of commercial affairs was of course increasingly assisted by print. Treatises on how to be a merchant proliferated. Commercial information about trade fairs, the arrival of ships and the prices of different commodities was increasingly available in print. In the 1540s, lists of the prices of commodities on the Antwerp

[31] Israel (1990b).
[32] Barbour (1950): Reinhartz (1987) ; Israel (1990a).
[33] Barbour (1928–9); Dawson (1932).

market were regularly published. The Frankfurt *Calendarium* or *Mess-relationen* (published from 1588 onwards) gave information about the trade fairs of the city. From 1618 onwards, Dutch newspapers gave economic information, including details about the arrival in Spain of silver from the New World. *Lloyd's News* (London, 1696–), concentrated on news about ships. Specialized newspapers such as the *Gazette Universelle de Commerce* (founded in Copenhagen in 1757) gave news about the prices of certain commodities and about the arrival and departure of ships.[34] Dictionaries of commerce were an increasingly common form of reference book from the late seventeenth century onwards, beginning with Jacques Savary's *Parfait negociant* (1675), a book dedicated to Colbert.

More confidential commercial information also found its way into print, with or without permission. The example of the Dutch historian Aitzema has already been quoted. Commercial documents were printed in other seventeenth-century Dutch treatises, including Commelin's history of the VOC (1646) and the history of the Dutch in Brazil by Barlaeus (1647), which drew on the archives of the West India Company.[35]

The publication of books was itself a trade which attracted the interest of businessmen who were already helping to finance printers in the fifteenth century.[36] Still more important, at least from the perspective of the present study, was the fact that print encouraged the commercialization of all kinds of knowledge. An obvious but significant consequence of the invention of printing was to involve entrepreneurs more closely in the process of spreading knowledge, 'the business of Enlightenment'.[37] Printers not infrequently commissioned new editions of classic texts, translations and reference books.

The frequent publication of different works on the same subject at much the same time is some indication of the intensity of competition between printers, like the claims on title-pages that the new edition was more accurate than its predecessors, or included more information, or was provided with a table of contents or an index that its rivals lacked. One example among many comes from the volume of missionary letters from Japan published in Leuven in 1570, which proclaims that it is the third edition 'more accurate and more detailed with an index' (*cum indice castigatior et auctior*).[38] The drive to produce ever larger and more detailed atlases, encyclopaedias and so on was fuelled by commercial competition.

[34] Morineau (1985), 42–55; Popkin (1990), 205; Sgard (1991).
[35] Harmsen (1994), 164.
[36] Balsamo (1973).
[37] Darnton (1979).
[38] Richardson (1994).

The point may be illustrated from the chronology of some leading reference books. Blaeu's *Atlas* of 1635 was followed almost immediately by his rival Jansson's *Atlas novus* of 1638; the legal and medical bibliographies compiled by Martin Lipen (1679) were followed by those of Cornelis de Beughem (1680–1); the collection of voyages edited by the Churchills (from 1704) by those of Harris (1705) and Stevens (1711); Postlethwayt's *Universal Dictionary of Trade* (1751–5) by Rolt's *A New Dictionary of Trade* (1756); and the revised *Encyclopaedia Britannica* (1777 onwards) by the revised Chambers (1778–).

Some printers were personally committed to intellectual movements such as humanism, the Protestant Reformation, or the Enlightenment. Others, though, are better described as mercenaries, working for Catholics and Protestant alike during the wars of religion. Some of these printers were already well aware of the importance of advertising, in other words the printing of information about goods and services in order to sell them, a practice which was developing in the seventeenth century. The Dutch news-sheets of the seventeenth century advertised books and the services of private tutors. In London around 1650, a newspaper would carry about six advertisements on the average; 100 years later, it would carry about fifty.[39] Among the items advertised in this way in England in the late seventeenth century were plays, race-meetings, quack doctors and 'Holman's Ink Powder' – perhaps the first brand name – for a product which was patented in 1688. Almanacs, which reached a particularly wide circle of readers, regularly carried advertisements. In England Gadbury's almanac for 1699 proclaimed the virtues of Dr Anderson's Scotch Pills, while a rival, Coley's, supported 'Buckworth's lozenges'.[40]

Books and journals often carried advertisements for other books and journals. Pages at the front or back advertised other works sold by the same printer (the modern distinction between printer and publisher was not yet the norm in this period). When Mencke's treatise *The Charlatanry of the Learned* was published in French translation at The Hague in 1721, the printer accompanied it with a twenty-nine-page list of the books he had in stock. In Italy, a separately printed catalogue of books with prices was produced as early as 1541. From the sixteenth century onwards, the Frankfurt Book Fair made particular titles known internationally (as it still does today). In the later seventeenth century, learned journals provided news about recent publications (below, 169). The practice of mailing booksellers'

---

[39] Dahl (1939); Sutherland (1986).
[40] Walker (1973).

catalogues to customers was established in the eighteenth century.[41] In France at the end of our period, a *catalogue des livres nouveaux* was published every week.

As potential profits rose, it became still more urgent to protect literary or intellectual property (discussed above, 149) by general laws. In Britain, for example, a Copyright Act was passed in 1709. One might interpret the passing of this Act as an attempt to solve the problem of the rival conceptions of knowledge as private and public. It was followed by an Engraver's Copyright Act in 1735, thanks to the efforts of William Hogarth, who had suffered more than most artists from the plagiarism of his work. In France, similar Copyright Acts to the British were passed after the Revolution, in 1791 and 1793.

However, plagiarism continued. So did illegal competition, known at the time as 'counterfeiting' (*contrefaçon*), or still more vividly as 'piracy', in other words, the publication of books of which others held the copyright. As case-studies in the commercialization of knowledge, including piracy, it may be illuminating to take a closer look at three cities which were major publishing centres: sixteenth-century Venice, seventeenth-century Amsterdam and eighteenth-century London.

SIXTEENTH-CENTURY VENICE

In the fifteenth century, more books were printed in Venice than in any other city in Europe (about 4,500 editions, which means something like 2,000,000 copies). Competition was vigorous and it was not unknown for printers to practise industrial espionage, acquiring the sheets of a book in the course of production in order to produce an almost simultaneous rival edition. No wonder that the first author's copyright was granted in Venice at this time.[42]

In the sixteenth century, Venice maintained its position as the leading publishing centre of Europe, with about 500 printing establishments producing 18,000,000 copies. One publisher alone, Gabriel Giolito, produced about 850 editions. Giolito opened branches of his bookshop in Bologna, Ferrara and Naples, and was perhaps the first bookseller to expand in this way. He seems to have been the first to publish books in a series, or as he called it, a 'necklace' (*collana*).[43]

---

[41] Raven (1993).
[42] Richardson (1999), 42, 69.
[43] Richardson (1999), 133.

The large number of printers in Venice was one of the attractions of the city for men of letters, since the market allowed them to make a living independent of patrons. Pietro Aretino was the most famous of a group of such men of letters, nicknamed *poligrafi* because they wrote so much and on such a wide variety of topics in order to survive – prose and verse, translations, adaptations from other writers, and especially works offering practical information, including a guide to Venice for visitors, conduct books and a treatise explaining how to write letters on different topics such as love and money. Some of the *poligrafi* served particular publishers (notably Giolito) as editors and proof-readers, new occupations which came into existence as the result of printing. They had equivalents in other places such as Paris and London, but Venice was the principal centre of professional writers in the sixteenth century.

Printed books were not simply commodities. They were given as well as sold, and these gifts, like dedications by authors to their friends or patrons, helped sustain social relationships.[44] Nevertheless, as was remarked by more than one contemporary, including the author of a treatise on the subject published in Venice in 1590, dedications were sometimes commercialized. Mercenary writers were following the lead of mercenary printers.[45]

SEVENTEENTH-CENTURY AMSTERDAM

In the seventeenth century, the Dutch Republic replaced Venice as an island of relative tolerance of religious diversity and also as a major centre and a major market of information, the 'magasin général' as Bayle called it in 1686.[46] The export of printed matter in Latin, French, English, German and other languages made an important contribution to the prosperity of this new nation. The first Hungarian encyclopaedia, for example, the *Magyar encyclopaedia* of Apáczai Csere János, was published in Utrecht in 1653.

The centre of this centre was the city of Amsterdam. By the second half of the seventeenth century, Amsterdam had become the most important centre of book production in Europe, as Venice had once been. Over 270 booksellers and printers were active there in the twenty-five years 1675–99. The Blaeu family alone published seven catalogues from 1633 onwards. As in Venice, maps and accounts of

---

[44] Davis (1983).
[45] Lucas (1989).
[46] Gardair (1984), 10.

voyages formed an important part of the printers' repertoire. Jan Tessing, for example, published a map of southern Russia in Amsterdam in 1699. Hendrick Doncker concentrated his production on travel books and maps. The biggest printing establishment in Amsterdam, that of Jan Blaeu (son of Willem) on the Bloemgracht, specialized in atlases. So did his rival Willem Jansson, who like Giolito opened branches, in his case in Leipzig and elsewhere.[47] The Italian Jesuit Martino Martini visited Amsterdam in 1653, as we have seen (54), in order to have his atlas of China printed by Blaeu.

Amsterdam printers, like the Venetians before them, specialized in printing in different languages. They printed English bibles and sold them in England more cheaply than the home product.[48] Till the end of the seventeenth century, 'English mariners depended on Dutch publishers for their charts and sailing directions, even of the coasts of England itself'.[49] They printed not only in Dutch, Latin, French, English and German, but in Russian, Yiddish, Armenian and Georgian as well.

The ethnic minorities of the city made an indispensable contribution to its economic success in this field.[50] Henri Desbordes, from Saumur, who moved to the Dutch Republic in 1681 and set up shop in the Kalverstraat a year later, is a good example of the contribution made to Amsterdam's economy by Calvinist refugees from Louis XIV's France. In 1698, when Peter the Great was trying to introduce scientific and technical knowledge into his dominions, the tsar hired Ilia Kopievski and other Russian émigrés to print technical books, maps and charts for the Russian market.[51]

The Dutch Republic has been described as 'the major European entrepôt' for information about East Asia in the 1650s and 1660s. The rest of the world was not forgotten. One of the leading printers in the republic, Elsevier, launched what may have been the first series of books with an academic editor. Johannes de Laet, a scholar who was also a director of the West India Company, was the editor in charge of a series of compendia of information (mentioned above, 77), about the organization and resources of different states of the world. Some he compiled himself, as in the cases of France, Spain, the Netherlands, the Ottoman Empire, India, Portugal and Poland; others he farmed out.[52]

---

[47] Koeman (1970).
[48] Hoftijzer (1987).
[49] Verner (1978).
[50] Dahl (1939); Davies (1952); Gibbs (1971); Bots (1983); Berkvens-Stevelinck et al. (1992).
[51] Shaw (1996), 164.
[52] Davies (1952); Davies (1954), 61ff; Kley (1971), 31.

De Laet was a Dutch equivalent of the Venetian *poligrafi*. Others included French Calvinists who came to the Dutch Republic after Louis XIV's Revocation of the Edict of Nantes had forced them to choose, in 1685, between conversion to Catholicism or emigration. Pierre Bayle, for example, who had migrated from the south of France to Rotterdam, edited a literary journal, the *News of the Republic of Letters*, which appeared in Amsterdam every month from 1684 onwards. Jacques Bernard arrived in 1688 and collaborated with Leclerc (Leclerc himself by contrast was from Switzerland, though he too arrived in Amsterdam at this time, in 1683). As we have seen (above, 29), the Calvinist diaspora contributed to the rise of journalism.

The Dutch popularizers of knowledge, the *broodschrijvers* as they were later known, remain to be studied as a group, unlike their counterparts in Venice, London or Paris.[53] Johannes de Laet was not alone in combining writing with other occupations. Caspar Barlaeus, for example, had an academic post but also translated an account of the Spanish in the New World and himself wrote an anonymous description of Italy and a history of the expedition of Johan Maurits of Nassau to Pernambuco. Isaak Commelin produced a guidebook to Amsterdam and a history of the voyages made by the VOC. Olfert Dapper, doctor of medicine, was the author of books on Africa and Asia. Arnoldus Montanus was pastor, schoolmaster, and writer of popular biographies and books on travel such as *The Wonders of the East*.

EIGHTEENTH-CENTURY LONDON

The British book market of the sixteenth and seventeenth centuries has been described as 'essentially provincial' by comparison with the Continent. Until the 1730s, the British imported rather than exported books. Until the middle of the eighteenth century, there was no large publishing house in Britain.[54] At the end of our period, however, the situation was changing, and changing rapidly. By 1777, London had seventy-two booksellers, said to be more than any other European city of the time (though Venice had ninety-six booksellers and printers in 1736).[55] The phrase 'the trade' was applied to booksellers as if they had become the traders *par excellence*. In 1725, Daniel Defoe had already declared that 'Writing . . . is become a very considerable Branch of the English commerce.' He compared booksellers to 'the Master Manufacturers' and writers to 'workmen'. It is worth adding

[53] Darnton (1982).
[54] McKenzie (1992); Raven (1992).
[55] Barber (1981).

that a few of these workmen were well paid. For the first time, a few authors, especially authors of non-fiction, received advances from their publishers large enough for them to begin to think of abandoning patrons and living from the proceeds of their writing. For example, Dr Johnson, whose hatred of patronage was notorious, received £1,575 in advance for his *Dictionary* in 1746.[56] David Hume received an advance of £1,400 for the third volume of his *History of Britain*, and William Robertson an advance of £3,400 for his *History of Charles V*. What appears to have been the largest advance of the century, in Britain at least, £6,000, was offered by Millar's successors, the partners William Strahan and Thomas Cadell, for the copyright of Dr John Hawkesworth's account of the discoveries of Captain Cook.[57] Dr Johnson's comment to Boswell on this publication was scathing: 'Sir, if you talk of it as an object of commerce, it will be gainful; if as a book that is to increase human knowledge, I believe there will not be much of that.'

We should not be too hasty to idealize the situation of eighteenth-century writers. For every successful man of letters there were scores or hundreds of literary workmen – and women – in poverty, in what was known as 'Grub Street' (as in sixteenth-century Venice and seventeenth-century Amsterdam).[58] They were the mercenaries, the 'hack' writers, as they were described on the analogy of hackney carriages, the taxis of the eighteenth and nineteenth centuries.

Even for the successful, the new freedom had its price. Johnson would probably have preferred to write his own books rather than compile a dictionary, and Pope to work on his own poems rather than translate Homer's. Hume wrote history because it sold better than philosophy, and if he were able to return to earth and consult the catalogue of the British Library, it is extremely unlikely that he would be happy to find himself listed as 'David Hume, historian'. All the same, some eighteenth-century men of letters enjoyed a greater degree of independence than their sixteenth-century predecessors the *poligrafi*, who lived by editing and proof-reading.

Let us now look at these changes from the printer's point of view. With expenses like these, the printers needed considerable capital, all the more so because after paying the advance and printing the book the publisher might suffer from piracy on the high seas of learning. Literary pirates tended to operate on the other side of the frontiers of centralized states, in zones where printers' privileges could not be

---

[56] Cochrane (1964).
[57] Cochrane (1964), 22–3, 40–5. Cf. Sher (1997).
[58] Rogers (1972).

enforced. Dublin was notorious in the mid-eighteenth century as a centre of pirated English editions, Geneva and other Swiss cities for books in French, and Amsterdam for books in both these languages. To survive in this increasingly competitive world, printers and booksellers made more frequent alliances, especially in Britain. In the seventeenth century, the Stationers' Company already had its 'joint stock'. In the eighteenth century, the 'conger' developed, a syndicate or system of alliances between firms to share risks and profits. Thus Johnson's *Dictionary* was financed by a group of five 'undertakers', including three well-known names, Thomas Longman, Andrew Millar and William Strahan.[59]

One way to raise money in advance was to publish by subscription. Eighty-seven English instances of publishing by subscription before 1700 have been discovered. John Ogilby, for example, published translations of Virgil and Homer in this way, disposing of unsold copies by lottery. He also used the device of a lottery to finance a description of China, the *Embassy from the East India Company* (1669).[60] The practice of subscription was still more common in the eighteenth century, especially for expensive books, and lists of subscribers were often printed in the volumes themselves in order to encourage others. More than 2,000 such lists have been discovered and it has been estimated that at least 100,000 individuals subscribed to books in eighteenth-century Britain.[61]

These methods were sometimes followed on the Continent. In Italy, for example, over 200 cases of publication by subscription are known for the first half of the eighteenth century, and the practice became more common thereafter. In the Dutch Republic, it is recorded as early as 1661. In Germany, on the other hand, the practice arrived late. F. G. Klopstock's description of the Republic of Letters, which appeared in 1773, was one of the first German books to be published in this way.[62]

In France, Montfaucon's multi-volume collection of images of the ancient world, *Antiquité Expliquée* (1716), was the first French publication to follow what the advertisement called 'the English model' (*la manière d'Angleterre*), in other words publishing by subscription. In the 1750s, a company with shareholders was founded in order to produce a multi-sheet map of France, which attracted some 650 subscribers. The *Encyclopédie* attracted nearly 4,000 subscribers to the

[59] Darnton (1979), 131–76; Feather (1994); Johns (1998).
[60] Clapp (1931, 1933).
[61] Wallis (1974), 273.
[62] Lankhorst (1990); Waquet (1993a).

first edition despite its price of nearly 1,000 livres.[63] As for the conger, the expense of publishing Montfaucon was borne by eight Paris printers, that of the *Encyclopédie* by four and that of the journal *Bibliothèque Universelle* in Amsterdam by three.[64]

NEWSPAPERS AND JOURNALS

Journals in particular, the *Journal Etranger* for example, relied on subscription. Although pamphlets about current events were already common in the sixteenth century, newspapers and journals, which began publication after 1600, were the literary genres which best illustrate the commercialization of information. The news was already viewed as a commodity in the seventeenth century. In his play *The Staple of News* (1626), mocking the rise of monopolies, Ben Jonson imagined the opening of a new office, 'a place of huge commerce', 'where all the news of all sorts shall be brought / And there be examined and then registered / And so be issued under the seal of the office / As staple news: no other news be current' (Act 1, scene 2). Jonson's attitude was shared by a Venetian intelligencer or 'reporter' (*reportista* was the local word) who wrote at the end of the eighteenth century that 'The news is a commodity which like all other goods is acquired either with money or by exchange.' Manuscript newsletters, containing all the news which was not fit to print, were commercial enterprises throughout the period. They allowed the writer or 'reporter' to make a living and on occasion sell the business to a successor.[65]

Printed news-sheets, first recorded in Germany in 1609, developed in the Dutch Republic in the early seventeenth century and had spread over most of Europe by the eighteenth century.[66] The first newspapers to appear in English and French, in 1620, were printed in Amsterdam under the title *The Corrant out of Italy, Germany etc.* and *Courant d'Italie, Alemaigne, etc.* The new genre was an immediate success, assisted by the outbreak of the Thirty Years War in central Europe in 1618 and by the Civil War in England in the 1640s, both of which were fully reported in the Dutch press.[67] From the 1660s onwards, a weekly paper in French, the *Gazette d'Amsterdam*, offered its readers not only information about European affairs but also frank criticisms of the Catholic Church and of the policies of the

---

[63] Wallis (1974); Darnton (1979), 254–63, 287–94; Pedley (1979); Pelletier (1990), 117–26.

[64] Martin (1957), 285; Martin and Chartier (1983–4), vol. 2, 30–3.

[65] Seguin (1964); Infelise (1997); Dooley (1999), 9–44.

[66] Harris (1987).

[67] Dahl (1939).

French government. Its rival, the *Gazette de Leyde*, went looking for news rather than waiting for it to arrive, and sent a correspondent to Paris in 1699 to cover the inauguration of a new statue of Louis XIV.

England also became a land of newspapers, some eighty years later than the Dutch Republic. An explosion of publications followed the lapsing of the Licensing Act in 1695. By 1704, London had nine newspapers, and by 1709 the number had risen to nineteen. Major provincial towns such as Bristol and Norwich also had their newspapers such as the *Bristol Postboy* (1702).[68]

More academic knowledge was spread by the learned journal, which appeared every month or two. The genre began in the 1660s with the *Journal des Savants* in Paris and the *Philosophical Transactions* of the Royal Society of London. In the later seventeenth century, Amsterdam was the place of publication of both the *Nouvelles de la République de Lettres*, published by Henri Desbordes, and the rival *Bibliothèque Universelle et Historique*, edited by Jean Leclerc. Desbordes's title was particularly well chosen. The point of publication in periodical form was precisely to provide news of the 'Republic of Letters', including obituaries of famous scholars and, for the first time, reviews of new books. That the learned journal might be good business is shown by the fact that the *Journal des Savants* was pirated in Amsterdam and 'Cologne', while the formula was imitated in Rome, Venice, Leipzig and elsewhere.

THE RISE OF REFERENCE BOOKS

The problem of finding information when it is needed, 'information retrieval' as it is now called, is an old one. It took new forms after the invention of printing, which in one sense simplified the problem and in another sense complicated it. Books made many items of information easier to find, provided that one first found the right book. Given the multiplication of books after 1500, that proviso has to be taken very seriously. The rise of the book review in the later seventeenth century was a response to a problem which had become increasingly acute.

Another attempt at a solution was the invention of the reference book. A dizzying variety of such books developed in the early modern period, especially in the eighteenth century. Encyclopaedias, dictionaries, atlases and bibliographies are only the most obvious members of the group. Dictionaries, rare in 1500, proliferated in the seventeenth

---

[68] Harris (1987).

and eighteenth centuries and were extended to include some non-European languages. Reference books of the period also included almanacs, herbals, chronologies and directories (in other words books of directions or rules). There were manuals of cases of conscience for confessors and penitents. There were catalogues of libraries, museums, booksellers and of course the Index of Prohibited Books, used by some readers as a catalogue of books which must be interesting since they were not allowed to be read.

Geographical works of reference proliferated. There were dictionaries of places or 'gazetteers' (so-called, from the early eighteenth century, because they helped readers to follow the stories in the newspapers). There were guidebooks to cities, regions, countries (notably the Elsevier series) or the world: the Italian priest Giovanni Botero's *Relationi universali*, published in the 1590s, or Pierre d'Avity's *Description* (1643), in four volumes, one for each of the four known continents. There were postal timetables and directories of addresses of tradesmen and others, ancestors of the telephone directory.[69]

Again, there were anthologies of anecdotes and collections of longer texts (travels, laws, treaties, or decrees of councils of the Church). There was also a range of how-to-do-it books giving instruction in such skills as calligraphy, carving, cooking, dancing, drilling, farming, letter-writing and so on. Over 1,600 guides for merchants printed between 1470 and 1599 have been identified, and more than double that number for the seventeenth century, while the eighteenth century witnessed the rise of multi-volume encyclopaedias of commerce and industry.[70]

The proliferation of reference books was already mocked by a man of letters, Melchior Grimm, in the mid-eighteenth century. 'The craze for dictionaries (*la fureur des dictionnaires*) has become so acute among us that someone has just printed a *Dictionary of Dictionaries*.' He was not exaggerating. Such a dictionary had been published in Paris in 1758 by a certain Durey de Noinville.

The titles of these reference books include 'atlas', 'axiomata', 'breviat' (or summary), 'castle', 'catalogue', 'commonplaces', 'compendium', 'corpus', 'dictionary' (or lexicon), 'directory', 'encyclopaedia', 'epitome', 'flowers' (*flores, polyanthea*, anthologies), 'forest' (*silva*), 'garden', 'glossary', 'gold mine' (*aurofodina*, Drexel, 1638), 'guide', 'handbook' (following the classical tradition of the *enchiridion* and the *manuale*), 'inventory', 'itinerary', 'key' (*clavis*), 'library', 'marrow' (*medulla*), 'mirror' (*speculum*), 'promptuarium', *recueil*, 'repertory',

[69] Goss (1932).
[70] Perrot (1981); Hoock and Jeannin (1991–3); Elkar (1995).

'summary', 'theatre', 'treasury', 'tree' and 'vade mecum'. Over time it is possible to detect a move from the concrete (flowers, gardens and trees) to the more abstract.

Among the most successful books were the priest Louis Moréri's historical dictionary (with twenty-four editions in French and sixteen in translation between 1674 and 1759) and the Cambridge don John Eachard's geographical dictionary, *The Gazetteer's Interpreter*, which reached its seventeenth edition in 1751 and was translated into French, Spanish, Italian and Polish before 1800. Some German guides to the world of scholarship were also publishing successes, notably Daniel Morhof's *Polyhistor* (1688), a guide to libraries, conversation and to 'all disciplines', which had reached its fifth – much expanded – edition by 1747, and Burkhard Struve's introduction to scholarship (*res literaria*) and to the use of libraries, first published in 1704 and in its sixth, enlarged edition in 1768.

Proliferation also led to specialization. Bibliography, for example, began with the aim of being universal, at least in the field of scholarship and in Latin. National bibliographies followed, such as La Croix du Maine's *Bibliothèque Françoise* (1584). A little later, in the early seventeenth century, came subject bibliographies, using categories such as theology, law, medicine, history (below, 187) and politics (in 1734, the French scholar Nicolas Lenglet would publish the first – select – bibliography of novels). An increasing number of reference books were produced for particular sections of the public, such as the clergy, merchants, physicians, lawyers, women and so on. Preachers, for example, could turn to Francisco Labata's *Apparatus concionatorum* (above, 95), or to the French Jesuit Vincent Houdry's *Bibliothèque des Prédicateurs* (1712). Both works went through several editions, and Houdry's was translated into Italian and also into Latin in order to reach a more international market.

ENCYCLOPAEDIAS

Encyclopaedias became more numerous, larger, more weighty and more expensive in this period. Moréri's historical dictionary, which first appeared in one volume, rose to ten tomes in the course of nearly a century. The German journalist Johann Georg Krünitz compiled an economic encyclopaedia in sixteen volumes (1771–2). Zedler's *Lexikon* ran to thirty-two volumes, the French *Encyclopédie* to thirty-five, and its Swiss rival the *Dictionnaire raisonné des connaissances humaines* to fifty-eight volumes (1770–80). Krünitz's work was regularly updated and expanded to reach 242 volumes by 1858.

This very expansiveness generated a need for the complementary opposite, the 'portable' reference book like the *Lexicon genealogicum portatile* (1727), the *Dictionnaire portatif des prédicateurs* (1757), *Dictionnaire domestique portatif* (1762), *Dictionnaire portatif d'Italie* (1777), *Dictionnaire portatif des femmes* (1788) and the *Dictionnaire géographique portatif* (1790). Attempts were made to cater for general readers and to sell them encyclopaedias on the grounds that it was impossible to read the newspaper without their aid, or even to converse intelligently (hence the idea of the *Konversationslexikon*).

Some enterprising publishers turned to new methods of production. Compiling encyclopaedias was becoming a specialized occupation. Reynier Leers of Rotterdam, the publisher of Furetière's *Dictionary* (1689), a one-man job competing with the official dictionary of French organized by the Académie Française, paid the refugee scholar Pierre Bayle a salary to support him while he was working on his *Historical and Critical Dictionary* (1697).[71] In similar fashion, the German polyhistor Carl Ludovici worked full-time for Zedler. Diderot's contract of 1747 specified that he was to receive 7,200 livres for editing the *Encyclopédie*, while d'Alembert, who did less of the work, was to receive 2,400.

The rise of collective research and writing was another new trend (cf chapter 3 above, 45). Jean Leclerc proposed the formation of an international committee of specialists to correct and enlarge Moréri. What scholars suggested, entrepreneurs put into practice. Zedler's *Lexikon* and the *Encyclopédie* were produced by teams of contributors (at least 135 of them in the case of Diderot's enterprise).[72] Multivolume encyclopaedias illustrate the commercialization of knowledge with particular clarity because large-scale enterprises required the investment of equivalent amounts of capital. Many of the famous encyclopaedias of the eighteenth century – Pivati's *Nuovo dizionario scientifico* in Venice, Zedler's *Lexicon* in Leipzig, the French *Encyclopédie* – were published by subscription. John Harris's *Lexicon technicum* (1704), published by a syndicate of ten booksellers or 'undertakers', listed nearly 900 subscribers.[73]

The two best-known British encyclopaedias of the time, Chambers's and the *Britannica*, both of which originated in Scotland, had a similar basis in subscriptions and in associations of booksellers to share expenses and profits, a system of partnership which has been

---

[71] Lankhorst (1983).
[72] Proust (1962); Lough (1968), 466–73; Quedenbaum (1977); Carels and Flory (1981).
[73] Garofalo (1980); Bradshaw (1981a).

compared to that of joint-stock companies (the shares were in fact bought and sold on occasion).

Ephraim Chambers published the first edition of his *Cyclopaedia* in 1728, in two folio volumes, at a price of 4 guineas. It had reached its fifth edition by 1746. The cost was shared between a number of publishers, including Thomas Longman, who bought shares from his partners until by 1740 he owned eleven sixty-fourths of the enterprise. In similar fashion William Strahan, who also owned shares in Johnson's *Dictionary*, had acquired five of the sixty-four units of Chambers by 1760.[74] As for the *Britannica*, it originated as the joint enterprise of the engraver Andrew Bell and the printer Colin McFarquhar. From the sale of the third edition Bell, the only surviving partner, received £42,000. However, the biggest success of all was probably the *Encyclopédie*, if we take into account not only the original Paris edition in folio but the reprints produced in Geneva, Lucca and Livorno, the quarto editions from Geneva and Neuchâtel, and the octavos from Lausanne and Berne, some 25,000 copies in all by 1789.[75]

The details provided earlier in this chapter suggest that the trade in knowledge was not new in the eighteenth century. What was new was that knowledge had become big business. The description of the *Encyclopédie* by one of its publishers, Charles Joseph Pancoucke, as 'a business matter' (*une affaire d'argent*) sums it up. The owner of seventeen journals, Pancoucke knew more than most about the process of selling knowledge.[76]

COMPARISONS AND CONCLUSIONS

The wider context for the developments in publishing described above, which may be summed up as 'the commercialization of the book', is what historians have come to call 'the consumer revolution' or 'the birth of a consumer society' in the eighteenth century, a shift particularly visible in England but extending to other parts of Europe and even beyond. Subscriptions, for example, were a device used for various purposes in this period: subscriptions to clubs, to plays, to lectures and so on. The 'commercialization of leisure' and the 'consumption of culture' were an important part of this revolution, including the rise of theatres, opera houses, and exhibitions of paintings, open to

[74] Bradshaw (1981b).
[75] Darnton (1979), 33–7.
[76] Darnton (1979), 26; Eisenstein (1992), 132.

anyone prepared to pay the price of a ticket.[77] Once again, acute
contemporaries noticed the trends long before historians. Adam Smith
once observed that in 'commercial society', the majority of 'any ordinary person's knowledge' had been purchased.

It may be illuminating to try to place the European trends described and analysed in this chapter in a wider context. The world of
Islam resisted print in this period, with very few exceptions such as
the press set up in Istanbul in the early eighteenth century, which
lasted for only a few years and produced no more than a handful of
books.[78] The most instructive comparisons are probably those with
East Asia, especially with Japan. Despite the growth of intercontin-
ental trade in this period, it is likely that the commercialization of
the book in Tokugawa Japan, linked to urbanization and the commercialization of leisure, ran parallel to trends in the West rather
than being connected to them.[79]

In Japan, from the seventeenth century onwards, there are signs of
a printing boom together with a rise of bookshops. This expansion
of the book trade was linked to the rise of new kinds of book, the
kana-zoshi, a term which might be translated as 'chap-books'. These
books, whether romances or guides to making a fortune, were written
not, as was customary, in Chinese characters, but in a more simple
syllabic script (kata-kana), enabling these relatively cheap publications to reach new kinds of reader, especially females, who had not
learned the Chinese characters.[80] By 1659 Kyoto booksellers' catalogues were giving information about authors, titles, publishers and
prices. By 1696, there were nearly 8,000 titles in circulation.

In China, the sixteenth-century Italian Jesuit missionary Matteo
Ricci, the individual best placed to make the comparison, commented
on the cheapness of books compared to his own country. Given the
size of the market for books in a country of over 100,000,000 people
using only one literary language, and the consequent possible economies of scale, Ricci's observation makes sense. Literacy was more
widespread in early modern China than historians used to believe. It
is true that to be considered an educated man one was supposed to
know some 30,000 ideograms, an achievement impossible without
years of study. On the other hand, it was possible to navigate one's
way through everyday life with a knowledge of two thousand characters, and there is evidence that ordinary townspeople, male and

[77] Plumb (1973); McKendrick, Brewer and Plumb (1982); Brewer and Porter (1993);
Bermingham and Brewer (1995).
[78] Robinson (1993).
[79] Shively (1991), 731.
[80] Kornicki (1998), 172.

female, often achieved this level.[81] Cheap publications, including almanacs and small encyclopaedias, abounded, the printers of the province of Fukien specializing in this end of the market. In other words, there was a trend to the 'commodification' of information in China as well as in Europe, although this trend seems to have stopped short of the encyclopaedia.

The Chinese encyclopaedic tradition goes back to the third century AD, and unlike the western classical tradition, it was continuous rather than interrupted. From the Ming period alone, 1368–1644, 139 encyclopaedias are known. Chinese encyclopaedias reached vast dimensions long before western ones. The early fifteenth-century *Yongle dadian* involved some 2,000 contributors and ran to more than 10,000 volumes, making it too expensive to print and so difficult to preserve (less than 4 per cent of it has survived). The early Qing period witnessed the publication in 1726, under imperial auspices, of an even grander enterprise, in print this time, *Qinding Gujin tushu jicheng*, with more than 750,000 pages, making it in all probability the longest printed book in the world. The point of the enterprise was to collect traditional knowledge, a point illustrated by the *Siku Quanshu*, a selection of some 3,500 books which were to be preserved in manuscript copies lodged in seven different places. The enterprise was carried out between 1772 and the late 1780s.[82]

The contrast between the organization, function and readership of Chinese and of western encyclopaedias deserves to be underlined. As early as the Tang dynasty, encyclopaedias were produced primarily to serve the needs of candidates in the examinations which led to posts in the imperial bureaucracy. The examinations took the form of essays, and the works of reference consisted mainly of quotations arranged by topic, allowing candidates with good memories to lard their answers with appropriate references to the literary classics. As for the *Tushu jicheng*, its imperial patronage, together with the small number of copies printed, suggests that it was produced essentially to help mandarins in their work. The contrast with Chambers, with Zedler and with the *Encyclopédie* will be obvious. In Korea, the control of printing by the government was even more thorough than in China, and the private production and sale of books was sometimes forbidden.[83]

The meaning of this contrast is necessarily a matter of speculation, but I would like to suggest that it may be regarded as a symptom or

---

[81] Rawski (1979); Rawski (1985), 17–28.
[82] Bauer (1966); Monnet (1996).
[83] Giesecke (1991), 124–9.

indicator of larger differences between two knowledge systems, between what might be called the bureaucratic organization of knowledge in China and the more entrepreneurial organization of knowledge in Europe, sometimes known as 'print capitalism'.[84] Returning to the language of Ernest Gellner (above, 7), we might say that in early modern China cognition was linked to coercion, in this case to mandarins rather than soldiers, the pen (more exactly the writing-brush) rather than the sword.

In early modern Europe, on the other hand, cognition was linked ever more closely to production via printing, and this led to a more open system of knowledge. The invention of printing effectively created a new social group with an interest in making knowledge public. This is not to say that information was made public only for economic reasons; as the previous chapter suggested, political rivalries sometimes led to one government disclosing the secrets of another. All the same, the market in information was growing in importance throughout the early modern period. Even 'pure' or academic knowledge was affected by this trend, as we have seen.

A similar point was made in a characteristically vivid way by Thorstein Veblen when he described the 'higher learning' of his time in the United States as 'matter-of-fact' and 'mechanistic' in the style of contemporary business and technology. It was, he claimed, a 'highly-sterilized germ-proof system of knowledge'.[85] The selection, organization and presentation of knowledge is not a neutral, value-free process. On the contrary, it is the expression of a world-view supported by an economic as well as a social and political system.

---

[84] Anderson (1983).
[85] Veblen (1918), 7.

8

ACQUIRING KNOWLEDGE: THE READER'S SHARE

To enter the palace of learning at the great gate, requires an expense
of time and forms; men of much haste and little ceremony are content
to get in by the back-door.

Swift

Knowledge is of two kinds. We know a subject ourselves,
or we know where we can find information upon it.

Johnson

THE last chapter concentrated on the production of knowledge for profit and its relation to the rise of the eighteenth-century 'consumer society'. It is time to turn to the consumers themselves, the ways in which they acquired or appropriated knowledge and the uses they found for it.

In the field of knowledge, individual consumption is relatively well documented. Inventories of goods often list the contents of libraries title by title. The practice of publishing by subscription discussed in chapter 7 (above, 167) led to the publication of lists of subscribers which give historians some impression of the nature of the reading public in different places and times and for different kinds of book. It is fascinating to find, for example, that the subscribers to John Harris's *Lexicon technicum* (above, 172) ranged from Isaac Newton and the classical scholar Richard Bentley to a shipwright and a watchmaker, or that the subscribers to the *Encyclopédie*, often perceived as an anticlerical enterprise, included substantial numbers of French clergymen.[1]

Subscription lists are also a vivid reminder of the problem of the limitations to individual access to knowledge at this time. Only a tiny proportion of the population could afford to subscribe to a folio encyclopaedia or even to a journal. Public or quasi-public libraries existed, as we have seen (chapter 4, 67), but access to them was

---

[1] Trenard (1965–6); Shackleton (1970).

limited, most obviously by the individual's location, with the inhabitants of Rome and Paris enjoying considerable advantages over everyone else (above, 68). Jean Barbeyrac, a French writer on law, wished in 1716 that he were living in Berlin rather than Lausanne because access to libraries was better there. The English historian Edward Gibbon worked in the public libraries of Lausanne and Geneva in 1763 and deplored the lack of a public library in London (he was admitted a reader at the British Museum in 1770, soon after it opened).[2]

The sociology as well as the geography of libraries is also relevant to the history of the acquisition of knowledge. Access to early modern libraries depended on the attitudes of the librarian and his staff. For example, the correspondence of foreign scholars is full of complaints about the difficulty of gaining access to the Marciana in Venice. In his treatise on libraries, Gabriel Naudé noted that only the Bodleian in Oxford, the Ambrosiana in Milan and the Augustinian library in Rome allowed free entrance to scholars (the Bodleian is known to have been used by some 350 foreign readers between 1620 and 1640). The seventeenth-century English traveller Richard Lassels also noted with pleasure that the Ambrosiana 'opens its doors to all comers and goers, and suffers them to read what book they please', and that in Rome the university library and that of the Augustinians were 'open to all men every day, with a courteous gentleman to reach you any book'.

Public libraries multiplied in the period and so did the numbers of users and the numbers of books available on their shelves. For example, in 1648, eighty to a hundred scholars regularly used the Bibliothèque Mazarine in Paris on the days on which it was open. The Hofbibliothek in Vienna officially opened to readers in 1726, and the Bibliothèque Royale in Paris a decade later. By the late eighteenth century there were printed forms to use for ordering books, although the journalist Sébastien Mercier complained: 'This vast store is open only twice a week and for two and a half hours . . . the public is poorly served, with a disdainful air.'[3]

Lectures for a wider public than that of university students were becoming more frequent in London, Paris and elsewhere (above, 152). Museums, which for the most part housed private collections, were gradually becoming more open in the course of the period, at least to visitors from the upper classes, as surviving visitors' books make clear.[4]

---

[2] Keynes (1940), 18–19; Goldgar (1995), 13.
[3] Clarke (1970), 83.
[4] Findlen (1994), 129–46.

All the same, it is appropriate for this chapter to focus on the acquisition of knowledge via the reading of books and periodicals. Periodicals deserve a special mention because they made learning easier. As the Italian *philosophe* Cesare Beccaria once observed – in the pages of the journal *Il Caffé* – periodicals spread knowledge more widely than books, just as books spread knowledge more widely than manuscripts. Some readers are in awe of books and prefer not to have them in the house. The periodical, on the other hand, is more reader-friendly. 'It presents itself like a friend who just wants to say a word in your ear.'

READING AND RECEPTION

The acquisition of knowledge is obviously dependent not only on the possibility of access to stores of information, but also on the individual's intelligence, assumptions and practices. The history of ways of listening and even of ways of viewing has not been studied in any depth, but the history of reading has attracted a good deal of attention in the last couple of decades, and it has led, for instance, to a new way of writing the history of science.[5]

The new approach has also generated a number of debates, notably the debate over the rise of what is known as 'extensive reading', in other words browsing, skimming or consulting. One historian has claimed that a 'reading revolution' took place in Germany in the later eighteenth century, in the sense of a shift from intensive to extensive reading. Another has described a more gradual and a more general shift 'from intensive and reverent reading to a more extensive, nonchalant reading style', the result of the proliferation and the consequent 'desacralization' of the book. It was in the mid-eighteenth century that Dr Johnson asked his interlocutor with his usual force, 'Sir, do you read books *through*?'[6]

However, extensive reading was not a new discovery. In ancient Rome the philosopher Seneca, in his second letter to Lucilius, was already advising his pupil not to browse in books, which he compared to toying with one's food. Francis Bacon developed the same common comparison between reading and eating in his essay 'Of Studies', when he distinguished three ways of using books: 'Some books are to be tasted, others to be swallowed, and some few to be chewed and digested.' Bacon's advice reminds us that it was perfectly

---

[5] Sherman (1995); Blair (1997); Johns (1998).
[6] Engelsing (1969, 1974); Chartier (1987).

possible for the same person to practise different styles of reading in the seventeenth century, just like many of us today. The preface to John Harris's technical dictionary claimed that the book was 'useful to be read carefully over, as well as to be consulted like other dictionaries occasionally'.

Intensive reading was encouraged in schools and universities, where close familiarity with certain texts such as Aristotle, Cicero, the Bible and the Corpus of Roman law was often required from students. To acquire this familiarity the students might practise the classical art of 'artificial memory', making an effort to associate whatever they wanted to remember with vivid and dramatic images which were located in imagined 'places' such as a church or a theatre.[7]

Centuries before Marcel Proust and his contemporary the sociologist Maurice Halbwachs, the power of associations and the importance of location for the act of remembering was clearly recognized. It was perhaps for this reason that Sir Robert Cotton described the major sections of his library by the names of Roman emperors whose busts were placed on the book-cases. Joseph Williamson, a secretary of state in the reign of Charles II, organized his papers in a similar way.[8]

Alternatively, the students might take notes on texts. The fact that this practice still persists does not mean that we can take it for granted or assume that it is unchanging. A history of note-taking, if it ever comes to be written, would make a valuable contribution to intellectual history. This history might include notes on lectures, a number of which have survived from the sixteenth and seventeenth centuries, and notes on travels, often made for educational reasons by young noblemen on the Grand Tour.[9]

Notes might be taken in the texts themselves, with the reader underlining passages or writing in the margin a heading or the words 'note well' (*nota bene*), sometimes symbolized by the image of a pointing finger. Marginalia of this kind were sometimes inserted by printers in order to make the student's task easier. Alternatively, notes might be taken in special notebooks. Well-organized scholars might keep different notebooks for different subjects, as Montesquieu did with his notes on history, geography, law, politics, mythology and so on. By the eighteenth century, if not before – how else could bibliographers like Conrad Gesner have operated? – notes were being taken on slips of paper or *fiches*, which had the advantage that they could be rearranged in different combinations whenever necessary. Since

---

[7] Rossi (1960); Yates (1966).
[8] Marshall (1994), 42–3.
[9] Kearney (1970), 60–3, 137, 151; Grafton and Jardine (1986), 15, 18–20, 85n, 164–6, 170–3; Stagl (1980).

slips of paper were liable to damage, some scholars preferred to take their notes on the back of playing-cards, the ancestor of the card-index system so important in intellectual life until the recent arrival of the personal computer.[10]

The practice of note-taking was taught in schools by the sixteenth century, if not before: it may be significant that the word 'notes' in this sense, like the term 'digest' in the sense of a summary, is recorded in English only in the sixteenth century. Frequently advised was the keeping of what were known at this time as 'commonplace books', notebooks which were organized in systematic form, often in alphabetical order of 'topics' or 'commonplaces' (*loci communes, lieux communs*, etc.). As we have seen (above, 95), this was a common way of ordering knowledge. Associated with the 'places' of artificial memory, commonplaces helped writers to produce new texts and readers to assimilate them with a minimum of effort, whether these readers were students, lawyers composing speeches or preachers with sermons to deliver.

The last group, for example, might turn to the collection of sermon outlines already circulating in print in the fifteenth century and nick-named 'Sleep Well' (*Dormi secure*) because it alleviated anxiety over next Sunday's sermon; or to Francisco Labata's *Instrument for Preachers* (1614), discussed in chapter 5 (above, 171); or to Vincent Houdry's eight-volume *Preachers' Library* (1712). Houdry's book, which had expanded to twenty-three volumes by its fourth edition, was an alphabetical list of topics for sermons, mainly moral topics such as 'affliction' or 'ambition', complete with appropriate references to the Bible, the fathers of the Church, theologians and preachers. Its derivation from the tradition of commonplaces is revealed by the author's habit of considering pairs of opposed qualities together, humility alongside pride and so on.

The 'places' included abstract concepts such as comparisons and opposites, which helped readers organize information and so retrieve it when they needed it. As recommended by writers on education such as Erasmus and Vives, the topics also included moral qualities such as prudence, justice, fortitude and temperance, sometimes paired with the opposite vice. Under these headings, the students were supposed to note striking examples from Homer, Virgil and other classics in order to use them in arguments for or against a particular line of conduct. Since the same examples frequently recurred, the idea of the 'commonplace' gradually shifted from active to passive, from a scheme for organizing information to what we call a verbal cliché.[11]

---

[10] Shackleton (1961), 229–38.
[11] Schmidt-Biggemann (1983); Blair (1992, 1996); Moss (1996).

The moral-rhetorical approach embodied in the commonplace books and taught in schools and universities influenced modes of reading in early modern Europe and may therefore be used by scholars to reconstruct these modes. Take history, for example. A number of treatises were devoted to the art of reading books on history. Jean Bodin's *Method for the Easy Comprehension of History* (1566), with its chapter 'On the order of reading historical treatises', is the most famous example of the genre. In his third chapter, 'On the proper arrangement of historical material', Bodin advises his readers to keep a commonplace book of the examples they come across when reading about the past, dividing them into four types, 'base, honourable, useful and useless'.

The study of history was generally justified on moral grounds. Readers of Livy, Tacitus or Guicciardini were supposed to look out for moral examples, good examples to follow and bad examples to avoid. The frequent moral reflections offered by historians ancient and modern helped readers in their task. Printed marginalia drew attention to these reflections, which were sometimes listed in a separate index of maxims or *gnomologia*. It would therefore appear that the sixteenth-century public read its history in a very different way from many readers today, concerned as it was with morals rather than facts, and attending to the general features of a situation at the expense of the specific.

History was also read with the precepts of rhetoric very much in mind. Sixteenth-century historians, like those of ancient Greece and Rome, offered a good deal of their explanations in the form of speeches placed in the mouths of counsellors, generals or ambassadors, and arguing for or against a particular course of action or exhorting the troops to fight. The professional writer François de Belleforest, a French equivalent of the Venetian *poligrafi*, once published a book called *Harangues* (1573), an anthology of speeches taken from leading ancient and modern historians, each speech preceded by a summary of the argument and followed by an account of its effect. An elaborate index which included maxims and commonplaces increased what might be called the reference value of the work.

REFERENCE BOOKS

If commonplace books encouraged intensive reading, its complementary opposite, extensive reading, was stimulated by the rise of reference books. This literary genre or cluster of genres has already been discussed from the point of view of the producer (above, 169). It is time to approach reference books from the demand side and to ask what they provided for whom and how they were used.

A reference book might be defined as a book designed not to be read 'from cover to cover' but rather to be 'consulted' by someone who 'looks up' or 'refers to' the book in search of a specific item of information, a short cut to knowledge. The essential point was neatly made by Jonathan Swift in a passage quoted as epigraph to this chapter as 'the back-door' to 'the palace of learning'.

It might reasonably be argued that from the reader's point of view, there is no such thing as a reference book, since any book, even a novel, can be consulted, and any book, even the encyclopaedia, can be read. The larger the book, the less likely that it will be read from cover to cover. Rather than thinking of a fixed corpus of objects, we should define reference books through the practices of readers.

Take the case of Baldassare Castiglione's *Book of the Courtier*, for example. It is likely that the author of this dialogue, first published in 1528, intended to explore a range of questions about education and life at court rather than to offer clear and definite answers. At all events, the original folio edition, lacking even a division into chapters, is one in which it was and is difficult to find anything quickly. However, the book became a best-seller which went through about 125 editions in various languages in the century which followed its publication. Surviving copies show that some readers used the book as a source of information about good behaviour or even of anecdotes to tell in company. Some of the printers exploited the possibility and facilitated information retrieval by dividing the book into chapters and providing it with a full apparatus of marginalia, index and detailed table of contents, thus transforming it into a kind of reference book.[12]

Changes in the physical format of books in the early modern period make it increasingly clear that many of them were designed for some uses other than close or intensive reading. Indexes and lists of contents became increasingly frequent. The term 'table of contents' was often to be taken literally, since the list of chapters might be replaced or supplemented by a synopsis in the form of bracketed tables of the kind discussed in chapter 5 (above, 97), tables which made it possible for a reader to take in the structure of the treatise virtually at a glance. Robert Burton's *Anatomy of Melancholy*, for example, uses this technique to display the definition, species, causes and symptoms of melancholy. The symptoms were divided into mental and physical, the causes into general or particular, natural or supernatural and so on.

---

[12] Burke (1995c).

Again, the use of parallel columns in chronological tables assisted the reader in the task of 'synchronizing' different systems of time reckoning (Jewish, Christian, Muslim and so on), and thus revealing 'anachronisms'. Parallel with the rise of statistics (above, 135) the increasing importance of tables of figures may be noted, whether the subject of the book is astronomy, history or political economy. Tables facilitated comparisons and contrasts. Diagrams and other illustrations, frequent in many kinds of treatise from the herbal to the drill manual, allowed readers to use books without paying very much attention to the text. New reading skills or modes of literacy were increasingly required to make sense of maps, tables of figures and so on.

The proliferation of books raised the problem of how to compare different accounts of the same phenomenon without wasting time. A book-wheel, designed to hold a series of open volumes, made the task of collation somewhat easier. A wheel of this kind, dating from the late sixteenth century, is still preserved in the Herzog-August library at Wolfenbüttel.

Certain kinds of book were organized in such a way as effectively to resist attempts to read them from cover to cover. Dictionaries, for example, or atlases and gazetteers, or catalogues (of stars, plants or books), or anthologies of maxims or proverbs such as the book through which Erasmus made his reputation, the *Adagia*, or indeed encyclopaedias, especially if they were arranged in alphabetical order.

ALPHABETICAL ORDER

As d'Alembert pointed out in his introduction to the *Encyclopédie* (above, 115), there are essentially two ways of arranging information in encyclopaedias (in the West at least). In the first place, what he called the 'encyclopaedic principle', in other words thematic organization, the traditional tree of knowledge. In the second place, what he called the 'dictionary principle', in other words alphabetical order of topics.

Alphabetical order had been introduced in the eleventh-century Byzantine encyclopaedia known as 'Suidas'. Indexes of this kind were used by Cistercians and others in the thirteenth century.[13] The famous library of the abbey of Saint-Victor in Paris was catalogued alphabetically in the early sixteenth century, while Erasmus arranged his famous collection of proverbs, the *Adagia* (1500) in the same way.

---

[13] Witty (1965); Daly (1967); Brincken (1972); Rouse and Rouse (1982, 1983).

Gesner's *Library* (1545) listed books in alphabetical order, while his *History of Animals* (1551–) listed animals alphabetically. The Catholic *Index of Prohibited Books* followed the same principle.[14] It was even applied to some museums: the collection assembled by the Farnese family at their great house at Caprarola, for instance, was arranged in drawers labelled A to N.

Alphabetical ordering became an increasingly common practice in the seventeenth century.[15] Thomas James, librarian of the Bodleian Library at Oxford, wanted the library catalogue, published in 1605, to be arranged in alphabetical order, although the founder, Sir Thomas Bodley, insisted on the traditional organization by disciplines, and James had to be content with making an alphabetical index (the 1620 version of the catalogue was arranged alphaetically).[16] Gazetteers bore titles such as *ABC de tout le monde* (1651). The library of the statesman Jean-Baptiste Colbert included 'alphabetical tables' listing important kinds of manuscript, such as maps and treaties.[17] Famous examples of reference books organized in this way include Laurentius Beyerlinck's *Theatre of Human Life* (1631), a rearrangement of Zwinger's thematic encyclopaedia; Louis Moréri's *Great Historical Dictionary* (1674), which went through many editions; and Pierre Bayle's riposte to Moréri, the *Critical and Historical Dictionary* (1697). Apparently Bayle even wrote the articles in his dictionary in alphabetical order.[18] In the mid-eighteenth century, Samuel Richardson provided his readers with the earliest known index to a work of fiction. By the end of the century, libraries were beginning to catalogue their holdings on cards (originally the backs of playing cards) so as to permit the insertion of new items in alphabetical order.[19]

However, obvious as the principle may seem today, it was only very slowly that alphabetical organization (as opposed to topical organization accompanied by an alphabetical index) replaced older systems. The collection of proverbs which Erasmus had published in alphabetical order in 1500 was republished, organized by topic, in 1596. Alphabetical order was still unusual enough at the end of the seventeenth century for the editor of a reference book about the Muslim world, Barthélemy d'Herbelot's *Oriental Library* (1697), to find it necessary to apologize for it in his preface, declaring that the method 'does not produce as much confusion as one might imagine'

---

[14] Taylor (1945), 89–198; Hopkins (1992).
[15] Serrai (1988–92).
[16] Clement (1991), 274.
[17] Saunders (1991).
[18] Lieshout (1993), 292.
[19] Wellisch (1991), 319.

– Gibbon complained all the same in his *Decline and Fall of the Roman Empire* (chapter 51) that he could not 'digest' the alphabetical order of Herbelot's book. The preface to the *Encyclopaedia Britannica* (1771) criticized both Chambers and the *Encyclopédie* for what it describes as 'the folly of attempts to communicate science under the various technical terms arranged in an alphabetical order'.[20]

The conflict between the two systems makes a good illustration of the problems raised by presenting the history of knowledge as a story of progress. The change from the thematic system to the alphabetical system is no simple shift from less to more efficiency. It may reflect a change in world-views (above, 115), a loss of faith in the correspondence between the world and the word. It also corresponds to a change in modes of reading.

It is clear enough that the traditional encyclopaedias described in chapter 5 were unsuitable for rapid consultation by readers who were in search of particular items. Alphabetical order saves time. However, this solution to the problem of information retrieval, the 'Suidas solution' as we might call it, also had its price. The Canadian communications theorist Harold Innis once complained how 'encyclopaedias may tear knowledge apart and pigeonhole it in alphabetical boxes'.[21] They both express and encourage the modern fragmentation of knowledge. The 'confusion' which Herbelot mentioned was more than a simple failure by readers to adapt to the requirements of a new system.

After all, the traditional thematic, organic or holistic arrangement of knowledge has great and obvious advantages. It encourages 'intensive' readers to notice what d'Alembert called 'l'enchaînement des connaissances', in other words the links between the different disciplines or specialities, the system underlying them. Medieval and Renaissance encyclopaedias were designed to be read rather than consulted (though they might, like Reisch's volume, include an alphabetical index).

The arbitrariness of alphabetical order could be and was counteracted by means of cross-references to other entries on related topics. As Leibniz pointed out, the system had the advantage of presenting the same material from different points of view. The work involved in following up such references, with or without mechanical aids such as the Wolfenbüttel book-wheel, is a useful reminder that 'reference reading' is not, or not necessarily, a soft option. As one English writer, Myles Davies, complained in 1716 in his *Athenae Britannicae*,

---

[20] Yeo (1991, 1996).
[21] Innis (1980).

'not one reader in a hundred takes the pains to turn backwards and forwards, as such appendicular References require.' However, some of the cross-references in the *Encyclopédie* surely achieved their subversive aims without being followed up; it was sufficient for an article on the Eucharist to end with the recommendation, 'see cannibals'.

AIDS TO HISTORICAL RESEARCH

To offer a more vivid picture of the way in which more resources were available in each successive century to someone seeking knowledge on a particular topic, we might take the example of history itself. Imagine a scholar concerned to discover the date of a particular event, for example, or some information about an individual who lived centuries before, or the text of a document.

In 1450, such a scholar would have had to depend entirely on manuscript sources. A hundred years later, he would have been able to consult a few works of reference. For geography, for instance, he could go to Sebastian Münster's *Cosmography* (1540). For bibliography, he could refer to Gesner (above, 93) or the list of ecclesiastical writers compiled by the German abbot Johannes Trithemius and published in 1494. On the histories of individual countries, he could turn to the work of the expatriate Italian humanists Paolo Emili on France (published 1516–20), Luca Marineo on Spain (1533), Polydore Vergil on England (1534), and Antonio Bonfini on Hungary (1543). After 1550 it was possible to consult Giorgio Vasari's biographies of Italian artists; after 1553, the historical dictionary compiled by the French scholar-printer Charles Estienne; and after 1566, Bodin's *Method*, which was among other things a bibliographical essay covering the whole field of history.

By 1650, the situation had changed dramatically, as private letters between scholars were increasingly supplemented as sources of information by periodicals and specialized reference books.[22] Bodin was supplemented by the Oxford don Degory Wheare's *Method of Reading Histories* (1623) and by the more detailed historical bibliography of the German pastor Paul Bolduan (1620). The atlases of Abraham Ortelius (1570), Gerard Mercator (1585–95) and the Blaeu family (1635 onwards) simplified the problem of finding the cities and regions discussed in historical texts. Chronological tables of world history could be found in a number of books, including the famous studies by Joseph Scaliger (1583) and the French Jesuit Denis Petavius (1627).

---

[22] Pomian (1973).

If information about individuals was needed, it was by now possible to turn, for instance, to the Swiss Heinrich Pantaleon's lives of famous Germans (1565), entitled 'Prosopography'; the Frenchman Gabriel du Preau's dictionary of heretics (1569), in alphabetical order from the 'Adamites' to Zwingli; the painter Karel van Mander's biographies of Dutch artists (1603); and Melchior Adam's lives of German theologians, lawyers and physicians, published in the 1620s. For genealogical problems, reference could be made to Henninger's *Theatre of Genealogies* (1598). For facts and figures about particular countries, one could turn to the description of the world by Giovanni Botero, available from the 1590s, or from the 1620s onwards, to the Elsevier series discussed in chapter 7 (above, 164). Collections of documents included volumes devoted to the decrees of German emperors and to the texts of German and Bohemian chroniclers. Works in foreign languages could be decoded with the help of dictionaries. Rare before 1550, a hundred years later these now indispensable reference books included Spanish–English, Italian–English, French–English, French–Spanish, German–Latin, German–Polish, Latin–Swedish, and a number of dictionaries of four, seven or even eleven languages, including Croat, Czech and Hungarian.

By 1750, given access to a reasonably large library, the scholar might consult a whole shelf of competing chronologies, including that of the Englishman John Marsham and the critical study published by a group of French Benedictines, *The Art of Verifying Dates* (1750). Atlases now included the six-volume edition of Blaeu (1655), the specialized *Historical Atlas* of Châtelain (1705), and Bruzen de la Martinière's ten-volume *Great Geographical and Critical Dictionary* (1726–39). The rival historical dictionaries of Moréri (1674) and Bayle (1697) were available in a number of editions. Anonymous and pseudonymous writers could be tracked down with the help of a number of dictionaries beginning with that of Placcius in 1674. Biographical dictionaries included one devoted to the lives of scholars, Mencke's *Lexicon of the Learned* (1715), as well as Jean-Pierre Nicéron's voluminous *Memoirs of Illustrious Men* (forty-three volumes, 1727–45).

Many more texts of documents such as treaties, medieval chronicles or the decrees of Church councils were now available in sets of folio volumes edited by such scholars as the Englishman Thomas Rymer (twenty volumes), or the Italians Ludovico Muratori (twenty-eight volumes) and Archbishop Giovanni Domenico Mansi (thirty-one volumes). Archaic forms of Latin were less of an obstacle after the publication of a glossary by the French scholar Charles Du Cange (1678). Bibliographies of books on history now included Cornelis de

Beughem's four-volume *Historical Bibliography* (1685–) and Burkhard Struve's *Select Historical Bibliography* (1705), both compiled by German scholars; and two French productions, Louis-Ellies Du Pin's *Universal Library of Historians* (1707) and Nicolas Lenglet's *Method of Studying History* (1713), an essay in the tradition of Bodin. New books on history – and many other subjects – could be found by browsing in the pages of learned journals such as the *Nouvelles de la République des Lettres* or the *Acta Eruditorum* of Leipzig.

INDIVIDUAL APPROPRIATIONS

It is clear that many reference books were intended for a particular section of the market, for clergy, lawyers, doctors, women and so on. For example, in the German-speaking world in particular, there was a rise of encyclopaedias intended in the first instance for female readers.[23]

To reconstruct the manner in which early modern readers acquired knowledge and put it to use, case-studies of individuals are also necessary. It is illuminating to learn which reference books were acquired by owners of small libraries. The inventories of books left by sixteenth-century students and teachers of the university of Cambridge, for example, include a number of references to dictionaries (notably that of Antonius Calepinus) and encyclopaedias (especially that of Gregor Reisch).[24] There remains the more important but more elusive problem of the way in which reference books were used. Philip II of Spain has been caught in the act of using Ortelius's atlas to identify villages in France in preparation for the sailing of the Spanish Armada in 1588.[25] Again, discussing the decline of the population in his *Political Restoration of Spain* (1619), the theologian Sancho de Moncada made recurrent references to Botero's work. The reading practices of a few well-known scholars, including Jean Bodin, John Dee, Gabriel Harvey and Johann Kepler have also been studied in some detail, and a careful analysis has been made of the different channels through which the Boston patrician Samuel Sewall acquired information in the early eighteenth century.[26]

A particularly well-documented case of an avid reader is that of the polymath Peiresc. Nicolas-Claude Fabri de Peiresc was a magistrate

---

[23] Woods (1987).
[24] Leedham-Green (1987), nos. 71, 82, 92.
[25] Parker (1992), 137; Parker (1998), 24.
[26] Brown (1989), 16–41; Grafton and Jardine (1986); Grafton (1992); Sherman (1995); Blair (1997).

of extremely broad intellectual interests. Living in Provence a generation before the rise of the learned journal, Peiresc was dependent on an international network of friends for news of the Republic of Letters, of 'people of curiosity like us' (*gens curieux comme nous*) as he called them. His voluminous correspondence, much of which has been published, is stuffed with references to new books, editions of the fathers of the Church, a history of the Arabs, the latest treatise by Galileo, the Elsevier series of descriptions of Poland and other states, the anthologies of travelogues edited by Richard Hakluyt and Samuel Purchas, and, not least, newsletters or gazettes in manuscript or print, from Venice, Amsterdam, Rome and elsewhere.

Peiresc did not learn from books alone. He was also an enthusiastic collector of objects such as Roman coins and Egyptian mummies, which reminds us that knowledge could be acquired by a number of means and warns us not to place too much stress on reading alone. Collections of curiosities illustrate the appropriation of knowledge with particular clarity. It may therefore be useful to cast an eye over the contents of a famous private museum of the seventeenth century, mentioned in an earlier chapter (106), and housing the collection belonging to Manfredo Settala, a noble clergyman of Milan. A catalogue of the collection was published in the seventeenth century. The catalogue is obviously no substitute for the objects themselves, but it was, after all, the means by which most people learned of the collections even at the time.

A contemporary engraving of Settala's museum gives the impression of apparently inexhaustible variety. Alligators and fish hang from the ceiling, urns and busts are ranged along the floor, and the centre of the room is filled with drawers. The catalogue reinforces this impression of a museum as microcosm (above, 107), containing specimens of everything in the world. One might also describe a museum of this kind as a kind of school, teaching the viewer about the uses of materials such as wood, metal, earthenware and so on as well as about the products of different parts of the world; silver from Potosì, porcelain from China, bows and arrows from the Ottoman Empire and Brazil, mummies from Egypt, Chinese and Japanese texts written in ideograms and so on. The references in the catalogue to books, such as González de Mendoza on China, or to donors, such as the archbishop of Milan (who gave Settala a Japanese vase), suggest that the owner at least viewed the objects in their historical and geographical contexts as well as as examples of different materials (as discussed in chapter 5, 107).[27]

---

[27] Findlen (1994), 42–4.

FROM MONTAIGNE TO MONTESQUIEU

Since an earlier chapter of this book emphasized the importance of major cities such as Rome and Paris, it may be illuminating to consider individuals who lived in the countryside. By the later sixteenth century, there is evidence of English country gentlemen acquiring and exchanging historical information.[28] The case of Peiresc has just been discussed. To perceive change within the period, one might compare and contrast two well-travelled French gentlemen with good libraries and wide interests, both of whom lived in the country near Bordeaux but a century and a half apart: Montaigne and Montesquieu.

When Montaigne retired to his estate, he made sure that the tower in which he meditated and wrote was well furnished with books. He is known to have used 271 books: only three on law, six on medicine and sixteen on theology, but nearly 100 on history, ancient and modern.[29] Like a good Renaissance man, Montaigne knew the Greek and Latin classics well, and was particularly fond of the moral works of Seneca and Plutarch. He was interested in the history of his own region, and made considerable use of the humanist Jean Bouchet's *Annales d'Aquitaine*. On the history of France, he read the chronicles of Jean Froissart and the memoirs of the diplomat Philippe de Commynes; on Italy, the famous history by Francesco Guicciardini. Montaigne made use of the *Method* of his contemporary Jean Bodin, as well as the same author's comparative study of political systems, *Six Livres de la république*. His interest in the world beyond Europe was nourished by the history of China by the Spanish missionary Juan González de Mendoza and by a handful of books on the Americas – the Spaniard Francisco López de Gómara and the Italian Girolamo Benzoni on the Spanish conquests, the cosmographer André Thevet and the missionary Jean de Léry on Brazil.

As for Montaigne's mode of reading, it was – despite the originality of so many of his observations – typical of his period, at least in the sense that he looked at books with an eye for moral exempla. Although he expressed contempt for what he called 'pâtés of commonplaces' (*pastissages de lieux communs*), it is likely that he kept a commonplace book as well as annotating volumes in his possession. His copy of the life of Alexander by Quintus Curtius, for instance, contains notes in the margin on topics such as 'armed chariots', 'Amazons' and 'words of Darius'. Montaigne's early essays read like an expansion of extracts taken from his favourite authors and arranged

---

[28] Levy (1982).
[29] Villey (1908), vol. 1, 244–70.

under moral categories, and the practice of 'commonplacing' affected both the title and the content of his later essays as well.[30]

Montesquieu's more systematic studies drew on the much wider range of books which had become available by his time. The library of his country house at La Brède contained some 3,000 volumes. His notebooks, most of them known only by their titles, were mentioned earlier in this chapter. One which has survived, the so-called *Spicilège*, reveals something about Montesquieu's modes of acquiring information. It includes notes to himself about books to buy, including the collections of travelogues edited by John Harris and the Churchills. It also refers to knowledge obtained through conversation, for example with a French Jesuit missionary who had returned from China.

The notebook shows Montesquieu reading famous works of history such as Niccolò Machiavelli on Florence, Pietro Giannone on Naples and Gilbert Burnet on England, as well as cutting out passages from newspapers such as the *Gazette d'Amsterdam*, especially when they gave commercial information such as the arrival in Lisbon of ships from Rio de Janeiro with a cargo of diamonds. In one case the notes are detailed, that of Kaempfer's famous description of Japan (above, 60), and they reveal something of Montesquieu's principles of selection, notably his interest in the Japanese mode of subsistence, rice agriculture, as an explanation of their relatively dense population. The notebook, supplemented by Montesquieu's letters, shows his familiarity with a shelf of works of reference such as the historical dictionaries of Moréri and Bayle, Chambers's *Cyclopaedia* and the law dictionaries compiled by the French jurist Pierre-Jacques Brillon.[31]

Without ignoring or ironing out either the idiosyncrasies or the originality of Montaigne and Montesquieu, it may be argued that the contrast between these neighbours is, among other things, a contrast between a sixteenth-century and an eighteenth-century manner of reading. Montaigne's manner was intensive, allowing him to quote passages from memory (as the minor inaccuracies show), and it focused on moral exempla. Montesquieu by contrast often looked books up rather than reading them through, and he read with an eye for facts, including statistics.

ACQUIRING KNOWLEDGE OF OTHER CULTURES

What Montaigne and Montesquieu had in common was a lively interest in other cultures, even if they relied on different sources. Many

---

[30] Villey (1908), vol. 2, 10, 52; Goyet (1986–7); Moss (1996), 212–13.
[31] Dodds (1929), 81, 94–5, 99–100; Shackleton (1961), 229–38.

leading European thinkers of the seventeenth and eighteenth centuries shared this curiosity. In France, one thinks of Voltaire, Diderot and Rousseau; in Britain, of John Locke and Adam Smith; and in Germany, of Leibniz, who wrote to the Electress Sophie Charlotte in 1697 that he meant to put a notice on his door, 'bureau d'adresse pour la Chine', so that people would know that they could apply to him for the latest news on this topic.

Generally speaking, educated Europeans acquired their knowledge of the world outside Europe from a relatively narrow range of books, a corpus which gradually changed over the course of the period. Around 1600, for example, one might, like Montaigne, read González de Mendoza on China, López de Gómara on Mexico and Jean de Léry on Brazil, supplemented by the Italian Jesuit Matteo Ricci's account of the China mission and that of his colleague Luis Frois on a similar mission to Japan. On Africa, there were descriptions of the north by Leo the African (Hassan al-Wazzân), a Muslim who was kidnapped by pirates and taken to Rome, and of the Congo by Duarte Lopes (available in Italian, Latin, Dutch and English). On the Ottoman Empire, which was widely feared, there was a whole shelf of books, including a first-hand account of the mission by the Flemish diplomat Ogier Ghiselin de Busbecq, available in Latin, German, Czech, Spanish, French and English.

By the early eighteenth century, far more information was available and the most frequently cited books had changed. There was less interest in the Ottoman Empire since the threat of invasion had subsided. China, on the other hand, had become a fashion, and Montesquieu was not alone in turning to the four volumes of the French Jesuit Jean-Baptiste du Halde's *Description de la Chine* (1735) to learn about it. Interest in Japan was also increasing, encouraged by the detailed account by Engelbert Kaempfer which was in English in 1727 and in French in 1729. Kaempfer was read with attention not only by Montesquieu but also by the German historian of philosophy Johann Jacob Brucker, by Jean-Jacques Rousseau and by Diderot and other contributors to the *Encyclopédie*.[32]

On Africa, the account by the Portuguese traveller, Duarte Lopes was now joined by that of the Jesuit missionary Jerónimo Lobo on Abyssinia, printed in summary form in 1673 (and inspiring Samuel Johnson's novel *Rasselas* a century later). From 1704 onwards, these descriptions could be supplemented by the Dutch merchant Willem Bosman's description of Guinea, divided into the gold coast, the slave coast and the ivory coast. It was only in the middle of the eighteenth

---

[32] Nakagawa (1992), 247–67.

century that detailed information about the interior of Africa began to be available.[33]

South America was also the object of increasing interest. Voltaire had thirteen books on the region in his library, including Charles-Marie de La Condamine's account of his official mission to Peru and his subsequent journey down the Amazon. La Condamine's work was cited with respect by the naturalist Buffon, the *philosophe* Holbach and William Robertson, principal of Edinburgh University and author of a successful *History of America* (1777).[34]

Readers without the time or inclination to read monographs such as these could always consult an encyclopaedia such as Moréri, Bayle or the *Encyclopédie,* although these works of reference were not at their most reliable where Asia, Africa and America were concerned.[35]

Given what was said earlier about systems of note-taking, it may be appropriate to sum up the early modern general reader's knowledge of the world beyond Europe in a series of commonplaces about slaves, despots, barbarians and cannibals. For example, the Ottoman Empire evoked the idea of new sultans killing their brothers on their accession as well as that of the harem or seraglio.[36] India meant naked philosophers ('gymnosophists') and juggernauts. A lecture at the university of Caen in 1663 described Calicut as follows: 'The inhabitants do not know the use of bread, they reject chastity and sometimes exchange their wives.'[37]

A number of readers appear to have paid particular attention to exotic methods of writing. Texts written in Arabic, Ethiopian, Chinese and Japanese were displayed in the museums of Settala and Worm. Mexico was associated with the use of pictograms or 'hieroglyphics', Peru with the use of the *quipu,* a mnemonic system based on knots. Mexican pictograms appeared in print for the first time in 1625 in a collection of travels edited by Samuel Purchas. The Dutch scholar Johannes de Laet used the Purchas edition for the account of Mexican culture given in his *New World* (1633). The Jesuit polymath Athanasius Kircher also used Purchas in the chapter on Mexico in his ambitious comparative study of hieroglyphics, *The Egyptian Oedipus* (1652–4).

To examine the western reader's knowledge of the world beyond Europe in a little more detail, we may take the cases of Japan and China. In 1500, few Europeans would have known that Japan existed at

---

[33] Santos Lopes (1992).
[34] Duchet (1971), 69, 72, 93, 109–110.
[35] Switzer (1967); Miller (1981).
[36] Grosrichard (1979).
[37] Brockliss (1987), 155.

all, although Marco Polo's travels had recently been printed for the first time, in Latin translation. Marco Polo mentioned a large island that is called 'Cipangu', with well-mannered inhabitants and 'gold in great abundance', but gave little more information. The letters of the Spanish missionary Francisco Xavier emphasized the Japanese sense of honour, an idea which rapidly became commonplace. The orientalist Guillaume Postel, for instance, in his *Merveilles* (1553) presented 'Giapan' as a country which was effectively Christian before the missionaries arrived. Postel made use of information from 'Schiabier', as he called him, and also from other Jesuit sources, presenting 'Xaca' (in other words, Buddha) as Christ and the emperor as 'sovereign pontiff'.[38]

Botero also followed Jesuit sources in stressing the Japanese sense of honour and gravity, which he compared to that of Spaniards; the frequency of earthquakes in that country; and the Japanese taste for water mixed with 'a precious powder which they call cha', in other words tea. Over the years the commonplaces gradually multiplied. In 1669, for instance, the Royal Society published in its *Philosophical Transactions* 'Some Observations concerning Japan made by an ingenious person that hath many years resided in that country', reduced to twenty points including the assertions that 'They write downward. Their government is despotic . . . Their left hand is the more honourable.' Serious gaps in knowledge remained, however, and at the end of the seventeenth century a leading French cartographer, Delisle, was still discussing whether or not Japan was an island.

In the case of China, commonplaces were particularly numerous. They include the idea that the Chinese emperor was a mere figurehead; that (as Vico's friend the philosopher Paolo Mattia Doria put it in his treatise on *Civil Life* of 1709) the Chinese were an unwarlike people who defended themselves against barbarians by allowing them to conquer them and then taming them; that the Chinese made use of writing before the West, with ideograms instead of the alphabet; that they had invented gunpowder, and perhaps printing as well. Montaigne had noted that printing and gunpowder were a thousand years older in China than in Europe, and the history of printing by the scholar-bookseller Prosper Marchand (1740) discussed its possible diffusion from East to West.

The Oxford don Robert Burton, a well-read man but no specialist in oriental studies, referred to China on a number of occasions in his *Anatomy of Melancholy* (1620). Burton was especially impressed by the position of the mandarins, the *literati* as he called them (above,

---

[38] Bernard-Maître (1953); Lach (1965), 657, 660n; Lach (1977), 267–8.

31). He also commented on the lack of beggars in China; the practice of suicide out of shame for failing examinations; and the contrast between Chinese and western medicine. In China, according to Burton (on the basis of Matteo Ricci), 'the physicians give precepts quite opposite to ours . . . they use altogether roots, herbs and simples in their medicines and all their physic is in a manner comprehended in an herbal: no science, no school, no art, no degree, but, like a trade, every man in private is instructed of his master' (Book 2, part 4, section 1, 5).

If they were not commonplace already, Burton's remarks soon became commonplaces and further points were added to the list. Reviewing a recent book on China in 1666, the *Philosophical Transactions* noted that the Chinese 'prize highly the root ginseng' and prescribe the use of tea as a medicine. In the course of the seventeenth century Chinese philosophy as well as Chinese medicine attracted western attention, and Confucius was placed by the side of Socrates as an exemplar of pagan virtue.[39]

The appropriation of exotic knowledge naturally included a process of domesticating or stereotyping. Even western observers in the 'field' perceived unfamiliar cultures in terms of stereotypes. Some, like those of American cannibals and oriental despots, exaggerated the cultural distance between the foreign culture and that of the observer. Others did the exact opposite. In Calicut, for example, the Portuguese mariner Vasco da Gama entered an Indian temple and viewed it as a church, the combination of Brahma, Vishnu and Shiva appearing to him as an image of the Holy Trinity. Xavier saw 'hidalgos' and 'universities' in Japan, while the Japanese emperor looked to him very much like a pope. The Jesuits took their Aristotelian categories with them to China and so interpreted the principles of Yin and Yang as 'matter' and 'form'. Readers at home were in no position to criticize these stereotypes. Their books of commonplaces often turned into anthologies of prejudices.

All the same, we cannot assume that early modern readers believed all they read about the world outside Europe or about anything else for that matter. The reliability of knowledge was the subject of debate – or more precisely, of a number of debates – to be discussed in the following chapter.

---

[39] Pinot (1932); Lach and Kley (1993).

9

TRUSTING AND DISTRUSTING KNOWLEDGE: A CODA

The old sceptics that would never profess that they had found a truth,
showed yet the best way to search for any . . . he that avoids their
disputing levity yet . . . takes to himself their liberty of enquiry, is in the
only way that in all kinds of studies leads and lies open even to the
sanctuary of truth.

Selden

THE reliability of knowledge cannot be taken for granted. In
different cultures and different periods, the criteria of reliability vary and change.[1] One of the most important intellectual
trends in early modern Europe was the rise of scepticism of various
kinds concerning claims to knowledge. To measure such a trend is
impossible, to explain it would be presumptuous. The following
account, which is obviously and indeed necessarily both simplification
and speculation, should itself be read with some degree of scepticism.

As a preliminary step, it may be useful to distinguish a 'high',
general or philosophical scepticism from a 'low', specific or practical
scepticism. At the practical level, Jean Bodin, for example, was critical of the Italian historian Paolo Giovio: 'Many things he reported
of the empires of the Persians, the Abyssinians and the Turks, but
whether they are true, not even he knew, since he accepted rumours.'
One might compare Samuel Johnson's reaction to Montesquieu's
Esprit des Lois, conveyed to Boswell in his usual abrupt manner in
the course of a visit to Skye in 1773: 'Whenever he wants to support
a strange opinion, he quotes you the practice of Japan or of some
distant country of which he knows nothing.' The interaction between
a 'high' philosophical scepticism and a more everyday or practical
distrust of claims to knowledge will be one of the major themes of
this chapter.

---

[1] Ziman (1978).

197

THE REVIVAL OF PYRRHONISM

At a more general level there was considerable interest in philosophical scepticism or 'Pyrrhonism', named after the Greek philosopher Pyrrho of Elis. Pyrrho's works have been lost, like those of other Pyrrhonists, such as Carneades. However, a summary of their claims was provided by a later Greek text, the 'Outlines' (*Hypotyposes*) of Sextus Empiricus, arguing from the diversity of points of view that judgement should be suspended on all claims to knowledge which go beyond appearances.[2] The text of Sextus Empiricus was rediscovered in Renaissance Italy. It was published in France in 1562 and translated into Latin there in 1569. The text was known to Montaigne, inspiring his famous motto, 'Que sais-je?', the question mark suggesting that he was sceptical even about scepticism. Montaigne's disciple Pierre Charron, on the other hand, preferred the more dogmatically negative 'Je ne sais'. By the early seventeenth century there was a group of French scholars, the so-called *libertins érudits*, who found these ideas attractive.[3]

It has been argued that the appeal of sceptical doctrines in sixteenth- and seventeenth-century Europe was a reaction to what has been called the 'intellectual crisis of the Reformation', on the grounds that in the controversies between Catholics and Protestants over the grounds for religious belief, Scripture or the tradition of the Church, each side was more successful in attacking its opponents than in defending its own position.[4] The argument is a plausible one. However it began, though, scepticism came to extend well beyond religious matters.

For example, a seventeenth-century French writer, François La Mothe Le Vayer, argued that works of history could not be trusted because the same events looked different from diverse points of view, national as well as religious. The problem, according to La Mothe, was essentially that of partiality, that of Spaniards, for example, or Catholics magnifying the successes and minimizing the failures of their own party. Pierre Bayle agreed, and went so far as to say that he read modern historians to inform himself about their prejudices rather than about the facts. Indeed, the problem of partiality, interest or 'bias' was one of the main issues discussed in treatises on historical writing in the seventeenth century.[5]

---

[2] Popkin (1960).
[3] Pintard (1943); Gregory et al. (1981).
[4] Popkin (1960), 1–16.
[5] Borghero (1983); Völkel (1987); Burke (1998b).

Another problem exercising scholars was that of distinguishing between genuine and forged texts in the past. Were the narratives of the Trojan War which circulated under the names of 'Dares' and 'Dictys' genuine or spurious? Were the writings attributed to 'Hermes Trismegistus', which appeared to foretell Christian doctrines, really produced in ancient Egypt, or were they written after the birth of Christ? Were all the texts attributed to the fathers of the Church really written by Augustine, Ambrose and so on? Come to that, how reliable was the attribution of the Greek and Roman classics to Plato, Homer, Virgil, Horace and so on? A French Jesuit of the early eighteenth century, Jean Hardouin, was notorious for his doubts about the authorship of most of the classics. His views were generally rejected as an exaggeration, but other scholars shared his scepticism about the authorship of specific ancient texts.[6] A famous case was that of the so-called 'Letters of Phalaris' (a tyrannical ruler of Sicily in ancient times), letters which were exposed as a later forgery by the English scholar Richard Bentley in 1699. The arch-sceptic Jean Hardouin was not completely out of step with his time. The debates over authenticity encouraged the production of a number of reference works unmasking anonymous and pseudonymous authors, such as the book *On Anonymous Writings* (1674) by the German polyhistor Vincent Placcius.

If the testimonies were not authentic, what of the stories they told? Scholars began to question whether Aeneas had ever visited Italy (since Virgil was writing fiction) and whether anything could be known about the early centuries of ancient Roman history (since the historian Livy was writing much later than the events he narrated).

Another major arena in which claims to knowledge were debated was natural philosophy, especially in the seventeenth century. In this domain, scepticism was encouraged by the discovery of a world beyond that of appearances – a world of atoms, for example – and the controversies about the nature of this world which followed. In this context, John Donne's much-quoted phrase that 'the new philosophy puts all in doubt' is particularly appropriate. In France, the natural philosophers Pierre Gassendi and Marin Mersenne, for example, professed a moderate or 'mitigated' scepticism concerning the essences of things, allowing a 'knowledge of appearances' (*scientia apparentiae*), based on description but excluding explanation.[7] In Naples, the physician Leonardo di Capoa argued against the certainty of medical knowledge.

---

[6] Yates (1964), 398–431; Sgard (1987); Grafton (1990).
[7] Gregory (1961), 41.

In London, Robert Boyle expressed his views through a character named 'Carneades' in his dialogue the *Sceptical Chymist* (1661). Boyle used Montaigne's term 'essay' to describe his writings precisely in order to emphasize their tentative quality, just as he used phrases such as 'it is not improbable' in order to imply what he called 'a diffidence [distrust] of the opinions I incline to'.[8] Another Fellow of the Royal Society, Joseph Glanvill, published an essay in defence of a moderate scepticism entitled *The Vanity of Dogmatising*. John Locke argued in his discussion of 'Knowledge and Opinion' in his *Essay Concerning Human Understanding* (1690) that 'our faculties are not fitted to penetrate into the internal fabric and real essences of bodies' (Book 4, chapter 12). Locke's point about the limitations of human faculties is reminiscent of Gassendi, while his use of the term 'essay', with the implication that his conclusions are only provisional, placed him, like Boyle and Glanvill, in the tradition of Montaigne.

PRAGMATIC SCEPTICISM

This movement of philosophers was accompanied by a gradual rise of practical or pragmatic scepticism which probably affected far more people in the long run. The authority of the ancients, especially Aristotle, was criticized and so was the very notion of intellectual 'authority' in the universities and elsewhere. The term 'critical', employed earlier to describe what we would call 'textual' or literary criticism, became a more general, positive and fashionable term in the late seventeenth and early eighteenth centuries. One sign of the change was the prevalence of the adjective 'critical' in book titles, including Richard Simon's *Critical History of the Old Testament* (1678), Pierre Bayle's *Historical and Critical Dictionary* (1697), Pierre Lebrun's *Critical History of Superstitious Practices* (1702) and the Spanish monk Benito Feijóo's *Universal Critical Theatre* (1726–).

Pragmatic scepticism was encouraged not only by philosophical debates, but also by the spread of printed matter, an information explosion which has been one of the major themes of this study. The printing press put rival assertions into a much wider circulation than ever before: Montaigne, for example, read as we have seen, the pro-Spanish López de Gómara and the anti-Spanish Benzoni on the Spanish conquests, and the Catholic André Thevet and the Protestant Jean de Léry on Brazil. Again, he noted drily in his *Essays* (book 3, chapter 7) that he had been reading two Scottish treatises on political

---

[8] Van Leeuwen (1963); Shapin and Schaffer (1985), 67.

theory at much the same time and found that their views of monarchy could not have been more opposed: 'The democrat puts the king lower than a carter; the monarchist places him well above God in power and sovereignty.'

Awareness of the problem that different 'authorities' contradict one another was in no way new: in the twelfth century, the philosopher Peter Abelard's treatise 'Yes and No' (*Sic et Non*) had already exploited these contradictions. However, the multiplicity of books is likely to have made more people more aware of the many discrepancies between different descriptions of the same phenomenon or different accounts of the same event.[9]

Descriptions of travels were subjected to critical examination in a similar manner to narratives of events. As more travellers to distant places published accounts of what they had seen, contradictions between them became apparent. Some travellers criticized the inaccuracies of others, as the Dominican missionary João dos Santos criticized the description of Africa by Duarte Lopes, or even denounced earlier writers as liars who had never been to the places they claimed to have seen. Some travelogues were exposed as fictions, from the travels of 'Sir John Mandeville', which Richard Hakluyt deliberately omitted from the second edition of his famous collection, to George Psalmanazar's *Historical and General Description of Formosa* (1704).

Psalmanazar was a Frenchman who came to England and attempted to pass himself off as a native of Formosa. His *Description* included information from earlier accounts of the island, but added some bold inventions of his own, from the statement that Formosa belonged to Japan to a description of the local alphabet. Before his fraud was detected, Psalmanazar was invited to visit the Royal Society and to dine with Sir Hans Sloane, while his book was translated into French and German. When Gilbert Burnet, bishop of Salisbury, asked the impostor to prove that he was Formosan, Psalmanazar retorted by asking Burnet how he could prove himself an Englishman in Formosa, given that he looked just like a Dutchman. All the same, his fraud was exposed by a Jesuit writing in 1705 in one of the new learned periodicals, the *Journal de Trévoux*.[10]

Apart from the detection of impostors, critics of travel writing were increasingly concerned to note the extent to which even genuine travellers made use of or copied earlier texts instead of making observations with a fresh eye. In other words, here too there were attempts to weigh different testimonies. What made travel-criticism urgent was

[9] Eisenstein (1979), 74.
[10] Rennie (1995), esp. 54, 75, 73; Stagl (1995), 171–207.

the fact that the Royal Society and similar associations in Europe relied on travellers' observations of natural phenomena in other parts of the world. They might try to guide the observations of their collaborators by composing and even printing questionnaires, but the problem of evaluating the testimonies remained. In his study of the effects of cold, for example, Boyle used the testimony of Samuel Collins, a physician who visited Russia in the 1660s.

The use of oral tradition as a historical source declined in the seventeenth century, owing to the increasing doubts about its reliability voiced by historians. The English antiquary John Aubrey linked the decline of 'the old fables' about fairies to the rise of printed matter, which according to him 'came in fashion . . . a little before the civil wars'.[11]

Pamphlets and above all newspapers had the same effect. In the sixteenth century, rival pamphlets, for example the thousands of pamphlets published in the course of the German Reformation or the Dutch revolt against Spain, demolished one another's arguments in the presence of a wide public. To use a favourite expression of the period, each side 'unmasked' the lies and the true motives of the other, thus encouraging readers to treat the arguments of all parties with suspicion, a point noted by Karl Mannheim (above, 5) in the course of a similar situation in the 1930s.

Discrepancies between different reports of the same events soon after they happened are likely to have made even more early modern readers into practical sceptics. As an Englishman commented in 1569, 'We have every day several news, and sometimes contraries, and yet all put out as true.'[12] The rise of the news-sheet in the seventeenth century made the unreliability of reports of the 'facts' more obvious to more people than ever before, since rival and discrepant accounts of the same events, battles for example, arrived in major cities on the same day and could easily be compared and contrasted. The very honesty of early newspapers, in which later issues corrected the errors of hasty reporting in earlier issues, is likely to have trained many readers to look at the news with a critical eye. Historians of the later seventeenth century not infrequently dismissed one another's work by comparing it either to 'romances' or 'gazettes', two terms which were virtually synonyms in this context.[13]

Historians are notorious for making too much use of dramatic expressions such as 'crisis' and 'revolution', thus debasing their intel-

---

[11] Shapin and Schaffer (1985), 39; Woolf (1988); Shapin (1994), 251–2; Fox (1999), 258.
[12] Shaaber (1929), 241.
[13] MacDonald and Murphy (1990), 306; Dooley (1999) 3, 81, 88, 119ff.

lectual currency. All the same, the reasons listed above make it not unreasonable to speak of a 'crisis of knowledge' in late seventeenth-century Europe, along the lines of the 'intellectual crisis of the Reformation' quoted above or the famous phrase coined by the intellectual historian Paul Hazard to refer to the period 1680–1715, 'the crisis of European consciousness'.[14] 'Crisis' was originally a medical term referring to the 'critical' moment of an illness, at which the patient's recovery or death hung in the balance. Adapting the term but attempting to be as precise as possible, we may use it to refer to a relatively short period of confusion or turbulence which leads to a transition from one intellectual structure to another.

Whether or not there was a crisis of consciousness in the later seventeenth century, there was certainly a consciousness of crisis. Philosophers and others were searching for a solution to the problem of knowledge, and they found two possibilities, two methods.

THE GEOMETRICAL METHOD

One was the geometrical method, associated with René Descartes, who had already found the solution to his own sceptical crisis by this means, as he recounts in his *Discourse on Method* (1637), deducing his intellectual system from a minimum number of axioms. This solution had considerable appeal in France and elsewhere. In the preface to his history of the French Academy of Sciences, published in 1709, Bernard de Fontenelle made a memorable claim for this approach. 'The geometrical spirit', he wrote, 'is not so closely attached to geometry that it cannot be taken and transported to other domains of knowledge [*à d'autres connaissances*]. A book on morals, politics or criticism, or even, perhaps, on eloquence, would be finer, other things being equal, if it was by the hand of a geometrician.'

Fontenelle's claim may seem exaggerated today, but he was not alone in believing that the geometrical method was applicable well beyond the sphere of mathematics. For example, the Jansenist Pierre Nicole wrote a 'geometrical essay' on the theology of grace. In his *Demonstration of the Gospel* (1679), Pierre-Daniel Huet, bishop of Avranches, tried to establish the truth of Christianity as a historical religion on the basis of 'axioms' such as the following: 'Every historical work is truthful, if it tells what happened in the way in which the events are told in many books which are contemporary or more or less contemporary to the events narrated.'

---

[14] Hazard (1935).

Enthusiasm for the geometrical method was not confined to France. Spinoza, for example, described his *Ethics* on the title-page as 'proved by the geometrical method' (*ordine geometrico demonstrata*) In his *Essay Concerning Human Understanding* (1690), John Locke made a similar claim, including morality with mathematics 'amongst the sciences capable of demonstration'. In his *Rules of Historical Evidence* (1699), John Craig, a follower of Isaac Newton, discussed historical method in the form of axioms and theorems such as the following: 'the reliability of sources varies with the distance of the source from the event recorded.'

Leibniz was sceptical of the general application of the geometrical method, but he did hope for a kind of universal mathematics which would allow philosophers who disagreed to sit down and calculate the truth. The means to this end would be the devising of a 'general language' or 'alphabet of thoughts' (*alphabetum cognitionum*). The belief in such a universal language was not uncommon in the seventeenth century. One of the best-known attempts was made by an English bishop who was also a Fellow of the Royal Society, John Wilkins. Inspired by mathematics and the characters used to write Chinese, Wilkins's *Essay towards a Real Character and a Philosophical Language* (1668) offered a system of signs which referred directly to things, not to words.[15]

THE RISE OF EMPIRICISM

Besides the geometrical method, there were other attempts to escape from intellectual crisis. One, which did not attract much attention at the time, although it became famous later, was formulated by Giambattista Vico in his *New Science* (section 331). This was the principle of the 'verum-factum', the 'truth beyond all question: that the world of civil society has certainly been made by men, and that its principles are therefore to be found within the modifications of our own human mind'.

Another response to crisis was the development of the method of experiment, viewed 'as a systematic means of generating natural knowledge', at least in certain domains.[16] Bacon's theory of 'putting nature to the question' and Boyle's practice – his air-pump, for example – were exemplary in this respect. Systematic experiment was not a seventeenth-century invention. After all, a thirteenth-century

---

[15] Rossi (1960), 235–58; Slaughter (1982); Eco (1995), esp. 238–59, 269–88.
[16] Shapin and Schaffer (1985), 3.

philosopher had used crystal balls and flasks of water in order to explain the rainbow in terms of both the reflection and the refraction of the sun's rays. What was new was the spread of the experimental method and its increasing acceptability as a 'knowledge-making practice'.[17]

Unfortunately it was impossible to study the whole of the natural world through experiment, let alone the social world. A method which worked for physics or chemistry could not be universalized. Astronomy and botany, for example, required other methods. However, there was always induction or empiricism, a method (discussed in chapter 1, 16) which might be described as a weaker or less systematic version of experiment, which had the advantage of a more general application.

It may seem odd to describe empiricism as a reaction to scepticism, in other words as an invention or discovery which took place in a particular period. It probably seems self-evident that empiricism or induction is a universal method, which most of us use just as Molière's character Monsieur Jourdain spoke prose, without realizing it. A recent essay on the history of truth suggests that there are only four reasons for accepting statements as true – feeling, authority, reason and sense-perception. Although 'all four categories have always been around', the balance between them varies with cultures and periods.[18] In the early modern period this balance was tilting towards a combination of reason and sense-perception (sometimes direct, sometimes mediated through instruments such as the telescope and the microscope). What was new was an increasingly acute consciousness of method, linked to the use of scientific instruments, to the increasingly systematic collection of particular facts, and to the rise of practical handbooks – nothing makes one so conscious of one's method as having to describe it in writing.

To return to the high ground of philosophy. Despite his interest in specimens of plants or political systems, Aristotle had dismissed knowledge of particulars, claiming in his *Posterior Analytics* that 'knowledge depends upon the recognition of the universal'. Particulars were a proper object for description (*historia*), as in the case of Aristotle's own *History of Animals*, on the basis of which generalizations might be made, but they did not provide true knowledge in themselves. Physicians from Hippocrates to Galen took the knowledge of particulars more seriously, and the term 'empirics' was coined in ancient Greece to refer to a medical school opposed to the 'dogmatists'. So

---

[17] Crombie (1953), 233–7; Shapin (1996), 96–117.
[18] Fernández-Armesto (1997), 4–5.

far as epistemology was concerned, however, the empirics were taken less seriously than Aristotle.

From the sixteenth century onwards, on the other hand, the knowledge of particulars or details (*cognitio singularium*) came to be given greater weight than before in a number of intellectual domains, from medicine to history, as well as being defended by philosophers from Bacon to Locke. 'Empiricism' itself received this name in the eighteenth century.[19]

Details, as Carlo Ginzburg has argued in a famous essay, came to be taken seriously because they were 'clues' to something larger.[20] Physicians had long been diagnosing illness on the basis of apparently trivial 'symptoms'. In the sixteenth century, some natural philosophers began to take 'natural history' – in other words, observation and description – more seriously than before.[21] For example, the Italian botanist Pier Andrea Mattioli argued for the importance of the first-hand observation of 'minutiae'. In the seventeenth century, if not before, connoisseurs – including a physician, Giulio Mancini – diagnosed the authenticity of paintings on the basis of apparently minor details.[22] Observation, increasingly careful and precise thanks to observatories, telescopes, microscopes and other instruments, was playing a more important part in the processing or production of knowledge of the natural world – and the social world too for that matter, given the rise of treatises on the 'art of travel', in the sense of a technique for the observation of the customs of foreign countries.

If healing (including the practice of 'empirics': above, 16), was one model for the reconstruction of theories of knowledge, another was the practical activity of doing justice in courts of law. Analogies between the practice of lawyers and historians in assessing the reliability of witnesses became increasingly common. As the phrase went, 'testimonies should be weighed and not counted', in order to determine the extent of their independence. This weighing included a consideration of what the eighteenth-century lawyer Sir Geoffrey Gilbert called the 'credit or competency of witnesses'. The credit of witnesses was linked to their social status in the case of scientific experiments as well as courts of law, since the word of a gentleman was considered more trustworthy than that of a person of lower status.[23]

It is likely that the lawyers learned from the natural philosophers as well as the other way round and made more use of specialized

---

[19] Seifert (1976), esp. 97ff, 116ff; Hassinger (1978).
[20] Ginzburg (1978).
[21] Daston (1991), 340.
[22] Ginzburg (1978), 108–11.
[23] Shapin and Schaffer (1985), 58–9; Daston (1991), 349; Shapin (1994), esp. 65–125.

'expert' witnesses. The verification of claimed miracles was central to the process of canonizing saints, which became increasingly rigorous in the early modern period. The Rome of the 'trials' for sanctity was not so distant from the Rome of the Lincei.[24] An increasing concern for evidence is also visible in the witch-trials of the seventeenth and eighteenth centuries, in which judges who had no difficulty in accepting the existence of witches in principle often considered the charges against individuals to lack proper verification.

What we call 'textual criticism', the attempt to reconstruct an original text despite its progressive corruption by a succession of copyists, also developed in the sixteenth and seventeenth centuries. The language of the critics betrays the influence of the courts of law. Humanist editors such as Erasmus examined individual manuscripts of a particular author as so many 'witnesses' to the original text which they were attempting to reconstruct, assessing the extent to which their testimony was independent.[25]

Again, the word 'research' and its parallels in other languages (*recherche*, *indagine* and so on) seems to have been borrowed from legal searches and enquiries (above, 45). The term 'evidence' was to be found in the mouths of lawyers before it flowed regularly from the pens of philosophers or historians. The word 'fact' (in Latin, *factum*) was used in courts of law, in phrases such as 'an accessory after the fact', or 'matters of fact' (as distinct from 'matters of law'), before it entered treatises on historical or scientific method.[26] Historians and natural philosophers of this period themselves drew analogies between their own work and the practice of the courts. Robert Boyle, for instance, compared witnesses to experiments with witnesses in a trial for murder.[27] Some historians claimed to be writing with the impartiality of a judge, as in the case of Gottfried Arnold's *Impartial History of the Church and of Heretics* (1699–1700).

Reacting to the claims of the Pyrrhonists that historical knowledge was impossible, philosophers came to emphasize probability rather than certainty and to distinguish between different 'degrees of assent' as Locke put it. For example, it was reasonable to believe that 'a man called Julius Caesar' once lived in Rome, because this 'matter of fact' was vouched for by 'the concurrent testimony of unsuspected witnesses' (*Concerning Human Understanding*, Book 4, chapter 16). Historians and lawyers followed this lead. In his treatise on *The Law*

---

[24] Burke (1984).
[25] Kenney (1974).
[26] Seifert (1976), 163–78; Daston (1991), 345; Shapiro (1994).
[27] Shapin and Schaffer (1985), 56.

of Evidence (1759), Sir Geoffrey Gilbert adopted Locke's idea of 'degrees of assent' and discussed evidence according to what he called the 'scale of probability' (proof, verisimilitude and so on).[28]

THE RISE OF THE FOOTNOTE

The new importance given to particulars was associated with changes in scholarly practice at an everyday level. Among natural philosophers and bureaucrats, there was an increasing trust in numbers, associated with an ideal of impartial or impersonal knowledge (which would later be described as 'objectivity').[29] Among historians, the rise of induction was linked to the rise of the footnote.[30] The term 'footnote' should not be taken too literally. What was important was the spread of the practice of giving some kind of guide to the reader of a particular text where to go for evidence and for further information, whether this information was given in the text itself, in the margin ('sidenote'), at the foot ('bottom notes'), at the back, or in special appendices containing documents. In his *Dictionary*, Pierre Bayle used both marginal notes (giving references) and footnotes (including quotations and attacks on other scholars). The main point of these practices was to facilitate a return to the 'sources', on the principle that information, like water, was purer the closer it came to the fountain. The historical note, like the detailed description of an experiment, was designed to allow the reader to repeat the author's experience if he or she wanted.

The return to the sources (*ad fontes*) was a slogan of Renaissance humanists and Protestant reformers alike, and some sixteenth-century historians were careful to refer to the manuscripts on which they based their accounts of the past. As a common practice, however, footnoting goes back to the seventeenth century. John Selden, for example, filled the margins of his *History of Tithes* (1618) with references to the sources, explaining proudly in his preface that 'The testimonies were chosen by weight, not by number, taken only thence whither the margin directs, never at second hand'. Even less scholarly works, such as Sancho de Moncada's *Political Restoration of Spain* (1619), a tract for the times, regularly cited authorities in the margin, including reference books such as Botero's world geography as well as the Bible and the classics.

---

[28] Hacking (1975); Shapiro (1983), 30–1, 81–5.
[29] Gillispie (1960); Daston (1991).
[30] Lipking (1977); Grafton (1997).

The example of Selden and scholars like him was increasingly followed from the late seventeenth century onwards. In his essay on the reliability of historians (*De fide historica*, 1679), the German scholar Johannes Eisenhart stressed the importance of citing sources. From about this time onwards, historical monographs make a habit of giving references to 'original documents' and often make a point of saying that they are doing so. In a prefatory note, Louis Maimbourg proudly informed readers of his history of the Catholic League (1684), that he had given references to his sources, while Gabriel Daniel's *History of France* (1713), emphasized the value of his marginal notes 'to show readers the sources from which are derived the things they are told' (*les sources d'où l'on a tiré les choses qu'on leur raconte*).

As a test of changes in changing scholarly practice, we might use David Hume's apology to a disgruntled reader (Horace Walpole), for the lack of 'references on the margin' in his *History of England*. In a letter to Walpole written in 1758, Hume declared that he was 'seduc'd by the example of all the best historians' such as Machiavelli and Sarpi, without considering that the practice of giving references 'having been once introduc'd, ought to be follow'd by every writer'. Hume was indeed a little old-fashioned in this respect, since some historians had already been giving references to their sources in the early seventeenth century. The footnoting procedure still followed in so many historical studies – including this one – developed out of early modern debates about the problem of knowledge.

CREDULITY, INCREDULITY AND THE SOCIOLOGY OF KNOWLEDGE

The debates over probability and certainty within or between academic disciplines are relatively easy to document. Changes at the pragmatic level, to return to the distinction made earlier, are less visible. It is difficult indeed to answer the question whether ordinary people became less credulous in the late seventeenth century. One reason for the difficulty is that what counts as 'credulity' varies with the culture. However, the history of the word may have something to tell us, taking the example of English. Similar stories might be told about equivalent terms in Italian and French, and perhaps in other languages too.

In English, the term 'credulity' originally meant 'belief'. In the eyes of some early Christian writers, it was a virtue. The term turned pejorative in the course of the seventeenth century, as it came to refer to people who were too easily (or uncritically) disposed to believe. Joseph Glanvill, for example, wrote of 'an ungrounded credulity'.

Even the conservative cleric Meric Casaubon, in his treatise *Of Credulity and Incredulity* (1668), essentially an attack on atheism, took care to reject credulity in the sense of 'unadvised', 'rash', 'easy' or 'ungrounded' belief. Conversely, the term 'incredulity', originally pejorative, shifted its meaning from 'atheism' to a broader, vaguer form of disbelief in whatever was not 'credible'. Credulity and incredulity became complementary opposites, as in Casaubon, who called them 'vicious extremes', or in Henry Hallywell's *Melampronea: or, A Discourse of the Polity and Kingdom of Darkness* (1681), which steered a middle course between 'Atheistical Incredulity' on one hand and foolish or 'over-Fond' credulity' on the other.[31]

The increasingly frequent analyses of the causes of error and the obstacles to reaching the truth may be interpreted as both a by-product and a sign of the increasing concern with epistemology. In a famous passage of his *New Organon* (Book 1, sections 39–44), Francis Bacon distinguished four kinds of 'idol' which 'so beset men's minds that truth can hardly find entrance'. 'Idols of the Tribe' have their foundation in human nature, making man the measure of all things. 'Idols of the Cave', by contrast, are individual errors. 'Idols of the Theatre' are those which have entered minds 'from the various dogmas of philosophies', which Bacon dismissed as 'so many stage plays'. The most 'sociological' part of Bacon's analysis – to use a convenient anachronism – was that of the 'Idols of the Market-Place', 'formed by the intercourse and association of men with each other'. In the eighteenth century, Giambattista Vico offered his own analysis of idols, or as he put it, 'arrogance' (*boria*), notably the arrogance of nations, each assuming that they discovered civilization, and the arrogance of the learned, who believe their own ideas to be as old as the world (*New Science*, sections 124–8).

The analyses offered by Bacon and Vico are among the most original and perceptive offered in the early modern period and intellectual historians are surely right to pay them attention. However, in a social history of knowledge it is even more important to stress the rise of everyday forms of historical epistemology at this time. The language of 'partiality' or 'bias' became increasingly commonplace. The metaphors of 'masks', 'cloaks' or 'veils' was often employed in attempts to detect deception (hence Milton's description of the historian Paolo Sarpi as 'the Great Unmasker' of the Council of Trent). In the course of the 'intellectual crisis of the Reformation' discussed above and of the religious wars which followed it, some sceptical individuals

---

[31] Quoted Clark (1997), 183.

and groups asserted that the appeal to religion was no more than camouflage.

For example, members of the so-called *politique* party in France during the religious wars of the later sixteenth century claimed that the extremists, Catholics and Protestants alike, had political rather than religious motives. Thus the French magistrate Jacques-Auguste de Thou wrote of 'those who use religion to make a Spanish cloak to cover their ambition'. In similar fashion the royalist historian Edward Hyde condemned the opponents of Charles I in the English civil war in almost identical terms: 'religion was made a cloak to cover their treacherous designs'.

Looking back at human history over the long term, anticlericals such as Thomas Hobbes and James Harrington condemned what was coming in the later seventeenth century to be called 'priestcraft', whether it was Catholic or Protestant, or indeed Egyptian, Jewish or Muslim. The anonymous treatise published early in the eighteenth century, stigmatizing Moses, Christ and Muhammad as the 'three impostors' who were able to persuade the credulous of their special relationship with God, is the most famous example of a trend which continued into the Enlightenment and beyond.[32]

The explanation for all these kinds of deceit was usually given in terms of 'interests'. 'Interests' was a word which came into use in the later sixteenth century, and was employed ever more frequently in the seventeenth and eighteenth centuries whether to refer to politics or economics, public or private concerns, the interest of states or that of individuals.[33] Duke Henri de Rohan published a book on *The Interests of the Princes and States of Christendom* (1624). Enrico Davila's famous history of *The Civil Wars of France* (1630) explained them in his very first paragraph as conflicts of 'private interests' disguised by 'various pretexts' such as religion. John Selden offered a similar interpretation of the English civil war in a remark recorded in his 'table-talk' that 'The very arcanum of pretending religion in all wars is that something may be found out, in which all men may have interest. In this the groom has as much interest as the lord. Were it for land, one has a thousand acres, the other but one; he would not venture so far as he that had a thousand.'

A more general account of the relation between interests and beliefs was offered by the English bishop Edward Stillingfleet, in the introduction to his defence of Christianity, *Origins of the Sacred*

---

[32] Goldie (1987), esp. 212n; Berti (1992); Benitez (1993).
[33] Meinecke (1924–5); Gunn (1969); Hirschman (1977).

(1662). In his own version of Bacon's idols, attempting to explain 'why so few pretenders to knowledge do light on truth', Stillingfleet discussed what he called 'partiality', 'prejudice', 'bias', the coloured 'spectacles' of authority, custom and education, and the 'correspondency' between ideas and 'interests'.

Karl Mannheim was well aware of the relevance to the sociology of knowledge of the civil wars of the sixteenth and seventeenth centuries and the party struggles of eighteenth-century England. 'Basically', he argued, 'it was in political struggles that for the first time men became aware of the unconscious collective motivations which had always guided the direction of thought . . . The discovery of the social-situational roots of thought at first, therefore, took the form of unmasking.' Like other forms of knowledge, the sociology of knowledge is itself socially situated.[34]

Another text from the eighteenth century, which Mannheim does not discuss, takes us from civil wars to the battle of the sexes. *Woman Not Inferior to Man* (1739), published by 'Sophia, a Person of Quality', argued that the doctrine of female inferiority was an error to be explained in terms of male 'interest' or 'partiality'. In similar fashion, the French philosopher François Poulain de La Barre, in his *Equality of the Two Sexes* (1673), had attacked male 'prejudices' which were to be explained by 'interests'. The continuities between the twentieth-century sociology of knowledge and early modern attitudes deserve to be remembered.

---

[34] Mannheim (1936), 35, 56.

SELECT BIBLIOGRAPHY

The books relevant to this study are legion. The list below is confined to secondary works cited in the footnotes. Unless specified otherwise, the place of publication of books in English is London and of books in French, Paris.

Ackerman, J. (1949) 'Ars sine scientia nihil est', *Art Bulletin* 12, pp. 84–108.

Agrell, W. and B. Huldt (eds, 1983) *Clio Goes Spying*. Malmö.

Åkerman, S. (1991) 'The Forms of Queen Christina's Academies', in Kelley and Popkin, pp. 165–88.

Albertini, R. von (1955) *Das Florentinische Staatsbewusstsein im Übergang von der Republik zum Prinzipat*. Berne.

Albònico, A. (1992) 'Le *Relationi Universali* di Giovanni Botero', in *Botero e la Ragion di Stato*, ed. A. E. Baldini, pp. 167–84. Florence.

Alcoff, L. and E. Potter (eds, 1993) *Feminist Epistemologies*.

Alexandrov, D. A. (1995) 'The Historical Anthropology of Science in Russia', *Russian Studies in History* 34, pp. 62–91.

Alvar Ezquerra, A. (ed., 1993) *Relaciones topográficas de Felipe II*, 3 vols. Madrid.

Ambrosini, F. (1982) *Paesi e mari ignoti: America e colonialismo europeo nella cultura veneziana (secoli xvi–xvii)*. Venice.

Ames-Lewis, F. (ed., 1999) *Sir Thomas Gresham and Gresham College*.

Anderson, B. (1983) *Imagined Communities*, second edn, 1991.

Anderson, M. S. (1978) *Peter the Great*, second edn, 1995.

Aquilon, P. and H.-J. Martin (eds, 1988), *Le Livre dans l'Europe de la Renaissance*.

Armstrong, E. (1990) *Before Copyright: The French Book-Privilege System, 1498–1526*. Cambridge.

Arrow, K. (1965) 'Knowledge, Productivity and Practice', rpr. in his *Production and Capital* (Cambridge, Mass., 1985), pp. 191–9.

Aubert, R. et al. (1976) *The University of Louvain*. Leuven.

Baker, J. N. L. (1935) 'Academic Geography in the Seventeenth and Eighteenth Centuries', rpr. in his *The History of Geography* (Oxford, 1963), pp. 14–32.

Baldamus, W. (1977) 'Ludwig Fleck and the Sociology of Science', in *Human Figurations*, pp. 135–56.

213

Ballester, L. García (1977) *Medicina, ciéncia y minorías marginadas: los Moriscos.* Granada.

Ballester, L. García (1993) 'The Inquisition and Minority Medical Practitioners in Counter-Reformation Spain', in *Medicine and the Reformation*, ed. P. P. Grell and A. Cunningham, pp. 156–91.

Ballesteros Beretta, A. (1941) 'J. B. Muñoz: la creación del Archivo de Indias', *Revista de Indias* 2, pp. 55–95.

Balsamo, J. (1995) 'Les Origines parisiennes du *Tesoro Politico*', *Bibliothèque d'Humanisme et Renaissance* 57, pp. 7–23.

Balsamo, L. (1973) 'Tecnologia e capitale nella storia del libro', in *Studi per Riccardo Ridolfi*, ed. B. M. Biagiarelli and D. E. Rhodes (Florence), pp. 77–94.

Baratin, M. and C. Jacob (eds, 1996) *Le Pouvoir des bibliothèques.*

Barber, G. (1981) 'Who were the Booksellers of the Enlightenment?', in G. Barber and B. Fabian (eds), *The Book and the Book Trade in Eighteenth-Century Europe* (Hamburg), pp. 211–24.

Barbour, V. (1928–9) 'Marine Risks and Insurance in the Seventeenth Century', *Journal of Economic and Business History* 1, pp. 561–96.

Barbour, V. (1950) *Capitalism in Amsterdam in the Seventeenth Century.* Baltimore.

Barkan, O. L. (1958) 'Essai sur les données statistiques des registres de recensement dans l'empire ottoman', *Journal of the Economic and Social History of the Orient* 1, pp. 9–36.

Barker, P. and R. Ariew (eds, 1991) *Revolution and Continuity: Essays in the History and Philosophy of Early Modern Science.* Washington.

Barnes, B. (1977) *Interests and the Growth of Knowledge.*

Basalla, G. (1987) 'The Spread of Western Science', rpr. in Storey, pp. 1–22.

Baschet, A. (1870) *Les Archives de Venise.*

Baschet, A. (1875) *Histoire du dépôt des archives des affaires étrangères.*

Bassett, D. K. (1960) 'The Trade of the English East India Company in the Far East, 1623–1684', rpr. in *European Commercial Expansion in Early Modern Asia*, ed. O. Prakash (Aldershot, 1997), pp. 208–36.

Bauer, W. (1966) 'The Encyclopaedia in China', *Cahiers d'Histoire Moderne* 9, pp. 665–91.

Bautier, R. H. (1968) 'La Phase cruciale de l'histoire des archives', *Archivum* 18, pp. 139–49.

Bayly, C. A. (1996) *Empire and Information: Intelligence Gathering and Social Communication in India, 1780–1870.* Cambridge.

Bec, C. (1967) *Les Marchands écrivains*.

Becher, T. (1989) *Academic Tribes and Territories*.

Belenky, M. F. et al. (1986) *Women's Ways of Knowing*.

Beljame, L. (1881) *Le Public et les hommes de lettres*.

Bell, D. (1976) *The Cultural Contradictions of Capitalism*.

Bély, L. (1990) *Espions et ambassadeurs au temps de Louis XIV*.

Benitez, M. (1993) 'La Diffusion du "traité des trois imposteurs" au 18e siècle', *Revue d'Histoire Moderne et Contemporaine* 40, pp. 137–51.

Bentley, J. H. (1983) *Humanists and Holy Writ: New Testament Scholarship in the Renaissance*. Princeton.

Benzoni, G. (1978) *Gli affanni della cultura: intellettuali e potere nell'Italia della Controriforma e barocca*. Milan.

Berger, P. and T. Luckmann (1966) *The Social Construction of Reality*. New York.

Berkey, J. (1992) *The Transmission of Knowledge in Medieval Cairo*. Princeton.

Berkvens-Stevelinck, C. et al. (eds, 1992) *Le Magasin de l'Univers: The Dutch Republic as the Centre of the European Book Trade*. Leiden.

Bermingham, A. and J. Brewer (eds, 1995) *The Consumption of Culture 1600–1800*.

Bernard-Maître, H. (1953) 'L'Orientaliste Guillaume Postel et la découverte spirituelle du Japon en 1552', *Monumenta Nipponica* 9, pp. 83–108.

Berti, S. (1992) 'The First Edition of the *Traité des trois imposteurs*', in *Atheism from the Reformation to the Enlightenment*, ed. M. Hunter and D. Wootton (Oxford), pp. 182–220.

Besterman, T. (1935) *The Beginnings of Systematic Bibliography*. Oxford.

Biagoli, M. (1993) *Galileo Courtier*. Princeton.

Biggs, M. (1999) 'Putting the State on the Map: Cartography, Territory and European State Formation', *Comparative Studies in Society and History* 41, pp. 374–405.

Birn, R. (1983) 'Book Production and Censorship in France, 1700–15', in Carpenter, pp. 145–71.

Birn, R. (1989) 'Malesherbes and the Call for a Free Press', in Darnton and Roche, pp. 50–66.

Blair, A. (1992) 'Humanist Methods in Natural Philosophy: The Commonplace Book', *Journal of the History of Ideas* 53, pp. 541–52.

Blair, A. (1996) 'Bibliothèques portables: les recueils de lieux communs', in Baratin and Jacob, pp. 84–106.

Blair, A. (1997) *The Theatre of Nature: Jean Bodin and Renaissance Science*. Princeton.

Blum, R. (1963) 'Bibliotheca Memmiana: Untersuchungen zu Gabriel Naudé's *Advis*', in *Festschrift Carl Wehmer* (Amsterdam), pp. 209–32.

Blum, W. (1969) *Curiosi und Regendarii: Untersuchen zur Geheimen Staatspolizei der Spätantike*. Munich.

Blumenberg, H. (1966) *The Legitimacy of the Modern Age*, English translation, Cambridge, Mass., 1983.

Böhme, G. (1984) 'Midwifery as Science', in Stehr and Meja.

Böhme, G. and N. Stehr (eds, 1986) *The Knowledge Society*. Dordrecht.

Boislisle, A. M. de (1874) *Correspondance des Contrôleurs Généraux des Finances*.

Borghero, C. (1983) *La certezza e la storia: cartesianesimo, pirronismo e conoscenza storica*. Milan.

Bost, H. (1994) *Un intellectuel avant la lettre: le journaliste Pierre Bayle*. Amsterdam–Maarssen.

Bots, H. (1983) 'Les Provinces-Unies, centre de l'information européenne au dix-septième siècle', *Quaderni del '600 francese* 5, pp. 283–306.

Bots, H. and F. Waquet (1997) *La République des Lettres*.

Boulding, K. E. (1966) 'The Economics of Knowledge and the Knowledge of Economics', *American Economic Review* 56, pp. 1–13.

Bourdieu, P. (1972) *Outlines of a Theory of Practice*, English translation, Cambridge, 1977.

Bourdieu, P. (1984) *Homo Academicus*, English translation, Cambridge, 1984.

Bourdieu, P. (1989) *La Noblesse d'Etat*.

Boutier, J., A. Dewerpe and D. Nordman (1984) *Un tour de France royal*.

Bouwsma, W. J. (1973) 'Lawyers and Early Modern Culture', rpr. in his *A Usable Past: Essays in European Cultural History* (Berkeley and Los Angeles, 1990), pp. 129–53.

Bouza, F. (1988) 'La biblioteca del Escorial y el orden de los saberes en el siglo xvi', rpr. in his *Imagen y propaganda: capítulos de historia cultural del reinado de Felipe II* (Madrid), pp. 168–85.

Bouza, F. (1992) *Del escribano a la biblioteca. La civilización escrita europea en la Alta Edad Moderna*. Madrid.

Bowen, M. (1981) *Empiricism and Geographical Thought from Francis Bacon to Alexander von Humboldt*. Cambridge.

Boxer, C. R. (1936) *Jan Compagnie in Japan*.

Boxer, C. R. (1948) *Three Historians of Portuguese Asia*. Hong Kong.

Boxer, C. R. (1957) *The Dutch in Brazil, 1624–54*. Oxford.

Boxer, C. R. (1963) *Two Pioneers of Tropical Medicine*.

Brading, D. A. (1991) *The First America: The Spanish Monarchy, Creole Patriots and the Liberal State, 1492–1867*. Cambridge.

Bradshaw, L. E. (1981a) 'John Harris's *Lexicon Technicum*', in Kafker, pp. 107–21.

Bradshaw, L. E. (1981b) 'Ephraim Chambers' *Cyclopaedia*', in Kafker, pp. 123–40.

Brentjes, S. (1999) 'The Interests of the Republic of Letters in the Middle East', *Science in Context* 12, pp. 435–68.

Brewer, J. (1989) *The Sinews of Power*.

Brewer, J. and R. Porter (eds, 1993) *Consumption and the World of Goods*.

Briggs, R. (1991) 'The Académie Royale des Sciences and the Pursuit of Utility', *Past and Present* 131, pp. 38–88.

Brincken, A.-D. von den (1972) 'Tabula alphabetica', in *Festschrift Herman Heimpel*, vol. 2 (Göttingen), pp. 900–23.

Broc, N. (1975) *La Géographie des philosophes: géographes et voyageurs français au 18e siècle*.

Broc, N. (1980) *La Géographie de la Renaissance*.

Brocchieri, M. F. Beonio (1987) 'L'intellettuale', in *L'uomo medievale*, ed. J. Le Goff (Rome–Bari), pp. 203–33.

Brockliss, L. W. B. (1987) *French Higher Education in the Seventeenth and Eighteenth Centuries*. Oxford.

Brockliss, L. W. B. (1996) 'Curricula', in Ridder-Symoens, vol. 2, pp. 565–620.

Brown, H. (1934) *Scientific Organizations in Seventeenth-Century France*. Baltimore.

Brown, J. (1978) *Images and Ideas in Seventeenth-Century Spanish Painting*. Princeton.

Brown, R. D. (1989) *Knowledge is Power: The Diffusion of Information in Early America, 1700–1865*. New York.

Buck, P. (1977) 'Seventeenth-Century Political Arithmetic: Civil Strife and Vital Statistics', *Isis* 68, pp. 67–84.

Buck, P. (1982) 'People who Counted: Political Arithmetic in the Eighteenth Century', *Isis* 73, pp. 28–45.

Buisseret, D. (ed., 1992) *Monarchs, Ministers and Maps: The Emergence of Cartography as a Tool of Government in Early Modern Europe*. Chicago.

Burckhardt, J. (1860) *The Civilisation of the Renaissance in Italy*, English translation, revised edn, Harmondsworth 1990.

Burke, P. (1979) 'The Bishop's Questions and the People's Religion', rpr. in Burke (1987), pp. 40–7.

Burke, P. (1983) 'The Reform of European Universities in the Six-teenth and Seventeenth Centuries', *CRE Information*, pp. 59–67.

Burke, P. (1984) 'How to be a Counter-Reformation Saint', rpr. in Burke (1987), pp. 48–62.

Burke, P. (1985) 'European Views of World History from Giovio to Voltaire', *History of European Ideas* 6, pp. 237–51.

Burke, P. (1986) 'The Humanist as Professional Teacher', in *The Professional Teacher*, ed. J. Wilkes (Leicester), pp. 19–27.

Burke, P. (1987) *Historical Anthropology of Early Modern Italy*. Cambridge.

Burke, P. (1988) 'William Dell, the Universities, and the Radical Tradition', in *Reviving the English Revolution*, ed. G. Eley and W. Hunt, pp. 181–9.

Burke, P. (1990) *The French Historical Revolution: The Annales School 1929–89*. Cambridge.

Burke, P. (1992) *The Fabrication of Louis XIV*. New Haven.

Burke, P. (1995a) 'America and the Rewriting of World History', in *America in European Consciousness*, ed. K. O. Kupperman (Chapel Hill), pp. 33–51.

Burke, P. (1995b) 'The Jargon of the Schools', in *Languages and Jargons*, ed. P. Burke and Roy Porter (Cambridge), pp. 22–41.

Burke, P. (1995c) *The Fortunes of the Courtier: The European Reception of Castiglione's Cortegiano*. Cambridge.

Burke, P. (1998a) *Varieties of Cultural History*. Cambridge.

Burke, P. (1998b) 'Two Crises of Historical Consciousness', *Storia della Storiografia* no. 33, pp. 3–16.

Burke, P. (1998c) *The European Renaissance: Centres and Peripheries*. Oxford.

Burke, P. (1999a) 'Erasmus and the Republic of Letters', *European Review* 7, no. 1, pp. 5–17.

Burke, P. (1999b) 'The Philosopher as Traveller: Bernier's Orient', in *Voyages and Visions: Towards a Cultural History of Travel*, ed. J. Elsner and J.-P. Rubiés, pp. 124–37.

Burke, P. (2000a) 'Venice as a Centre of Information and Commun-ication', forthcoming in *Venice Reconsidered: The History and Civilization of an Italian City-State 1297–1997*, ed. J. Martin and D. Romano (Baltimore).

Burke, P. (2000b) 'Assumptions and Observations: Eighteenth-Century French Travellers in South America', forthcoming in *Invitation au Voyage*, ed. J. Renwick (Edinburgh).

Burke, P. (2001) 'Rome as a Centre of Information and Communica-tion', forthcoming in P. Jones and T. Worcester (eds), *Saints and Sinners* (Toronto).

Bustamante García, G. (1997) 'Francisco Hernández', in B. Ares Queija and S. Gruzinski (eds), *Entre dos mundos: fronteras culturales y agentes mediadores* (Seville), pp. 243–68.

Canone, E. (ed., 1993) *Bibliothecae Selectae da Cusano a Leopardi.* Florence.

Caracciolo Aricò, A. (ed., 1990) *L'impatto della scoperta dell'America nella cultura veneziana.* Rome.

Carels, P. E. and D. Flory (1981) 'J. H. Zedler's Universal Lexicon', in Kafker, pp. 165–95.

Carpenter, K. E. (ed., 1983) *Books and Society in History.* New York.

Carter, C. H. (1964) *The Secret Diplomacy of the Habsburgs, 1598–1625.* New York.

Castells, M. (1989) *The Informational City.* Oxford.

Cavaciocchi, S. (ed., 1992) *Produzione e commercio della carta e del libro, secc. xiii–xviii.* Florence.

Chabod, F. (1934) 'Giovanni Botero', rpr. in his *Scritti sul Rinascimento* (Turin, 1967), pp. 271–458.

Chaffee, J. W. (1985) *The Thorny Gates of Learning in Sung China: A Social History of Examinations.* Cambridge.

Chamberlain, M. (1994) *Knowledge and Social Practice in Medieval Damascus.* Cambridge.

Charle, C. (1990) *Naissance des 'intellectuels' 1880–1900.*

Chartier, R. (1982) 'Les Intellectuels frustrés au 17e siècle', *Annales: Economies, Sociétés, Civilisations* 37, pp. 389–400.

Chartier, R. (1987) *The Cultural Uses of Print in Early Modern France.* Princeton.

Chartier, R. (1992) *The Order of Books: Readers, Authors and Libraries in Europe between the Fourteenth and Eighteenth Centuries.* Cambridge.

Christianson, J. R. (2000) *On Tycho's Island: Tycho Brahe and his Assistants, 1570–1601.* Cambridge.

Church, W. F. (1972) *Richelieu and Reason of State.* Princeton.

Cipolla, C. M. (1972) 'The Diffusion of Innovations in Early Modern Europe', *Comparative Studies in Society and History* 14, pp. 46–52.

Cipolla, C. M. (1976) *Public Health and the Medical Profession in the Renaissance.* Cambridge.

Clanchy, M. (1979) *From Memory to Written Record: England 1066–1307.* Revised edn, Oxford, 1993.

Clapp, S. (1931) 'The Beginnings of Subscription in the Seventeenth Century', *Modern Philology* 29, pp. 199–224.

Clapp, S. (1933) 'The Subscription Enterprises of John Ogilby and Richard Blome', *Modern Philology* 30, pp. 365–79.

Clark, S. (1997) *Thinking with Demons: The Idea of Witchcraft in Early Modern Europe*. Oxford.

Clarke, J. A. (1966) 'Librarians of the King: The Bignon, 1642–1784', *Library Quarterly* 36, pp. 293–8.

Clarke, J. A. (1970) *Gabriel Naudé, 1600–53*. Hamden, Conn.

Clement, R. W. (1991) 'The Career of Thomas James', *Libraries and Culture* 26, pp. 269–82.

Cline, H. F. (1964) 'The *Relaciones Geográficas* of the Spanish Indies, 1577–1586', *Hispanic American Historical Review* 44, pp. 341–74.

Cobb, R. (1970) *The Police and the People*. Oxford.

Cochrane, J. A. (1964) *Dr Johnson's Printer: The Life of William Strahan*.

Codina Mir, G. (1968) *Aux sources de la pédagogie des Jésuites*. Rome.

Cohen, H. F. (1989) 'Comment', in *New Trends in the History of Science*, ed. R. P. W. Visser et al., Amsterdam–Atlanta, pp. 49–51.

Cohn, B. S. (1996) *Colonialism and its Forms of Knowledge*. Princeton.

Confino, M. (1962) 'Les Enquêtes économiques de la Société Libre d'Économie de Saint Petersbourg', *Revue Historique* 227, pp. 155–80.

Cormack, L. B. (1997) *Charting an Empire; Geography at the English Universities, 1580–1620*. Chicago.

Cortesão, A. (ed., 1944) *Tomé Pires, Suma Oriental*. London.

Costello, William T. (1958) *The Scholastic Curriculum at Early Seventeenth-Century Cambridge*. Cambridge, Mass.

Crane, D. (1972) *Invisible Colleges: Diffusion of Knowledge in Scientific Communities*. Chicago.

Crick, M. (1982) 'Anthropology of Knowledge', *Annual Review of Anthropology* 11, pp. 287–313.

Crombie, A. C. (1953) *Robert Grosseteste and the Origins of Experimental Science, 1100–1700*. Oxford.

Cropper, E. and C. Dempsey (1996) *Nicolas Poussin: Friendship and the Love of Painting*. New Haven.

Curtis, M. H. (1959) *Oxford and Cambridge in Transition, 1558–1642*. Oxford.

Curtis, M. H. (1962) 'The Alienated Intellectuals of Early Stuart England', *Past and Present* 23, pp. 25–41.

Curtius, E. R. (1948) *European Literature and the Latin Middle Ages*, English translation, 1954; second edn, New York, 1963.

D'Addario, A. (1990) 'Lineamenti di storia dell'archivistica', *Archivio Storico Italiano* 148, pp. 3–36.

Dahl, F. (1939) 'Amsterdam – Earliest Newspaper Centre of Western Europe', *Het Boek* 25, pp. 160–97.

Dahl, F. (1951) 'Les Premiers Journaux en français', in *Débuts de la presse française*, ed. Dahl et al. (Göteborg–Paris), pp. 1–15.

Dainville, F. de (1940) *La Géographie des humanistes*.

Daly, L. W. (1967) *Contribution to a History of Alphabetization in Antiquity and the Middle Ages*. Brussels.

Darnton, R. (1979) *The Business of Enlightenment*. Cambridge, Mass.

Darnton, R. (1982) *The Literary Underground of the Old Regime*. New York.

Darnton, R. (1984) 'Philosophers Trim the Tree of Knowledge: The Epistemological Structure of the *Encyclopédie*', in his *The Great Cat Massacre* (New York), pp. 191–214.

Darnton, R. and D. Roche (eds, 1989) *Revolution in Print: The Press in France 1775–1800*. Berkeley.

Daston, L. (1991) 'Baconian Facts, Academic Civility and the Prehistory of Objectivity', *Annals of Scholarship* 8, pp. 337–63.

Daston, L. (1992) 'Classifications of Knowledge in the Age of Louis XIV', in D. L. Rubin (ed.), *Sun King* (Washington), pp. 206–20.

Davids, K. (1995) 'Openness or Secrecy? Industrial Espionage in the Dutch Republic', *Journal of European Economic History* 24, pp. 334–48.

Davies, D. W. (1952) 'The Geographical Extent of the Dutch Book Trade in the 17th Century', *Library Quarterly* 22, pp. 200–13.

Davies, D. W. (1954) *The World of the Elseviers, 1580–1712*. The Hague.

Davis, N. Z. (1983) 'Beyond the Market: Books as Gifts in Sixteenth-Century France', *Transactions of the Royal Historical Society* 33, pp. 69–88.

Dawson, W. R. (1932) 'The London Coffeehouses and the Beginnings of Lloyds', *Essays by Divers Hands* 11, pp. 69–112.

Derber, C., W. A. Schwartz and Y. Magrass (1990) *Power in the Highest Degree: Professionals and the Rise of a New Mandarin Order*. New York.

Deutsch, K. (1953) *Nationalism and Social Communication*. New York.

Dieckmann, H. (1961) 'The Concept of Knowledge in the Encyclopédie', *Essays in Comparative Literature*, pp. 73–107.

Dierse, U. (1977) *Enzyklopädie*. Bonn.

Dionisotti, C. (1967) 'Chierici e laici', in his *Geografia e storia della letteratura italiana*, Turin, pp. 47–73.

Dodds, M. (1929) *Les Récits de voyage sources de l'Esprit des Loix de Montesquieu*.

Dooley, B. (1999) *The Social History of Scepticism: Experience and Doubt in Early Modern Culture.* Baltimore.

Doria, G. (1986) 'Conoscenza del mercato e sistema informativo: il know-how dei mercanti-finanzieri genovesi nei secoli xvi e xvii', in *La repubblica internazionale del danaro*, ed. A. da Maddalena and H. Kellenbenz (Florence), pp. 57–115.

Drayton, R. (1998) 'Knowledge and Empire', in *The Oxford History of the British Empire*, vol. 2: *The Eighteenth Century*, ed. P. Marshall (Oxford), pp. 231–52.

Drège, J.-P. (1991) *Les Bibliothèques en Chine au temps des manuscrits.* Paris.

Dreitzel, H. (1983) 'Hermann Conring und die politische Wissenschaft seiner Zeit', in Stolleis, pp. 135–72.

Duchet, M. (1971) *Anthropologie et histoire au siècle des lumières.*

Duke, A. C. and C. A. Tamse (eds, 1987) *Too Mighty to be Free: Censorship and the Press in Britain and the Netherlands.* Zutphen.

Dülmen, R. van (1978) 'Die Aufklärungsgesellschaften in Deutschland', *Francia* 5, pp. 251–75.

Dülmen, R. van (1986) *The Society of the Enlightenment*, English translation, Cambridge, 1992.

Durán, J. (1991) *Toward a Feminist Epistemology.* Savage, Md.

Durkheim, E. (1912) *The Elementary Forms of the Religious Life.* English translation, New York, 1961.

Durkheim, E. and M. Mauss (1901–2) *Primitive Classification.* English translation 1963.

Duyvendak, J. J. L. (1936) 'Early Chinese Studies in Holland', *T'oung Pao* 32, pp. 293–344.

Eamon, W. (1994) *Science and the Secrets of Nature: Books of Secrets in Early Modern Culture.* Princeton.

Echevarria Bacigalupe, M. A. (1984) *La diplomacia secreta en Flandres, 1598–1643.* Madrid.

Eco, U. (1995) *The Search for the Perfect Language.* Oxford.

Edney, M. (1997) *Mapping an Empire: The Geographic Construction of British India, 1765–1843.* Chicago.

Eisenstein, E. (1979) *The Printing Press as an Agent of Change*, 2 vols. Cambridge.

Eisenstein, E. (1992) *Grub Street Abroad.* Oxford.

Elias, N. (1939) *The Civilising Process*, English translation, 2 vols, Oxford, 1978–82.

Elias, N. (1982) 'Scientific Establishments', in *Scientific Establishments and Hierarchies*, ed. N. Elias, H. Martins and R. Whitley (Dordrecht), pp. 3–69.

Elkanah, Y. (1981) 'A Programmatic Attempt at an Anthropology of Knowledge', in *Sciences and Cultures*, ed. E. Mendelsohn and Y. Elkanah, pp. 1–76.

Elkar, R. S. (1995) 'Altes Handwerk und ökonomische Enzyklopädie', in Eybl et al., pp. 215–31.

Elliott, J. H. (1986) *The Count-Duke of Olivares*. New Haven.

Elton, G. R. (1972) *Policy and Police*. Cambridge.

Engelsing, R. (1969) 'Die Perioden der Lesergeschichte in der Neuzeit', *Archiv für Geschichte des Buchwesens* 10, pp. 944–1002.

Engelsing, R. (1974) *Der Bürger als Leser. Lesergeschichte in Deutschland, 1500–1800*. Stuttgart.

Esmonin, E. (1964) *Etudes sur la France des 17e et 18e siècles*.

Ettinghausen, H. (1984) 'The News in Spain', *European History Quarterly* 14, pp. 1–20.

Evans, R. J. W. (1973) *Rudolf II and his World*. Oxford.

Eybl, F. et al. (eds, 1995) *Enzyklopädien der frühen Neuzeit*. Tübingen.

Feather, F. (1994) 'From Rights in Copies to Copyright', in *The Construction of Authorship*, ed. M. Woodmansee, Durham, NC, pp. 191–209.

Feingold, M. (1984) *The Mathematicians' Apprenticeship*. Cambridge.

Feingold, M. (1989) 'The Universities and the Scientific Revolution: The Case of England', in *New Trends in the History of Science*, ed. R. P. W. Visser et al., Amsterdam–Atlanta, pp. 29–48.

Feingold, M. (1991) 'Tradition versus Novelty: Universities and Scientific Societies in the Early Modern Period', in P. Barker and R. Ariew (eds, 1991) *Revolution and Continuity: Essays in the History and Philosophy of Early Modern Science* (Washington), pp. 45–59.

Feingold, M. (1997) 'The Mathematical Sciences and New Philosophies', in *History of the University of Oxford*, vol. 4, ed. Nicholas Tyacke (Oxford), pp. 359–448.

Feldhay, R. (1995) *Galileo and the Church: Political Inquisition or Critical Dialogue?* Cambridge.

Fernández-Armesto, F. (ed., 1995) *The European Opportunity*. Aldershot.

Fernández-Armesto, F. (1997) *Truth: A History and a Guide for the Perplexed*.

Field, A. (1988) *The Origins of the Platonic Academy of Florence*. Princeton.

Fiering, N. (1976) 'The Transatlantic Republic of Letters', *William & Mary Quarterly* 33, pp. 642–60.

Figueiredo, J. M. de (1984) 'Ayurvedic Medicine in Goa', rpr. in Storey, pp. 247–57.

Findlen, P. (1989) 'The Museum', *Journal of the History of Collections* 1, pp. 59–78.

Findlen, P. (1994) *Possessing Nature: Museums, Collecting and Scientific Culture in Early Modern Italy*. Berkeley.

Fleck, L. (1935) *Genesis and Development of a Scientific Fact*, English translation, Chicago, 1979.

Fleischer, C. H. (1986) *Bureaucrat and Intellectual in the Ottoman Empire*. Princeton.

Fletcher, J. M. (1981) 'Change and Resistance to Change: A Consideration of the Development of English and German Universities during the Sixteenth Century', *History of Universities* 1, pp. 1–36.

Flint, R. (1904) *Philosophy as Scientia Scientiarum and a History of the Classification of the Sciences*.

Fogel, M. (1989) *Les Cérémonies de l'information*.

Foucault, M. (1961) *Naissance de la clinique*.

Foucault, M. (1966) *Les Mots et les choses*.

Foucault, M. (1980) *Power/Knowledge*, ed. C. Gordon. Brighton.

Fox, A. (1999) 'Remembering the Past in Early Modern England', *Transactions of the Royal Historical Society* 9, pp. 233–56.

Frängsmyr, Tore, J. L. Heilbron and R. E. Rider (eds, 1990) *The Quantifying Spirit in the Eighteenth Century*. Berkeley–Los Angeles.

Fuller, S. (1992) 'Knowledge as Product and Property', in Stehr and Ericson, pp. 157–90.

Fumaroli, M. (1988) 'The Republic of Letters', *Diogenes* 143, pp. 129–52.

Gandt, F. de (1994) 'D'Alembert et la chaîne des sciences', *Revue de Synthèse* 115, pp. 39–54.

Gardair, J.-M. (1984) *Le 'Giornale de' letterati' de Rome (1668–81)*. Florence.

Garin, E. (1961) 'Ritratto del Paolo del Pozzo Toscanelli', rpr. in *Ritratti di umanisti* (Florence, 1967), pp. 41–68.

Garofalo, S. (1980) *L'enciclopedismo italiano: Gianfrancesco Pivati*. Ravenna.

Gasnault, P. (1976) 'Les travaux d'érudition des Mauristes au 18e siècle', in Hammer and Voss, pp. 102–21.

Gasparolo, P. (1887) 'Costituzione dell'Archivio Vaticano e suo primo indice sotto il pontificato di Paolo V', *Studi e documenti di storia e diritto* 8, pp. 3–64.

Geertz, C. (1975) 'Common Sense as a Cultural System', rpr. in his *Local Knowledge* (New York, 1983), pp. 73–93.

Geertz, C. (1979) 'Suq', in *Meaning and Order in Moroccan Society* (Cambridge), pp. 123–244.

Geertz, C. (1983) 'Local Knowledge: Fact and Law in Comparative Perspective', in his *Local Knowledge* (New York), pp. 167–234.

Gellner, E. (1974) *Legitimation of Belief*. Cambridge.

Gellner, E. (1988) *Plough, Sword and Book*.

Gellrich, J. M. (1985) *The Idea of the Book in the Middle Ages*. Ithaca.

George, M. D. (1926–9) 'The Early History of Registry Offices', *Economic History* 1, pp. 570–90.

Gerulaitis, L. V. (1976) *Printing and Publishing in Fifteenth-Century Venice*. Chicago.

Giard, L. (1983–5) 'Histoire de l'université et histoire du savoir: Padoue (xive–xvie siècles)', *Revue de Synthèse* 104–6, pp. 139–69, 259–98, 419–42.

Giard, L. (1991) 'Remapping Knowledge, Reshaping Institutions', in *Science, Culture and Popular Belief in Renaissance Europe*, ed. S. Pumfrey, P. L. Rossi and M. Slawinski (Manchester), pp. 19–47.

Gibbs, G. C. (1971) 'The Role of the Dutch Republic as the Intellectual Entrepot of Europe in the Seventeenth and Eighteenth Centuries', *Bijdragen en Mededelingen betreffende de Geschiedenis van de Nederlanden* 86, pp. 323–49.

Gibbs, G. C. (1975) 'Some Intellectual and Political Influences of the Huguenot Emigrés in the United Provinces c.1680–1730', *Bijdragen en Mededelingen betreffende de Geschiedenis van de Nederlanden* 90, pp. 255–87.

Giddens, A. (1985) *The Nation-State and Violence*. Cambridge.

Giesecke, M. (1991) *Der Buchdruck in der frühen Neuzeit: Eine historische Fallstudie über die Durchsetzung neuer Informations- und Kommunikationstechnologien*. Frankfurt.

Gilbert, F. (1965) *Machiavelli and Guicciardini*. Princeton.

Gilbert, N. W. (1960) *Renaissance Concepts of Method*. New York.

Gillispie, C. C. (1960) *The Edge of Objectivity: An Essay in the History of Scientific Ideas*. Princeton.

Gillispie, C. C. (1980) *Science and Polity in France at the End of the Old Regime*. Princeton.

Ginzburg, C. (1976) 'High and Low: The Theme of Forbidden Knowledge in the 16th and 17th Centuries', *Past and Present* 73, pp. 28–41.

Ginzburg, C. (1978) 'Clues: Roots of an Evidential Paradigm', rpr. in his *Myths, Emblems, Clues*, English translation (1990), pp. 96–125.

Ginzburg, C. (1996) 'Making Things Strange: The Prehistory of a Literary Device', *Representations* 56, pp. 8–28.

Ginzburg, C. (1997) *Occhiacci di legno: nove riflessioni sulla distanza*. Milan.

Glass, D. V. (1973) *Numbering the People: The Eighteenth-Century Population Controversy and the Development of Census and Vital Statistics in Britain*. Farnborough.

Golder, F. A. (ed., 1922) *Bering's Voyages*, 2 vols. New York.

Goldgar, A. (1995) *Impolite Learning*. New Haven.

Goldie, M. (1987) 'The Civil Religion of James Harrington', in *The Languages of Political Theory in Early-Modern Europe*, ed. Anthony Pagden (Cambridge), pp. 197–222.

Goldstein, T. (1965) 'Geography in Fifteenth-Century Florence', rpr. in Fernández-Armesto (1995), pp. 1–22.

Goldthwaite, R. A. (1972) 'Schools and Teachers of Commercial Arithmetic in Renaissance Florence', *Journal of European Economic History* 1, pp. 418–33.

Goodman, D. C. (1988) *Power and Penury: Government, Technology and Science in Philip II's Spain*. Cambridge.

Goodman, D. (1994) *The Republic of Letters: A Cultural History of the French Enlightenment*. Ithaca.

Goodman, G. K. (1967) *Japan: the Dutch Experience*, revised edn, 1987.

Goody, J. (1978) *The Domestication of the Savage Mind*. Cambridge.

Goody, J. (1996) *The East in the West*. Cambridge.

Goss, C. W. F. (1932) *The London Directories, 1677–1855*.

Goyet, F. (1986–7) 'A propos de "ces pastissages de lieux communs": le rôle de notes de lecture dans la genèse des *Essais*', *Bulletin de la Société des Amis de Montaigne*, parts 5–8, pp. 11–26, 9–30.

Goyet, F. (1996) *Le sublime du 'lieu commun': l'invention rhétorique dans l'antiquité et à la Renaissance*.

Grafton, A. (1990) *Forgers and Critics*. Princeton.

Grafton, A. (1992) 'Kepler as a Reader', *Journal of the History of Ideas* 53, pp. 561–72.

Grafton, A. (1997) *The Footnote: A Curious History*.

Grafton, A. and L. Jardine (1986) *From Humanism to the Humanities: Education and the Liberal Arts in Fifteenth- and Sixteenth-Century Europe*.

Granet, M. (1934) *La Pensée chinoise*.

Grant, E. (1996) *The Foundations of Modern Science in the Middle Ages*. Cambridge.

Greengrass, M. (1998) 'Archive Refractions: Hartlib's Papers and the Workings of an Intelligencer', in Hunter, pp. 35–48.

Gregory, T. (1961) *Scetticismo e empirismo: studio su Gassendi*. Bari.

Gregory, T. et al. (eds, 1981) *Ricerche su letteratura libertina e letteratura clandestina nel '600*. Florence.

Grosrichard, A. (1979) *Structure du serail: la fiction du despotisme asiatique dans l'occident classique.*

Grossman, M. (1975) *Humanism in Wittenberg 1485–1517.* Nieuwkoop.

Grove, R. (1991) 'The Transfer of Botanical Knowledge between Asia and Europe, 1498–1800', *Journal of the Japan–Netherlands Institute* 3, pp. 160–76.

Grove, R. (1996) 'Indigenous Knowledge and the Significance of South West India for Portuguese and Dutch Constructions of Tropical Nature', *Modern Asian Studies* 30, pp. 121–44.

Guénée, B. (1980) *Histoire et culture historique dans l'occident médiéval.*

Gunn, J. A. W. (1969) *Politics and the Public Interest in the Seventeenth Century.*

Gurvitch, G. (1966) *The Social Frameworks of Knowledge*, English translation, Oxford, 1971.

Guy, R. K. (1987) *The Emperor's Four Treasuries: Scholars and the State in the Late Ch'ien-Lung Era.* Cambridge, Mass.

Haase, E. (1959) *Einführung in die Literatur des Refuge: Der Beitrag der französischen Protestanten zur Entwicklung analytischer Denkformen am Ende des 17. Jht.* Berlin.

Habermas, J. (1962) *The Structural Transformation of the Public Sphere*, English translation, Cambridge, 1989.

Hacking, I. (1975) *The Emergence of Probability.* Cambridge.

Hahn, R. (1971) *The Anatomy of a Scientific Institution: The Paris Academy of Sciences, 1666–1803.* Berkeley.

Hahn, R. (1975) 'Scientific Careers in Eighteenth-Century France', in M. P. Crosland (ed.), *The Emergence of Science in Western Europe*, pp. 127–38.

Hall, A. R. (1962) 'The Scholar and the Craftsman in the Scientific Revolution', in *Critical Problems in the History of Science*, ed. M. Clagett (Madison), pp. 3–32.

Hall, M. B. (1965) 'Oldenburg and the Art of Scientific Communication', *British Journal of the History of Science* 2, pp. 277–90.

Hall, M. B. (1975) 'The Royal Society's Role in the Diffusion of Information in the Seventeenth Century', *Notes and Records of the Royal Society* 29, pp. 173–92.

Hammer, K. and J. Voss (eds, 1976) *Historische Forschung im 18. Jht.* Bonn.

Hammermeyer, L. (1976) 'Die Forschungszentren der deutschen Benediktinern und ihre Vorhaben', in Hammer and Voss, pp. 122–91.

Hammerstein, N. (1972) *Jus und Historie: ein Beitrag zur Geschichte des historischen Denkens an deutschen Universitäten im späten 17. und im 18. Jht.* Göttingen.

Hankins, J. (1990) *Plato in the Italian Renaissance*, 2 vols. Leiden.

Hankins, J. (1991) 'The Myth of the Platonic Academy of Florence', *Renaissance Quarterly* 44, pp. 429–75.

Hannaway, O. (1975) *The Chemists and the Word: The Didactic Origins of Chemistry.* Baltimore.

Hannaway, O. (1986) 'Laboratory Design and the Aims of Science: Andreas Libavius and Tycho Brahe', *Isis* 77, pp. 585–610.

Hannaway, O. (1992) 'Georgius Agricola as Humanist', *Journal of the History of Ideas* 53, pp. 553–60.

Haraway, D. (1988) 'Situated Knowledge', *Feminist Studies* 14, pp. 575–99.

Harley, J. B. (1988) 'Silences and Secrecy: The Hidden Agenda of Cartography in Early Modern Europe', *Imago Mundi* 40, pp. 57–76.

Harley, J. B. and D. Woodward (eds, 1992) *The History of Cartography*, vol. 2, part 1. Chicago.

Harley, J. B. and D. Woodward (eds, 1994) *The History of Cartography*, vol. 2, part 2. Chicago.

Harmsen, A. J. E. (1994) 'Barlaeus's Description of the Dutch Colony in Brazil', in *Travel Fact and Travel Fiction*, ed. Z. von Martels (Leiden), pp. 158–69.

Harris, J. R. (1985) 'Industrial Espionage in the Eighteenth Century', *Industrial Archaeology Review* 7, pp. 127–38.

Harris, J. R. (1992) 'The First British Measures against Industrial Espionage', in *Industry and Finance in Early Modern History*, ed. Ian Blanchard et al.

Harris, J. R. (1996a) 'A French Industrial Spy: The Engineer Le Turc in England in the 1780s', *Icon* 1, pp. 16–35.

Harris, J. R. (1996b) 'Law, Industrial Espionage and the Transfer of Technology from 18thc Britain', in *Technological Change*, ed. R. Fox (Amsterdam), pp. 123–36.

Harris, M. (1987) *London Newspapers in the Age of Walpole.*

Harris, S. J. (1996) 'Confession-Building, Long-Distance Networks, and the Organisation of Jesuit Science', *Early Modern Science* 1, pp. 287–318.

Harris, S. J. (1998) 'Long-Distance Corporations, Big Sciences and the Geography of Knowledge', *Configurations* 6, pp. 269–304.

Harris, S. J. (1999) 'Mapping Jesuit Science: The Role of Travel in the Geography of Knowledge', in O'Malley and Bailey, pp. 212–40.

Haskell, F. (1993) *History and its Images: Art and the Interpretation of the Past*. New Haven.

Hassinger, E. (1978) *Empirisch-rationaler Historismus*. Berne–Munich.

Hathaway, N. (1989) 'Compilatio: from Plagiarism to Compiling', *Viator* 20, pp. 19–44.

Hazard, P. (1935) *The European Mind, 1680–1715*, English translation, 1953.

Heath, M. J. (1983) 'Montaigne, Lucinge and the *Tesoro Politico*', *Bibliothèque d'Humanisme et Remaissance* 45, pp. 131–5.

Heckscher, W. S. (1958) *Rembrandt's Anatomy of Dr Nicholas Tulp: An Iconological Study*. New York.

Heers, J. (1976) 'L'Enseignement à Gênes et la formation culturelle des hommes d'affaires en Méditerranée à la fin du Moyen Âge', *Etudes Islamiques* 44, pp. 229–44.

Helms, M. W. (1988) *Ulysses' Sail*. Princeton.

Henningsen, G. and J. Tedeschi (eds, 1986) *The Inquisition in Early Modern Europe: Studies on Sources and Methods*. Dekalb, Ill.

Herlihy, D. and C. Klapisch (1978) *Les Toscans et leurs familles*.

Hess, A. (1974) 'Piri Reis and the Ottoman Response to the Voyages of Discovery', *Terrae Incognitae* 6, pp. 19–37.

Hill, C. (1965) *Intellectual Origins of the Scientific Revolution*. Oxford.

Hill, C. (1972) *The World Turned Upside Down: Radical Ideas During the English Revolution*, second edn, Harmondsworth, 1975.

Hirschman, A. (1977) *The Passions and the Interests: Political Arguments for Capitalism before its Triumph*. Princeton.

Hoftijzer, P. G. (1987) *Engelse boekverkopers bij de Beurs*. Amsterdam–Maarssen.

Holmes, G. (1977) 'Gregory King and the Social Structure of Preindustrial England', *Transactions of the Royal Historical Society* 27, pp. 41–65.

Hoock, J. (1980) 'Statistik und Politische Ökonomie', in Rassem and Stagl, pp. 307–23.

Hoock, J. and P. Jeannin (eds, 1991–3) *Ars mercatoria*, 2 vols. Paderborn.

Hopkins, J. (1992) 'The 1791 French Cataloging Code and the Origins of the Card Catalogue', *Libraries and Culture* 27, pp. 378–404.

Houghton, W. E., Jr (1942) 'The English Virtuoso in the Seventeenth Century', *Journal of the History of Ideas* 3, pp. 51–73 and 190–219.

Hucker, C. O. (ed., 1968) *Chinese Government in Ming Times*. New York.

Huff, T. E. (1993) *The Rise of Early Modern Science*. Cambridge.
Huisman, F. (1989) 'Itinerant Medical Practitioners in the Dutch Republic: The Case of Groningen', *Tractrix* 1, pp. 63–83.
Hulshoff Pol, E. (1975) 'The Library', in Lunsingh Scheurleer and Posthumus Meyjes, pp. 395–460.
Hunter, M. C. W. (1981) *Science and Society in Restoration England*. Cambridge.
Hunter, M. C. W. (1982) *The Royal Society and its Fellows*, second edn, Oxford, 1994.
Hunter, M. C. W. (1989) *Establishing the New Science: The Experience of the Early Royal Society*. Woodbridge.
Hunter, M. C. W. (ed., 1998) *Archives of the Scientific Revolution: The Formation and Exchange of Ideas in 17th-Century Europe*. Woodbridge.
Hutchinson, T. W. (1988) *Before Adam Smith: The Emergence of Political Economy, 1662–1776*. Oxford.
Iliffe, R. (1992) 'In the Warehouse: Privacy, Property and Priority in the early Royal Society', *History of Science* 30, pp. 29–68.
Im Hoff, U. (1982) *Das gesellige Jahrhundert: Gesellschaft und Gesellschaften im Zeitalter der Aufklärung*. Munich.
Im Hoff, U. (1994) *The Enlightenment*. Oxford.
Impey, O. and A. Macgregor (eds, 1985) *The Origins of Museums*. Oxford.
Infelise, M. (1997) 'Professione reportista. Copisti e gazzettieri nella Venezia del '600', in *Venezia: Itinerari per la storia della città*, ed. S. Gasparri, G. Levi and P. Moro (Bologna), pp. 193–219.
Infelise, M. (1999a) 'Le Marché des informations à Venise au 17e siècle', in H. Duranton and P. Rétat (eds, 1999) *Gazettes et information politique sous l'ancien régime* (Saint-Etienne), pp. 117–28.
Infelise, M. (1999b) *I libri proibiti da Gutenberg all'Encyclopédie*. Rome–Bari.
Innes, J. (1987) *The Collection and Use of Information by Government, circa 1690–1800*. Unpublished.
Innis, H. A. (1950) *Empire and Communications*. Oxford.
Innis, H. A. (1980) *The Idea File of Harold Innis*. Toronto.
Isaievych, I. (1993) 'The Book Trade in Eastern Europe in the Seventeenth and Eighteenth Centuries', in Brewer and Porter, pp. 381–92.
Israel, J. (1990a) 'The Amsterdam Stock Exchange and the English Revolution of 1688', *Tijdschrift voor Geschiedenis* 103, pp. 412–40.
Israel, J. (1990b) 'Een merkwaardig literair werk en de Amsterdamse effectenmarkt in 1688', in *De 17de eeuw* 6, pp. 159–65.

Itzkowitz, N. (1972) *Ottoman Empire and Islamic Tradition.* Princeton.

Jacob, C. (1992) *L'Empire des cartes.*

Jacob, C. (1996) 'Navigations alexandrines', in Baratin and Jacob, pp. 47–83.

Jacob, C. (1999) 'Mapping in the Mind', in *Mappings*, ed. D. Cosgrove, pp. 24–49.

Jardine, L. (1983) 'Isotta Nogarola', *History of Education* 12, pp. 231–44.

Jardine, L. (1985) 'The Myth of the Learned Lady in the Renaissance', *Historical Journal* 28, pp. 799–820.

Jardine, N., J. A. Secord and E. Spary (eds, 1996) *Cultures of Natural History.* Cambridge.

Johannisson, K. (1990) 'The Debate over Quantification in Eighteenth-Century Political Economy', in Frängsmyr, Tore et al. pp. 343–62.

Johansson, E. (1977) 'The History of Literacy in Sweden', rpr. in *Literacy and Social Development in the West*, ed. H. J. Graff (Cambridge, 1981), pp. 151–82.

Johns, A. (1998) *The Nature of the Book: Print and Knowledge in the Making.* Chicago.

Jukes, H. A. L. (ed., 1957) *Thomas Secker's Articles of Enquiry.* Oxford.

Julia, D. (1986) 'Les Institutions et les hommes (16e–18e siècles)', in Verger, pp. 141–97.

Kafker, F. A. (ed., 1981) *Notable Encyclopaedias.* Oxford.

Kahn, D. (1967) *The Code-Breakers: The Story of Secret Writing.* New York.

Kany, C. E. (1932) *Life and Manners in Madrid, 1750–1800.* Berkeley.

Kapp, V. (ed., 1993) *Les Lieux de mémoire et la fabrique de l'oeuvre.*

Karamustafa, A. T. (1992) 'Military, Administrative and Scholarly Maps and Plans', in Harley and Woodward vol. 2, part 1, pp. 209–27.

Kearney, H. (1970) *Scholars and Gentlemen: Universities and Society in Preindustrial Britain, 1500–1700.*

Keene, D. (1952), *The Japanese Discovery of Europe.*

Keens-Soper, H. M. A. (1972) 'The French Political Academy, 1712', *European Studies Review* 2, pp. 329–55.

Kelley, D. R. (1971) 'History as a Calling: The Case of La Popelinière', in A. Molho and J. A. Tedeschi, eds, *Renaissance Studies in Honor of Hans Baron* (Florence), pp. 773–89.

Kelley, D. R. (1980) 'Johann Sleidan and the Origins of History as a Profession', *Journal of Modern History* 52, pp. 577–98.

Kelley, D. R. (ed., 1997) *History and the Disciplines*. Rochester.

Kelley, D. R. and R. H. Popkin (eds, 1991) *The Shapes of Knowledge from the Renaissance to the Enlightenment*. Dordrecht.

Kelly, C. M. (1994) 'Later Roman Bureaucracy: Going through the Files', in *Literacy and Power in the Ancient World*, ed. A. K. Bowman and G. Woolf, Cambridge, pp. 161–76.

Kenney, E. J. (1974) *The Classical Text: Aspects of Editing in the Age of the Printed Book*. Berkeley.

Kenny, N. (1991) *The Palace of Secrets: Béroalde de Verville and Renaissance Conceptions of Knowledge*. Oxford.

Kenny, N. (1998) *Curiosity in Early Modern Europe: Word Histories*. Wiesbaden.

Keynes, G. (1940) *The Library of Edward Gibbon*. Second edn, 1980.

King, J. E. (1949) *Science and Rationalism in the Government of Louis XIV*. Baltimore.

King, M. L. (1976) 'Thwarted Ambitions: Six Learned Women of the Italian Renaissance', *Soundings* 59, pp. 280–300.

Kitchin, G. (1913) *Sir Roger L'Estrange*.

Klaits, J. (1971) 'Men of Letters and Political Reformation in France at the End of the Reign of Louis XIV: The Founding of the Académie Politique', *Journal of Modern History* 43, pp. 577–97.

Kley, E. J. Van (1971) 'Europe's "Discovery" of China and the Writing of World History', *American Historical Review* 76, pp. 358–85.

Klueting, H. (1986) *Die Lehre von Macht der Staaten*. Berlin.

Knorr-Cetina, K. (1981) *The Manufacture of Knowledge*. Oxford.

Knowles, M. D. (1958) 'Great Historical Enterprises: The Bollandists', *Transactions of the Royal Historical Society* 8, pp. 147–66.

Knowles, M. D. (1959) 'Great Historical Enterprises: The Maurists', *Transactions of the Royal Historical Society* 9, pp. 169–88.

Koeman, C. (1970) *Joan Blaeu and his Grand Atlas*. Amsterdam.

Koerner, L. (1996) 'Carl Linnaeus in his Time and Place', in Jardine, Secord and Spary, pp. 145–62.

Kolmar, L. (1979) 'Colbert und die Entstehung der Collection Doat', *Francia* 7, pp. 463–89.

Konvitz, J. (1987) *Cartography in France, 1660–1848*. Chicago.

Koran, R. (1874) *Der Kanzleienstreit*. Halle.

Kornicki, P. (1998) *The Book in Japan: A Cultural History from the Beginnings to the Nineteenth Century*. Leiden.

Koselleck, R. (1972) '*Begriffsgeschichte* and Social History', rpr. in his *Futures Past*, English translation, Cambridge, Mass., 1985, pp. 73–91.

Kristeller, P. O. (1951–2) 'The Modern System of the Arts', rpr. in his *Renaissance Thought*, II (New York, 1965), pp. 163–227.

Kristeller, P. O. (1955) 'The Humanist Movement', in his *Renaissance Thought* (New York, 1961), pp. 3–23.

Kühlmann, W. (1982) *Gelehrtenrepublik und Fürstenstaat*. Tübingen.

Kuhn, T. S. (1962) *The Structure of Scientific Revolutions*. Chicago.

Kusukawa, S. (1996) 'Bacon's Classification of Knowledge', in *The Cambridge Companion to Bacon*, ed. M. Peltonen (Cambridge), pp. 47–74.

Labrousse, E. (1963–4) *Pierre Bayle*, 2 vols. The Hague.

Labrousse, E. (1983) *Bayle*. Oxford.

Lach, D. (1965) *Asia in the Making of Europe*, part 1. Chicago.

Lach, D. (1977) *Asia in the Making of Europe*, part 2. Chicago.

Lach, D. and E. J. Van Kley (1993) *Asia in the Making of Europe*, part 3. Chicago.

Ladner, G. B. (1979) 'Medieval and Modern Understanding of Symbolism: A Comparison', *Speculum* 54, pp. 223–56.

Laeven, A. H. (1986) *Acta Eruditorum*. Amsterdam.

Lamb. U. (1969) 'Science by Litigation: A Cosmographic Feud', rpr. in her *Cosmographers and Pilots of the Spanish Maritime Empire* (Aldershot, 1995), III, pp. 40–57.

Lamb, U. (1976) 'Cosmographers of Seville', rpr. ibid., VI, pp. 675–86.

Lamo de Espinosa, E., J. M. González García and C. Torres Albero (1994) *La sociología del conocimiento y de la ciencia*. Madrid.

Landau, D. and P. Parshall (1994) *The Renaissance Print 1470–1550*. New Haven.

Lander, J. R. (1969) *Conflict and Stability in Fifteenth-Century England*.

Landes, D. S. (1998) *The Wealth and Poverty of Nations*.

Lankhorst, O. S. (1983) *Reinier Leers*. Amsterdam–Maarssen.

Lankhorst, O. S. (1990) 'Die snode uitwerkzels', *De 17de eeuw* 6, pp. 129–36.

Larrère, C. (1992) *L'Invention de l'économie au xviiie siècle*.

Latour, B. (1983) *Science in Action*.

Latour, B. (1986) 'Ces réseaux que la raison ignore: laboratoires, bibliothèques, collections', in Baratin and Jacob, pp. 23–46.

Law, J. (ed., 1986) *Power, Action and Belief: A New Sociology of Knowledge?*

Lawrence, S. C. (1996) *Charitable Knowledge: Hospital Pupils and Practitioners in Eighteenth-Century London*. Cambridge.

LeDonne, J. P. (1984) *Ruling Russia: Politics and Administration in the Age of Absolutism, 1762–1796*. Princeton.

Leedham-Green, E. (1987) *Books in Cambridge Inventories*, 2 vols. Cambridge.

Le Goff, J. (1957) *Intellectuals in the Middle Ages*, revised edn, 1985, English translation, Oxford, 1992.

Le Goff, J. (1977) *Time, Work and Culture in the Middle Ages*, English translation, Chicago, 1980.

Lemaine, G. et al. (eds, 1976) *Perspectives on the Emergence of Scientific Disciplines*. The Hague.

Lenoir, T. (1997) *Instituting Science*. Stanford.

Letwin, W. (1963) *The Origins of Scientific Economics: English Economic Thought, 1660–1776.*

Lévi-Strauss, C. (1962) *La Pensée Sauvage.*

Lévi-Strauss, C. (1964) *Le Cru et le cuit.*

Levy, F. (1982) 'How Information Spread among the Gentry, 1550–1640', *Journal of British Studies* 21, pp. 11–34.

Lieshout, H. H. M. van (1993) 'The Library of Pierre Bayle', in Canone, pp. 281–97.

Lieshout, H. H. M. van (1994) 'Dictionnaires et diffusion de savoir', in *Commercium Litterarium*, ed. H. Bots and F. Waquet (Amsterdam–Maarssen), pp. 131–50.

Lindey, A. (1952) *Plagiarism and Originality*. New York.

Lindqvist, S. (1984) *Technology on Trial: The Introduction of Steam Power Technology into Sweden, 1715–36.* Uppsala.

Lipking, L. (1977) 'The Marginal Gloss', *Critical Inquiry* 3, pp. 620–31.

Livingstone, D. N. (1995) 'The Spaces of Knowledge', *Society and Space* 13, pp. 5–34.

Long, P. O. (1991) 'Invention, Authorship, "Intellectual Property" and the Origin of Patents: Notes towards a Conceptual History', *Technology and Culture* 32, pp. 846–84.

Losman, A. (1983) 'The European Communications Network of Carl Gustaf Wrangel and Magnus Gabriel de la Gardie', in *Europe and Scandinavia*, ed. G. Rystad (Lund), pp. 199–206.

Lougee, C. C. (1976) *Le Paradis des femmes: Women, Salons and Social Stratification in Seventeenth-Century France*. Princeton.

Lough, J. (1968) *Essays on the Encyclopédie*. Oxford.

Lowood, H. E. (1990) 'The Calculating Forester', in Frängsmyr et al., pp. 315–42.

Lucas, C. (1989) 'Vers une nouvelle image de l'écrivain', in *L'Ecrivain face à son public*, ed. C. A. Fiorato and J.-C. Margolin, pp. 85–104.

Lugli, A. (1983) *Naturalia e Mirabilia. Il collezionismo enciclopedico nelle Wunderkammer d'Europa*. Milan.

Luhmann, N. (1990) 'The Cognitive Programme of Constructivism and a Reality that Remains Unknown', in *Self-Organisation*, ed. W. Krohn, G. Küpper and H. Novotny (Dordrecht), pp. 64–85.

Lukes, S. (1973) *Emile Durkheim.*

Lunsingh Scheurleer, T. H. and G. H. M. Posthumus Meyes (1975) *Leiden University in the Seventeenth Century.* Leiden.

Lux, D. S. (1991a) 'The Reorganisation of Science, 1450–1700', in Moran, pp. 185–94.

Lux, D. S. (1991b) 'Societies, Circles, Academies and Organisations', in Barker and Ariew, pp. 23–44.

McCarthy, E. D. (1996) *Knowledge as Culture: The New Sociology of Knowledge.*

McClellan, J. E., III (1985) *Science Reorganized: Scientific Societies in the Eighteenth Century.* New York.

MacDonald, M. and T. R. Murphy (1990) *Sleepless Souls: Suicide in Early Modern England.* Oxford.

Machlup, F. (1962) *The Production and Distribution of Knowledge in the United States.* Princeton.

Machlup, F. (1980–4) *Knowledge,* 3 vols. Princeton.

McKendrick, N., J. Brewer and J. H. Plumb (1982) *The Birth of a Consumer Society: The Commercialization of Eighteenth-Century England.*

McKenzie, D. F. (1992) 'The Economies of Print, 1550–1750: Scales of Production and Conditions of Constraint', in Cavaciocchi, pp. 389–426.

McKitterick, D. (1992) 'Bibliography, Bibliophily and the Organization of Knowledge', in *The Foundations of Scholarship,* ed. D. Vaisey and D. McKitterick (Los Angeles), pp. 29–64.

Macleod, R. (1987) 'On Visiting the "Moving Metropolis": Reflections on the Architecture of Imperial Science', rpr. in Storey, pp. 23–55.

Makdisi, G. (1981) *The Rise of Colleges: Institutions of Learning in Islam and the West.* Edinburgh.

Malherbe, M. (1994) 'Bacon, Diderot et l'ordre encyclopédique', *Revue de Synthèse* 115, pp. 13–38.

Mandosio, J.-M. (1993) 'L'Alchimie dans la classification des sciences et des arts à la Renaissance', in *Alchimie et philosophie à la Renaissance,* ed. J.-C. Margolin and S. Matton (Paris), pp. 11–42.

Mannheim, K. (1925) 'The Problem of a Sociology of Knowledge', English translation in his *Essays in the Sociology of Knowledge,* 1952, pp. 134–90.

Mannheim, K. (1927) Conservatism: A Contribution to the Sociology of Knowledge, English translation, 1986.

Mannheim, K. (1929) 'Competition as a Cultural Phenomenon', English translation in his *Essays in the Sociology of Knowledge,* 1952, pp. 191–229.

Mannheim, K. (1936) *Ideology and Utopia: an Introduction to the Sociology of Knowledge.*

Mannheim, K. (1952) 'The Problem of Generations', in his *Essays on the Sociology of Knowledge*, pp. 276–320.

Marini, G. (1825) 'Memorie istoriche degli archivi della S. Sede', rpr. in *Monumenta Vaticana*, ed. H. Laemmer (Freiburg), 1861, pp. 433–53.

Marsh, R. M. (1961) *The Mandarins: The Circulation of Elites in China, 1600–1900.* Glencoe.

Marshall, A. (1994) *Intelligence and Espionage in the Reign of Charles II.* Cambridge.

Martens, W. (1974) 'Die Geburt des Journalisten in der Aufklärung', in *Wolfenbütteler Studien zur Aufklärung*, vol. 1, ed. G. Schulz (Bremen), pp. 84–98.

Martin, H.-J. (1957) 'Les Bénédictins, leurs libraires et le pouvoir: notes sur le financement de la recherche au temps de Mabillon et de Montfaucon', *Revue Française de l'Histoire du Livre* 43, pp. 273–87.

Martin, H.-J. (1969) *Livre, pouvoirs et société à Paris au 17e siècle.*

Martin, H.-J. (1988) *Histoire et pouvoirs de l'écrit.*

Martin, H.-J. (1996) *The French Book: Religion, Absolutism, and Readership 1585–1715.* Baltimore.

Martin, H.-J. and R. Chartier (1983–4) *Histoire de l'édition française*, 2 vols.

Masseau, D. (1994) *L'Invention de l'intellectuel dans l'Europe du 18e siècle.*

Mattingly, G. (1955) *Renaissance Diplomacy.*

Mazauric, S. (1997) *Savoirs et philosophie à Paris dans la première moitié du 17e siècle: les conférences du bureau d'adresse de Théophraste Renaudot.*

Mazzone, U. and A. Turchini (eds, 1985) *Le visite pastorali.* Bologna.

Meier, H. (1966) *Die ältere deutsche Staats- und Verwaltungslehre.* Neuwied.

Meinecke, F. (1924–5) *Machiavellism*, English translation, 1957.

Meinel, C. (1988) 'Chemistry's Place in 18th-Century Universities', *History of Universities* 7, pp. 89–116.

Mendelsohn, E. (1977) 'The Social Construction of Scientific Knowledge', in *The Social Production of Scientific Knowledge*, ed. Mendelsohn (Dordrecht–Boston), pp. 3–26.

Merton, R. K. (1938) *Science, Technology and Society in Seventeenth-Century England*, revised edn, New York, 1970.

Merton, R. K. (1941) 'Karl Mannheim and the Sociology of Knowledge', rpr. in his *Social Theory and Social Structure*, revised edn, Glencoe, 1957, pp. 489–508.

Merton, R. K. (1945) 'The Sociology of Knowledge', ibid. pp. 456–88.

Merton, R. K. (1957) 'Priorities in Scientific Discovery', rpr. in his *Sociology of Science* (Chicago, 1973), pp. 286–324.

Merton, R. K. (1968) 'The Matthew Effect in Science', rpr. ibid., pp. 439–59.

Messick, B. (1993) *The Calligraphic State: Textual Domination and History in a Muslim Society*. Berkeley.

Metzger, T. (1973) *The Internal Organisation of Ch'ing Bureaucracy*.

Meyer, J. (1981) *Colbert*.

Middleton, W. E. K. (1971) *The Experimenters: A Study of the Accademia del Cimento*. Baltimore.

Miller, A. (1981) 'Louis Moréri's *Grand Dictionnaire Historique*', in Kafker, pp. 13–52.

Miller, D. P. (1996) 'Joseph Banks, Empire and "Centres of Calculation" in Late Hanoverian London', in *Visions of Empire*, ed. D. P. Miller and P. Reill (Cambridge), pp. 21–37.

Mills, C. W. (1940) 'The Language and Ideas of Ancient China', mimeo, rpr. in his *Power, Politics and People* (New York), pp. 469–520.

Mirot, L. (1924) *Roger de Piles*.

Miyazaki, I. (1963) *China's Examination Hell*, English translation, New York–Tokyo, 1976.

Money, J. (1993) 'Teaching in the Marketplace', in Brewer and Porter, pp. 335–80.

Monnet, N. (1996) 'L'Encyclopédisme en Chine', in Schaer, pp. 344–67.

Moore, W. E. and M. M. Tumin (1949) 'Some Social Functions of Ignorance', *American Sociological Review* 14, pp. 787–95.

Moran, B. T. (1991) 'Courts, Universities and Academies in Germany: An Overview, 1550–1750', in *Patronage and Institutions* (Woodbridge), pp. 169–94.

Morel-Fatio, A. (1913) *Historiographie de Charles V*.

Morgan, B. T. (1929) *Histoire du Journal des Savants depuis 1665 jusqu'en 1701*.

Morineau, M. (1985) *Incroyables gazettes et fabuleux métaux: les retours des trésors américains d'après les gazettes hollandaises*. Cambridge–Paris.

Moss, A. (1996) *Printed Commonplace Books and the Structuring of Renaissance Thought*. Oxford.

Moureau, F. (ed., 1995) *De bonne main: la communication manuscrite au 18e siècle*. Paris–Oxford.

Mundy, B. (1996) *The Mapping of New Spain: Indigenous Cartography and the Maps of the Relaciones Geográficas*. Chicago.

Murray, A. (1978) *Reason and Society in the Middle Ages.* Oxford.
Myers, R. and M. Harris (eds, 1992) *Censorship and the Control of Print in England and France, 1600–1910.* Winchester.
Nakagawa, H. (1992) 'L'Encyclopédie et le Japon', in his *Des lumières et du comparatisme: un regard japonais sur le 18e siècle,* pp. 237–68.
Nelles, P. N. (1997) 'The Library as an Instrument of Discovery', in Kelley, pp. 41–57.
Nigro, S. S. (1991) 'The Secretary', in *Baroque Personae,* ed. R. Villari, English translation (Chicago, 1995), pp. 82–99.
Nisard, C. (1860) *Les Gladiateurs de la république des lettres,* 2 vols.
Nordenmark, N. V. E. (1939) *Pehr Wilhelm Wargentin.* Uppsala.
Oakley, S. P. (1968) 'The Interception of Posts in Celle, 1694–1700', in *William III and Louis XIV,* ed. R. Hatton and J. S. Bromley (Liverpool), pp. 95–116.
Ollard, S. L. and P. C. Walker (eds, 1929–31) *Archbishop T. Herring's Visitation Returns,* 4 vols. York.
Olmi, G. (1992) *L'inventario del mondo.* Bologna.
O'Malley, J. and G. Bailey (eds, 1999) *The Jesuits.* Toronto.
Ong, W. (1958) *Ramus: Method and the Decay of Dialogue,* Cambridge, Mass.
Ophir, A. and Steven Shapin (1991) 'The Place of Knowledge', *Science in Context* 4, pp. 3–21.
Ornstein, M. (1913) *The Role of the Scientific Societies in the Seventeenth Century.* New York.
Palumbo, M. (1993a) 'La biblioteca lessicografica di Leibniz', in Canone, pp. 419–56.
Palumbo, M. (1993b) *Leibniz e la res bibliothecaria.* Rome.
Panofsky, E. (1953) 'Artist, Scientist, Genius', revised in *The Renaissance: Six Essays* (New York, 1962), pp. 123–82.
Pardo Tomás. J. (1991) *Ciencia y censura: la inquisición española y los libros científicos en los siglos xvi y xvii.* Madrid.
Pareto, V. (1916) *The Mind and Society,* English translation, 1935.
Parker, G. (1992) 'Maps and Ministers: The Spanish Habsburgs', in Buisseret, pp. 124–52.
Parker, G. (1998) *The Grand Strategy of Philip II.* New Haven.
Parker, I. (1914) *Dissenting Academies in England.* Cambridge.
Partner, P. (1980) 'Papal Financial Policy in the Renaissance and Counter-Reformation', *Past and Present* 88, pp. 17–62.
Partner, P. (1990) *The Pope's Men: The Papal Civil Service in the Renaissance.* Oxford.
Pearson, K. (1978) *The History of Statistics in the Seventeenth and Eighteenth Centuries.*

Pedersen, J. and G. Makdisi (1979) 'Madrasa', *Encyclopaedia of Islam*, vol. 5, pp. 1123–34. Leiden.

Pedersen, O. (1996) 'Tradition and Innovation', in Ridder-Symoens, pp. 452–88.

Pedley, M. S. (1979) 'The Subscription Lists of the *Atlas Universel* (1757): A Study in Cartographic Dissemination', *Imago Mundi* 31, pp. 66–77.

Pelletier, M. (1990) *La Carte de Cassini: l'extraordinaire aventure de la carte en France.*

Pels, D. (1996) 'Strange Standpoints: or How to Define the Situation for Situated Knowledge', *Telos* 108, pp. 65–91.

Pels, D. (1997) 'Mixing Metaphors: Politics or Economics of Knowledge', *Theory and Society* 26, pp. 685–717.

Perrot, J.-C. (1981) 'Les Dictionnaires de commerce au 18e siècle', *Revue d' Histoire Moderne et Contemporaine* 28, pp. 36–67.

Petrucci, A. (1995) 'Reading to Read', in *A History of Reading in the West*, ed. G. Cavallo and R. Chartier, English translation, Cambridge, 1999, pp. 345–67.

Phillips, H. (1997) *Church and Culture in Seventeenth-Century France.* Cambridge.

Phillips, P. (1990) *The Scientific Lady: A Social History of Women's Scientific Interests, 1520–1918.*

Picard, R. (1943) *Les Salons littéraires.*

Pinch, W. R. (1999) 'Same Difference in India and Europe', *History and Theory* 38, pp. 389–407.

Pinot, V. (1932) *La Chine et la formation de l'esprit philosophique en France, 1640–1740.*

Pintard, R. (1943) *Le Libertinage érudit dans la première moitié du 17e siècle*, revised edn, Geneva–Paris, 1983.

Pipes, R. (1960) 'The Historical Evolution of the Russian Intelligentsia', in Pipes, ed., *The Russian Intelligentsia*, pp. 47–62.

Plumb, J. H. (1973) *The Emergence of Leisure in the Eighteenth Century.* Reading.

Poelhekke, J. J. (1960) 'Lieuwe van Aitzema', rpr. in *Geschiedschrijving in Nederland*, ed. P. A. M. Geurts and A. E. M. Janssen (The Hague, 1981), pp. 97–116.

Pollard, G. and A. Ehrman (1965) *The Distribution of Books by Catalogue.* Cambridge.

Pomian, K. (1972) 'Les Historiens et les archives dans la France du 17e siècle', *Acta Poloniae Historica* 26, pp. 109–25.

Pomian, K. (1973) 'De la lettre au périodique: la circulation des informations dans les milieux des historiens au 17e siècle', *Organon* 9, pp. 25–43.

Pomian, K. (1987) *Collectors and Curiosities*, English translation, Cambridge, 1990.

Popkin, J. D. (1990) *Revolutionary News: The Press in France 1789–99*. Durham, NC.

Popkin, R. H. (1960) *History of Scepticism from Erasmus to Spinoza*, revised edn, Berkeley–Los Angeles, 1979.

Porter, R. (1989) *Health for Sale*.

Porter, R. (1996) 'The Scientific Revolution and Universities', in Ridder-Symoens, pp. 531–64.

Post, G. (1932) 'Masters' Salaries and Students' Fees in the Medieval Universities', *Speculum* 7, pp. 181–98.

Post, G., K. Giocarini and R. Kay (1955) 'The Medieval Heritage of a Humanist Ideal', *Traditio* 11, pp. 195–234.

Poster, M. (1990) *The Mode of Information*. Cambridge.

Potter, E. (1993) 'Gender and Epistemic Negotiation', in Alcoff and Potter, pp. 161–86.

Pred, A. (1973) *Urban Growth and the Circulation of Information*. New York.

Preto, P. (1994) *I servizi segreti di Venezia*. Milan.

Principe, L. M. (1992) 'Robert Boyle's Alchemical Secrecy: Codes, Ciphers and Concealment', *Ambix* 39, pp. 63–74.

Prodi, P. (1982) *The Papal Prince*, English translation, Cambridge, 1987.

Prosperi, A. (1981) 'Intellettuali e chiesa all'inizio dell'età moderna', in *Storia d'Italia, Annali*, vol. 4 (Turin), pp. 161–252.

Prosperi, A. (1996) *Tribunali di coscienza: inquisitori, confessori, missionari*. Turin.

Prosperi, A. (1997) 'Effetti involontari della censura', in *La censura libraria nell'Europa del secolo xvi*, ed. U. Rozzo (Udine), pp. 147–62.

Proust, J. (1962) *Diderot et l'Encyclopédie*.

Pulido Rubio, J. (1950) *El Piloto Mayor de la Casa de la Contratación de Sevilla*. Seville.

Pumfrey, S., P. L. Rossi and M. Slawinski (eds, 1991) *Science, Culture and Popular Belief in Renaissance Europe*. Manchester.

Quedenbaum, G. (1977) *Der Verleger J. H. Zedler*. Hildesheim.

Queller, D. (1973) 'The Development of Ambassadorial *Relazioni*', in *Renaissance Venice*, ed. J. R. Hale, pp. 174–96.

Raeff, M. (1983) *The Well-Ordered Police State*. New Haven.

Ranum, R. (1963) *Richelieu and the Councillors of Louis XIII*. Oxford.

Rassem, M. and J. Stagl (eds, 1980) *Statistik und Staatsbeschreibung in der Neuzeit*. Paderborn.

Rassem, M. and J. Stagl (eds, 1994) *Geschichte der Staatsbeschreibung: Ausgewählte Quellentexte, 1456–1813*. Berlin.

Raven, J. (1992) 'Book Distribution Networks in Early Modern Europe: The Case of the Western Fringe, c.1400–1800', in Cavaciocchi, pp. 583–630.

Raven, J. (1993) 'Selling Books across Europe c.1450–1800: An Overview', *Publishing History* 34, pp. 5–20.

Rawski, E. S. (1979) *Education and Popular Literacy in Ch'ing China*. Ann Arbor.

Rawski, E. S. (1985) 'Economic and Social Foundations', in *Popular Culture in Late Imperial China*, ed. D. Johnson, A. J. Nathan and E. S. Rawski (Berkeley) Los Angeles, pp. 3–33.

Reichardt, R. (1989) 'Prints: Images of the Bastille', in Darnton and Roche, pp. 223–51.

Reichmann, E. (1968) *Der Herrschaft der Zahl. Quantitatives Denken in der Deutschen Aufklärung*. Stuttgart.

Reinhartz, D. (1987) 'Shared Vision: Herman Moll and his Circle and the Great South Sea', *Terrae Incognitae* 19, pp. 1–10.

Reinhartz, D. (1994) 'In the Service of Catherine the Great: The Siberian Explorations and Map of Sir Samuel Bentham', *Terrae Incognitae* 26, pp. 49–60.

Reiss, T. J. (1997) *Knowledge, Discovery and Imagination in Early Modern Europe: The Rise of Aesthetic Rationalism*. Cambridge.

Rennie, N. (1995) *Far-Fetched Facts: The Literature of Travel and the Idea of the South Seas*. Oxford.

Repp, R. (1972) 'Some Observations on the Development of the Ottoman Learned Hierarchy', in *Scholars, Saints and Sufis*, ed. N. R. Keddie (Berkeley), pp. 17–32.

Repp, R. (1986) *The Müfti of Istanbul: A Study in the Development of the Ottoman Learned Hierarchy*.

Revel, J. (1991) 'Knowledge of the Territory', *Science in Context* 4, pp. 133–61.

Revel, J. (1996) 'Entre deux mondes: la bibliothèque de Gabriel Naudé', in Baratin and Jacob, pp. 243–50.

Rey, R. (1994) 'La classification des sciences', *Revue de Synthèse* 115, pp. 5–12.

Richardson, B. (1994) *Print Culture in Renaissance Italy: The Editor and the Vernacular Text, 1470–1600*. Cambridge.

Richardson, B. (1999) *Printing, Writers and Readers in Renaissance Italy*. Cambridge.

Richter, L. (1946) *Leibniz und Russland*. Berlin.

Ridder-Symoens, H. de (ed., 1992) *A History of the University in Europe: The Middle Ages*. Cambridge.

Ridder-Symoens, H. de (ed., 1996) *A History of the University in Europe: Universities in Early Modern Europe, 1500–1800.* Cambridge.

Ringer, F. K. (1969) *The Decline of the German Mandarins: The German Academic Community, 1890–1933.* Cambridge, Mass.

Ringer, F. K. (1990) 'The Intellectual Field, Intellectual History and the Sociology of Knowledge', *Theory and Society* 19, pp. 269–94.

Ringer, F. K. (1992) *Fields of Knowledge: French Academic Culture in Comparative Perspective, 1890–1920.* Cambridge.

Robinson, E. (1975) 'The Transference of British Technology to Russia, 1760–1820', in *Great Britain and her World, 1750–1914,* ed. B. M. Ratcliffe (Manchester), pp. 1–26.

Robinson, F. (1993) 'Technology and Religious Change: Islam and the Impact of Print', *Modern Asian Studies* 27, pp. 229–51, revised and enlarged as 'Islam and the Impact of Print in South Asia', in *The Transmission of Knowledge in South Asia,* ed. N. Crook (Delhi, 1996), pp. 62–97.

Roche, D. (1976) 'L'Histoire dans les activités des académies provinciales en France au 18e siècle', in Hammer and Voss, pp. 260–95.

Roche, D. (1978) *Le Siècle des lumières en province.* The Hague.

Roche, D. (1981) *The People of Paris,* English translation, Leamington, 1987.

Roche, D. (1982) 'L'Intellectuel au travail', rpr. in his *Les Républicains des lettres* (1988), pp. 225–41.

Roche, D. (1989) 'Censorship and the Publishing Industry', in Darnton and Roche, pp. 3–26.

Rochot, B. (1966) 'Le Père Mersenne et les relations intellectuelles dans l'Europe du 17e siècle', *Cahiers d'Histoire Mondiale* 10, pp. 55–73.

Rogers, P. (1972) *Grub Street.*

Romano, R. and A. Tenenti (1967) 'L'Intellectuel dans la société italienne des 15e et 16e siècles', in *Niveaux de culture,* ed. L. Bergeron, pp. 51–65.

Rosa, M. (1994) 'Un médiateur dans la République des Lettres: le bibliothécaire', in *Commercium Literarium,* ed. H. Bots and F. Waquet (Amsterdam–Maarssen), pp. 81–100.

Rose, M. (1988) 'The Author as Proprietor', *Representations* 23, pp. 51–85.

Rose, M. (1993) *Authors and Owners.* Cambridge, Mass.

Rosenthal, F. (1970) *Knowledge Triumphant.* Leiden.

Rossi, P. (1960) *Clavis Universalis: Arti Mnemoniche e Logica Combinatoria da Lullo a Leibniz.* Milan–Naples.

Rossi, P. (1962) *Philosophy, Technology and the Arts in the Early Modern Era*, English translation, New York, 1970.

Rothkrug, L. (1965) *Opposition to Louis XIV: The Political and Social Origins of the French Enlightenment*. Princeton.

Rouse, R. H. and M. A. Rouse (1982) 'Statim invenire: Schools, Preachers and New Attitudes to the Page', in *Renaissance and Renewal*, ed. R. L. Benson and G. Constable (Cambridge, Mass.), pp. 201–25.

Rouse, R. H. and M. A. Rouse (1983) 'La naissance des index', in Martin and Chartier vol. 1, pp. 77–86.

Rowen, H. H. (1987) 'Lieuwe van Aitzema', in *Politics and Culture in Early Modern Europe*, ed. P. Mack and M. Jacob (Cambridge), pp. 169–82.

Rubin, M. R. and M. T. Huber (1986) *The Knowledge Industry in the United States, 1960–1980*. New Haven.

Rüegg, W. (1992) 'The Rise of Humanism', in Ridder-Symoens, pp. 442–68.

Ruestow, E. G. (1973) *Physics at 17th and 18thc Leiden*. The Hague.

Said, E. (1978) *Orientalism*, second edn, 1995.

Salmond, A. (1982) 'Theoretical Landscapes: On Cross-Cultural Conceptions of Knowledge', in *Semantic Anthropology*, ed. D. Parkin, pp. 65–88.

Santos Lopes, M. dos (1992) *Afrika: eine neue Welt in deutschen Schriften des 16. und 17. Jht.* Stuttgart.

Santschi, C. (1978) *La Censure à Genève au 17e siècle*. Geneva.

Sardella, P. (1948) *Nouvelles et spéculations à Venise*.

Saunders, S. (1991) 'Public Administration and the Library of J.-B. Colbert', *Libraries and Culture* 26, pp. 282–300.

Sazonova, L. (1996) 'Die Entstehung der Akademien in Russland', in K. Garber and H. Wismann (eds), *Die europäischen Akademien* (Tübingen), pp. 966–92.

Schaer, R. (ed., 1996) *Tous les savoirs du monde: encyclopédies et bibliothèques, de Sumer au xxie siècle*.

Schaffer, S. (1996) 'Afterword', in *Visions of Empire*, ed. D. P. Miller and P. Reill (Cambridge), pp. 335–52.

Scheler, M. (1926) *Die Wissensformen und die Gesellschaft*. Leipzig.

Schiebinger, L. (1989) *The Mind has no Sex?* Cambridge, Mass.

Schilder, G. (1976) 'Organisation and Evolution of the Dutch East India Company's Hydrographic Office', *Imago Mundi* 28, pp. 61–78.

Schiller, H. I. (1986) *Information and the Crisis Economy*. New York.

Schiller, H. I. (1996) *Information Inequality: The Deepening Social Crisis in America*.

Schilling, H. (1983) 'Innovation through Migration', *Histoire Sociale* 16, pp. 7–34.

Schmidt-Biggemann, W. (1983) *Topica universalis: eine Modellgeschichte humanistischer und barocker Wissenschaft*. Hamburg.

Schmidt-Biggemann, W. (1996) 'New Structures of Knowledge', in Ridder-Symoens, pp. 489–530.

Schöffler, H. (1936) *Wirkungen der Reformation*, rpr. Frankfurt, 1960.

Schottenloher, K. (1933) 'Die Druckprivilegien', *Gutenberg Jahrbuch*, pp. 89–111.

Schottenloher, K. (1935) *Der Buchdrucker als neuer Berufstand des 15. und 16. Jahrhunderts*. Berlin.

Schulte-Albert, H. G. (1971) 'G. W. Leibniz and Library Classification', *Journal of Library History* 6, pp. 133–52.

Schumpeter, J. (1942) *Capitalism, Socialism and Democracy*.

Scott, J. (1991) 'Ignorance and Revolution: Perceptions of Social Reality in Revolutionary Marseilles', in *Interpretation and Cultural History*, ed. J. Pittock and A. Wear, pp. 235–68.

Sealy, R. J. (1981) *The Palace Academy of Henry III*. Geneva.

Seguin, J.-P. (1964) *L'Information en France avant le périodique, 1529–1631*.

Seifert, A. (1976) *Cognitio historica: die Geschichte als Namengeberin der frühneuzeitliche Empirie*. Berlin.

Seifert, A. (1980) 'Staatenkunde', in Rassem and Stagl, pp. 217–48.

Seifert, A. (1983) 'Conring und die Begründung der Staatenkunde', in Stolleis, pp. 201–16.

Serjeantson, R. (1999) 'Introduction' to Meric Casaubon, *Generall Learning* (Cambridge), pp. 1–65 [first edn of seventeenth-century text].

Serrai, A. (1988–92) *Storia della bibliografia*, 5 vols. Rome.

Serrai, A. (1990) *Conrad Gessner*, ed. M. Cochetti. Rome.

Seymour, W. A. (ed., 1980) *A History of the Ordnance Survey*. Folkestone.

Sgard, J. (ed., 1976) *Dictionnaire des journalistes (1600–1789)*. Grenoble.

Sgard, J. (1987) 'Et si les anciens étaient modernes . . . le système du P. Hardouin', in *D'un siècle à l'autre*, ed. L. Godard de Donville (Marseilles), pp. 209–20.

Sgard, J. (ed., 1991) *Dictionnaire des journaux, 1600–1789*, 2 vols.

Shaaber, M. (1929) *Some Forerunners of the Newspaper, 1476–1622*. Philadelphia.

Shackleton, R. (1961) *Montesquieu: An Intellectual and Critical Biography*. Oxford.

Shackleton, R. (1970) *The Encyclopaedia and the Clerks*. Oxford.

Shapin, S. (1982) 'History of Science and its Sociological Reconstructions', revised in *Cognition and Fact*, ed. R. S. Cohen and T. Schnelle (Dordrecht), pp. 325–86.

Shapin, S. (1988) 'The House of Experiment in Seventeenth-Century England', *Isis* 79, pp. 373–404.

Shapin, S. (1994) *A Social History of Truth: Civility and Science in Seventeenth-Century England*. Chicago.

Shapin, S. (1996) *The Scientific Revolution*. Chicago.

Shapin, S. and S. Schaffer (1985) *Leviathan and the Air-Pump: Hobbes, Boyle and the Experimental Life*. Princeton.

Shapiro, B. J. (1983) *Probability and Certainty in Seventeenth-Century England*. Princeton.

Shapiro, B. J. (1991) *Beyond Reasonable Doubt*. Berkeley.

Shapiro, B. J. (1994) 'The Concept "Fact": Legal Origins and Cultural Diffusion', *Albion* 26, pp. 1–26.

Shaw, D. J. B. (1996) 'Geographical Practice and its Significance in Peter the Great's Russia', *Journal of Historical Geography* 22, pp. 160–76.

Sher, R. B. (1997) '*Charles V* and the Book Trade: An Episode in Enlightenment Print Culture', in S. J. Brown (ed.) *William Robertson and the Expansion of Empire* (Cambridge), pp. 164–95.

Sherman, W. (1995) *John Dee: The Politics of Reading and Writing in the English Renaissance*. Amherst.

Shively, D. H. (1991) 'Popular Culture', in *Early Modern Japan*, ed. J. W. Hall (Cambridge), pp. 706–69.

Shteir, A. B. (1996) *Cultivating Women, Cultivating Science*. Baltimore.

Siebert, F. S. (1965) *Freedom of the Press in England, 1476–1776*. Urbana.

Slaughter, M. M. (1982) *Universal Language and Scientific Taxonomy in the Seventeenth Century*. Cambridge.

Smith, P. H. (1994) *The Business of Alchemy: Science and Culture in the Holy Roman Empire*. Princeton.

Smith, W. D. (1984) 'Amsterdam as an Information Exchange in the Seventeenth Century', *Journal of Economic History* 44, pp. 985–1005.

Solomon, H. M. (1972) *Public Welfare, Science and Propaganda*. Princeton.

Solt, L. F. (1956) 'Anti-intellectualism in the Puritan Revolution', *Church History* 25, pp. 306–16.

Soucek, S. (1992) 'Islamic Charting in the Mediterranean', in Harley and Woodward vol. 2, part 1, pp. 263–92.

Stagl, J. (1980) 'Die Apodemik oder "Reisekunst" als Methodik der Sozialforschung vom Humanismus bis zur Aufklärung', in Rassem and Stagl, pp. 131–202.

Stagl, J. (1995) *The History of Curiosity*. Chur.

Stark, W. (1960) *Montesquieu, Pioneer of the Sociology of Knowledge*.

Steensgaard, N. (1982) 'The Dutch East India Company as an Institutional Innovation', in *Dutch Capitalism and World Capitalism*, ed. M. Aymard (Cambridge–Paris), pp. 235–57.

Stegmann, J. (1988) 'Comment constituer une bibliothèque en France au début du 17e siècle', in Aquilon and Martin, pp. 467–501.

Stehr, N. (1992) 'Experts, Counsellors and Advisers', in Stehr and Ericson, pp. 107–55.

Stehr, N. (1994) *Knowledge Societies*.

Stehr, N. and R. V. Ericson (eds, 1992) *The Culture and Power of Knowledge*. Berlin–New York.

Stehr, N. and V. Meja (eds, 1984) *Society and Knowledge*. New Brunswick.

Stenzel, H. (1993) 'Gabriel Naudé et l'utopie d'une bibliothèque idéale', in Kapp, pp. 103–15.

Stevenson, E. L. (1927) 'The Geographical Activities of the *Casa de la Contratación*', *Annals of the Association of American Geographers* 17, pp. 39–52.

Stewart, L. (1992) *The Rise of Public Science: Rhetoric, Technology and Natural Philosophy in Newtonian Britain, 1660–1750*. Cambridge.

Stichweh, R. (1991) *Der frühmoderne Staat und die europäische Universität*. Frankfurt.

Stigler, G. J. (1961) 'The Economics of Information', *Journal of Political Economy* 69, pp. 213–25.

Stock, B. (1983) *The Implications of Literacy*. Princeton.

Stolleis, M. (1980) *Arcana Imperii und Ratio Status*. Göttingen.

Stolleis, M. (1983) 'Die Einheit der Wissenschaften – Hermann Conring', in *Hermann Conring (1606–1681)* (Berlin), pp. 11–34.

Storey, W. K. (ed., 1996) *Scientific Aspects of European Expansion*. Aldershot.

Strauss, G. (1975) 'Success and Failure in the German Reformation', *Past and Present* 67, pp. 30–63.

Stroup, A. (1990) *A Company of Scientists: Botany, Patronage and Community at the Seventeenth-Century Parisian Royal Academy of Sciences*. Berkeley–Los Angeles.

Sutherland, J. R. (1986) *The Restoration Newspaper*. Cambridge.

Switzer, R. (1967) 'America in the *Encyclopédie*', *Studies on Voltaire* 58, pp. 1481–99.

Taylor, A. R. (1945) *Renaissance Guides to Books*. Berkeley–Los Angeles.

Tega, W. (1984) *Arbor scientiarum*. Bologna.

Teixeira de Mota, A. (1976) 'Some Notes on the Organisation of Hydrographical Services in Portugal', *Imago Mundi* 28, pp. 51–60.

Teng, S.-Y. (1942–3) 'Chinese Influence on the Western Examination System', *Harvard Journal of Asiatic Studies* 7, pp. 267–312.

Teng, S.-Y. and K. Biggerstaff (1936) *An Annotated Bibliography of Selected Chinese Reference Works*, revised edn, Cambridge, Mass., 1950.

Tennant, E. C. (1996) 'The Protection of Invention: Printing Privileges in Early Modern Germany', in *Knowledge, Science and Literature in Early Modern Germany*, ed. G. S. Williams and S. K. Schindler (Chapel Hill), pp. 7–48.

Thiel-Horstmann, M. (1980) 'Staatsbeschreibung und Statistische Erhebungen im Vorkolonialen und Kolonialen Indien', in Rassem and Stagl, pp. 205–13.

Thomas, K. V. (1971) *Religion and the Decline of Magic: Studies in Popular Beliefs in Sixteenth and Seventeenth Century England*.

Thorndike, L. (1951) 'Newness and Novelty in Seventeenth-Century Science', *Journal of the History of Ideas* 12, pp. 584–98.

Thrift, N. (1985) 'Flies and Germs: A Geography of Knowledge', in *Social Relations and Spatial Structures*, ed. D. Gregory and J. Urry, pp. 366–403.

Thrift, N., F. Driver and D. Livingstone (1995) 'The Geography of Truth', *Society and Space* 13, pp. 1–3.

Toscani, I. (1980) 'Etatistisches Denken und Erkenntnis-theoretische Überlegungen in den Venezianischen Relationen', in Rassem and Stagl, pp. 111–25.

Trenard, L. (1965–6) 'Le Rayonnement de l'*Encyclopédie*', *Cahiers d'Histoire Moderne* 9, pp. 712–47.

Tucci, U. (1990) 'Ranke and the Venetian Document Market', in *Leopold von Ranke and the Shaping of the Historical Discipline*, ed. G. G. Iggers and J. M. Powell (Syracuse), pp. 99–108.

Turner, R. (ed., 1974) *Ethnomethodology*. Harmondsworth.

Tyacke, N. (1978) 'Science and Religion at Oxford before the Civil War', in *Puritans and Revolution*, ed. D. Pennington and K. V. Thomas (Oxford), pp. 73–93.

Unno, K. (1994) 'Cartography in Japan', in Harley and Woodward, vol. 2, pt 2, pp. 346–477.

Vandermeersch, P. A. (1996) 'Teachers', in Ridder-Simoens, pp. 210–55.

Van Leeuwen, H. G. (1963) *The Problem of Certainty in English Thought 1630–90*. The Hague.

Veblen, T. (1906) 'The Place of Science in Modern Civilisation', *American Journal of Sociology* 11, pp. 585–609.

Veblen, T. (1918) *The Higher Learning in America: A Memorandum on the Conduct of Universities by Businessmen.* New York.

Veblen, T. (1919) 'The Intellectual Pre-eminence of Jews in Modern Europe', *Political Science Quarterly* 34, pp. 33–42.

Venard, M. (1985) 'Le visite pastorali francesi dal xvi al xviii secolo', in Mazzone and Turchini, pp. 13–55.

Venturi, F. (1959) 'Contributi ad un dizionario storico', *Rivista Storica Italiana* 71, pp. 119–30.

Verger, J. (1997) *Les Gens de savoir en Europe à la fin du Moyen Age.*

Vericat, J. (1982) 'La "organizatoriedad" del saber en la España del siglo xvi', in *Homenaje a G. F. de Oviedo,* ed. F. de Solano and F. del Pino, 2 vols (Madrid), vol. 1, pp. 381–415.

Verner, C. (1978) 'John Seller and the Chart Trade in Seventeenth-Century England', in N. J. W. Thrower (ed.), *The Complete Plattmaker* (Berkeley), pp. 127–58.

Viala, A. (1985) *Naissance de l'écrivain.*

Villey, P. (1908) *Les Sources et l'évolution des Essais de Montaigne,* 2 vols.

Völkel, M. (1987) *'Pyrrhonismus historicus' und 'fides historica': die Entwicklung der deutschen historischen Methodologie unter dem Gesichtspunkt der historischen Skepsis.* Frankfurt.

Voss, J. (1972) *Das Mittelalter im historischen Denken Frankreichs.* Munich.

Voss, J. (1979) *Universität, Geschichtswissenschaft und Diplomatie im Zeitalter der Aufklärung: Johann Daniel Schöpflin (1694–1771).* Munich.

Voss, J. (1980) 'Die Akademien als Organisationsträger der Wissenschaften im 18. Jht', *Historisches Zeitschrift* 231, pp. 43–74.

Vucinich, A. (1963) *Science in Russian Culture: A History to 1860.* Stanford.

Walker, R. B. (1973) 'Advertising in London Newspapers 1650–1750', *Business History* 15 (1973) pp. 112–30.

Wallis, P. J. (1974) 'Book Subscription Lists', *The Library* 29, pp. 255–86.

Wallis, R. (ed., 1979) *On the Margins of Science: The Social Construction of Rejected Knowledge.* Keele.

Walzer, M. (1965) *The Revolution of the Saints: A Study in the Origins of Radical Politics.* Cambridge, Mass.

Wansink, H. (1975) *Politieke Wetenschappen aan de Leidse Universiteit.* Leiden.

Waquet, F. (1993a) 'Book Subscription Lists in Early Eighteenth-Century Italy', *Publishing History* 33, pp. 77–88.

Waquet, F. (1993b) 'Le *Polyhistor* de Daniel Georg Morhof, lieu de mémoire de la République des Lettres', in Kapp, pp. 47–60.

Weber, M. (1920) *Economy and Society*, English trans., 3 vols, New York, 1968.

Webster, C. (1975) *The Great Instauration: Science, Medicine and Reform, 1626–1660.*

Webster, F. (1995) *Theories of the Information Society.*

Wellisch, H. H. (1991) *Indexing from A to Z*, revised edn, New York, 1995.

Wells, J. M. (1966) *The Circle of Knowledge.*

Wernham, R. B. (1956) 'The Public Records', in *English Historical Scholarship*, ed. L. Fox, pp. 11–30.

Wiener, N. (1948) *Cybernetics.*

Williams, A. (1979) *The Police of Paris, 1718–89.* Baton Rouge.

Wilson, A. M. (1972) *Diderot.* New York.

Wilterdink, N. (1977) 'Norbert Elias's Sociology of Knowledge', in *Human Figurations*, pp. 110–26.

Winch, D. (1990) 'Economic Knowledge and Government in Britain: Some Historical and Comparative Reflexions', in M. O. Furner and B. Supple (eds), *The State and Economic Knowledge* (Cambridge), pp. 40–70.

Winch, D. (1993) 'The Science of the Legislator: The Enlightenment Heritage', in M. Lacey and M. O. Furner (eds), *The State and Social Investigation in Britain and the United States* (Cambridge), pp. 63–91.

Withers, C. W. J. (1998) 'Towards a History of Geography in the Public Sphere', *History of Science* 36, pp. 45–78.

Witty, F. J. (1965) 'Early Indexing Techniques', *The Library Quarterly* 35, pp. 141–8.

Wood, P. (1993) *The Aberdeen Enlightenment: The Arts Curriculum in the Eighteenth Century.* Aberdeen.

Woodmansee, M. (1984) 'The Genius and the Copyright: Economic and Legal Conditions for the Emergence of the Author', *Eighteenth-Century Studies* 17, pp. 425–48.

Woods, J. M. (1987) 'Das "Gelahrte Frauenzimmer" und die deutsche Frauenlexika 1631–1743', in *Res Publica Litteraria*, ed. Sebastian Neumeister and Conrad Wiedemann, 2 vols (Wiesbaden), pp. 577–88.

Woolf, D. R. (1988) 'History, Folklore and Oral Tradition in Early Modern England', *Past and Present* 120, pp. 26–52.

Woolgar, S. (ed., 1988) *Knowledge and Reflexivity.*

Worsley, P. (1956) 'Emile Durkheim's Theory of Knowledge', *Sociological Review*, 47–61.

Worsley, P. (1997) *Knowledges: What Different Peoples Make of the World*.

Yardeni, M. (1973) 'Journalisme et histoire contemporaine à l'époque de Bayle', *History and Theory* 12, pp. 208–29.

Yardeni, M. (1985) 'Naissance du journalisme moderne', in her *Le Refuge protestant*, pp. 201–7.

Yates, F. (1947) *French Academies of the Sixteenth Century*.

Yates, F. (1964) *Giordano Bruno and the Hermetic Tradition*.

Yates, F. (1966) *The Renaissance Art of Memory*.

Yates, F. (1979) *The Occult Philosophy in the Elizabethan Age*.

Yazaki, T. (1968) *Social Change and the City in Japan*. Tokyo.

Yee, C. D. K. (1994a) 'Chinese Maps in Political Culture', in Harley and Woodward, vol. 2, pt 2, pp. 71–95.

Yee, C. D. K. (1994b) 'Traditional Chinese Cartography and the Myth of Westernisation', in Harley and Woodward, vol. 2, pt 2, pp. 170–202.

Yeo, R. (1991) 'Reading Encyclopaedias: Science and the Organisation of Knowledge in British Dictionaries of Arts and Sciences, 1730–1850', *Isis* 82, pp. 24–49.

Yeo, R. (1996) 'Ephraim Chambers' Cyclopaedia (1728) and the Tradition of Commonplaces', *Journal of the History of Ideas* 57, pp. 157–75.

Zacharias, T. (1960) *Joseph Emmanuel Fischer von Erlach*. Vienna.

Zedelmaier, H. (1992) *Bibliotheca Universalis und Bibliotheca Selecta: das Problem der Ordnung des gelehrten Wissens in der frühen Neuzeit*. Cologne.

Zhang, L. (1998) *Mighty Opposites: From Dichotomies to Differences in the Comparative Study of China*. Stanford.

Ziegler, W. (1981) 'Tentativi di Accademia in ambito monastico nella Germania del xviii secolo', in L. Boehm and E. Raimondi (eds), *Università, accademie in Italia e Germania dal '500 al '700* (Bologna), pp. 355–78.

Zilfi, M. C. (1988) *The Politics of Piety: The Ottoman Ulema in the Post-classical Age*. Minneapolis.

Zilsel, E. (1926) *Die Entstehung des Geniebegriffes*. Tübingen.

Zilsel, E. (1941a) 'Problems of Empiricism', in *The Development of Rationalism and Empiricism* (Chicago), pp. 53–94.

Zilsel, E. (1941b) 'Origins of William Gilbert's Scientific Method', *Journal of the History of Ideas* 2, pp. 1–32.

Ziman, J. (1978) *Reliable Knowledge*. Cambridge.

Znaniecki, F. (1940) *The Social Role of the Man of Knowledge*. New York.

INDEX

Deshima, 59–60

detachment, 2, 18, 22, 26, 32, 51

Deutsch, Karl (born 1912), Czech-American political scientist, 116

Dewey, John (1859–1952), American philosopher, 3, 105

Dewey, Melville (1851–1931), American librarian, 105

dictionaries, 76

Diderot, Denis (1713–84), French encyclopaedist, 17, 25, 29, 48, 77, 111, 115, 143, 151, 172, 193

Dissenting academies, 45

distanciation *see* detachment

Dodoens, Rembert (1516–85), Dutch botanist, 38, 101

Domesday Book, 118

Domínguez, Francisco (late 16th century) Portuguese cosmographer, 132

Doni, Antonfrancesco (1513–74), Italian writer, 103

Doria, Paolo Mattia (1662–1746), Italian philosopher, 195

Dorpat (Tartu), 69

Dousa, Janus (1545–1604), Dutch humanist, 38

Dryden, John (1631–1700), English poet and historian, 27, 48

Dublin, 47, 111, 167

Du Cange, Charles du Fresne, sieur (1610–88), French scholar, 25, 188

Du Halde, Jean-Baptiste (1674–1743), French Jesuit, 77, 193

Du Pin, Louis-Ellies (1657–1719), French priest and scholar, 189

Durie, John (1596–1680), English divine, 56, 110, 114, 152

Durkheim, Emile (1858–1917), French anthropologist and sociologist, 3, 7, 81

Eachard, John (*c.* 1636–97), Master of Catherine Hall Cambridge, 171

East India Company (British), 16, 66–7, 156

East India Company (Dutch), 59–60, 63–4, 76, 157–8

East India Company (French), 126, 157

Ecluse, Charles de l' (1526–1609), Flemish naturalist, 38

economics, 1, 15, 101–2

Edwards, Jonathan (1703–56), New England clergyman, 58

Egypt, 190, 194

Eisenhart, Johannes (1643–1707), German professor, 209

Elias, Norbert (1897–1990), German sociologist, 7, 22, 33, 91

Elsevier family, Dutch printers, 164, 190

Emili, Paolo (*c.* 1460–1529), Italian historian, 187

empiricism, 16, 205–6

experiment, 39, 46

encyclopaedias, 12–13, 93–6, 102, 109–10, 171–3, 175, 184, 186–7

Encyclopédie, 11, 16–17, 28–9, 48, 85–6, 111, 115, 143, 151, 167, 172, 184, 186–7, 193–4

Erasmus, Desiderius (*c.* 1466–1536), Netherlands humanist, 22, 24, 36, 55, 85, 95, 185, 207

Eratosthenes (*c.* 276–*c.* 194 BC), Greek astronomer and geographer, 75

Erfurt, 111

Escorial, 68

Espinasse, Julie de l' (1752–76), salon hostess, 48

Esquivel, Pedro de (late 16th century), Spanish mathematician, 132

Ethiopia, 63, 107, 194

Euler, Leonhard (1707–83), German mathematician, 70

Evelyn, John (1620–1706), English virtuoso, 107, 109

Evreinov, Ivan (died 1724), Russian explorer, 127

experiment, 204–5

Lightning Source UK Ltd.
Milton Keynes UK
UKOW032011130712

195939UK00006B/104/P

9 780745 624853